THE
LOST BOYS
of
SOHO

WILLIAM HAMPSON

This book represents the authors account, experiences, and present recollections over time. Names, characteristics, descriptions, dates, and locations have been changed to protect both personal and commercial identity/reputation/interests. Any similarity to real persons/business, living or dead/trading, is coincidental and not intended by the author.

No part of this book may be reproduced, or stored in a retrieval system, or transmitted in any form or by any means, electronic, mechanical, photocopying, recording, or otherwise, without express written permission of the author.

Copyright © 2022 William Hampson

All rights reserved.

ISBN: 9798794735666

DEDICATED FOR

Dr. ALAN McGOWAN & 56 DEAN STREET
for overseeing my HIV care.

TERRENCE HIGGINS TRUST
for your support and advice as a PLWHIV

JAMES B.
for being there.

SHADE FOR

THE LOST BOYS of SOHO
"I realised I finally had a family".

You argue, you bitch, you stab each other in the back,
a 'family' in every sense of the word.
Big love
x

CONTENTS

1	THE JOB VACANCY READ:	1
2	COLLECT GLASSES & WIPE TABLES	8
3	"LEMON'AIDS"	13
4	I HAVEN'T GOT COVID	19
5	I'M POSITIVE, I'M NEGATIVE	29
6	TO ISOLATE, OR NOT TO ISOLATE?	36
7	THE BURNER PHONE	43
8	LAST FOUR DIGITS	48
9	GIN, LIME & SODA	56
10	"WE CALL HER BUBBLES, EVERYBODY DOES"	64
11	IT'S ONLY HIS SECOND SHIFT	71
12	STICKS & STONES	79
13	BATTERED SAUSAGE & CHIPS	86
14	LOST BOY	93
15	FETISH SOCIAL	100
16	I'M U=U TOO	109
17	'THE ATMOSPHERE CHANGED'	119
18	BAGEL BOY	130
19	VAJAZZLED	141
20	MURDER OF A UNICORN	147
21	DODGY DEALINGS	155

22	NO PRIDE	168
23	LIAR, LIAR, PANTS ON FIRE!	178
24	LEMONADE-GATE	187
25	"JUST A FRIENDSHIP FOR ME"	198
26	GAGGING FOR 'IT'!	207
27	"SAY PLEASE"!	213

U=U

Undetectable = Untransmittable

People on effective HIV treatment CANNOT pass on the virus, FACT!

If everyone knew this simple and powerful message, we could bring an end to stigma around HIV. Not only that, but we could stop HIV transmissions altogether.

We know that while amazing medical progress has been made, knowledge of HIV hasn't kept up with that progress. Stigma that affects people living with HIV also stops others from getting tested. The more people who test and get onto effective treatment, the fewer HIV transmissions will happen.

- Terrence Higgins Trust

THE JOB VACANCY READ:

It was a slightly overcast day in May 2021 and I was making my way through the unusually quiet streets of Soho. I'd been invited to a job interview I'd only applied for the day before. I spotted the vacancy online which read: "'Bar Person for Soho Gay Bar', no experience necessary as full training will be given. Must have exciting personality and be outgoing"!

I'd had 11 interviews in my usual sector of hospitality: Hotel Management the day before. I had left every interview dressed in my Ted Baker suit, quirky, bright socks and bow tie looking up to the sky, pleading "please don't be successful"!

My heart was not in returning to my old routine and after the year I'd had I wanted something entirely different. Something fresh and exiting, casual, but most of all a routine. When I arrived for the interview having squeezed into a pair of skinny jeans and a hoodie, I was greeted by Adam the Deputy who seemed somewhat socially awkward but nice enough.

We both wore face masks observing Covid-19 restrictions and as he tried to make conversation, we ascended the wooden stairs of the pub. Even wearing a face mask, I could smell the warm stale stench of beer and dust. Adam was making small talk although I couldn't understand a word, he said so just assumed it was the usual pleasantries. I just threw back with "…and how are you? Been busy"?

We sat in two very worn brown leatherette wingback chairs overlooking Old Compton Street. As I gingerly plonked myself down on the chair it creaked and then snapped, and I let out a small squeal. From behind his mask Adam concerned, asked, "are you ok dear"? I quipped, "I am, but not sure about your chair I think my fat arse may have taken out a few springs"!

Giggling uncomfortably Adam sat cross legged resting a wooden clipboard against his knee and said he would run through the standard interview questions. I thought it seemed very formal for a pub, but then I quickly determined it was due to a lack of interview experience on Adam's behalf. It was clear he was unable or perhaps nervous to be able to naturally interview a candidate without the aid of a script. Rather than me asking the usual questions at the end of the interview, I asked Adam the same question he'd asked me to gauge if this would be a decent place to not only work, but progress.

Adam shared he had just finished his management training online during the national covid-19 lockdown. This resulted in his recent promotion as Deputy Manager. At the end of the half hour interview Adam said, "I'd like to offer you the job". This slightly threw me as even in my usual sector of hospitality I'd progress bar staff to a second interview. Anyhow, I thought 'in for a penny, in for a pound, why not' and accepted on the spot and said I would be available to start in a few days.

It was 10am Wednesday and arriving at the pub, it appeared closed as it didn't open until lunch time. I knocked and peered through the window and the guy inside looked at me with some distain before he continued with what he was doing. I telephoned the pub from the pavement and shared with the same guy that answered that I was here for my first day. The guy came out to open a side gate to let me in while scowling in an unfriendly manner.

"Hi love, are you William"? This short, bearded, muscly but dumpy chap with blonde hair and sparkly blue eyes enquired. I said that I was, and he continued "nice to meet you my love, I am Jack one of the Deputies here". He seemed pleasant enough despite his scowl and once I'd assured myself, he wasn't about to rip off my head I began to warm to him. Not that I was at all nervous, I don't do nerves. Although I was perhaps wary at working in an all-male, gay environment that no doubt had its fair share of drama and toxicity.

I've been around the gay community as it is more politically correct to say these days, as opposed to 'the gays' long enough to know they will look you up and down while making a preconceived judgement. I'd made no effort to tart myself up, not even for my first day as I knew it would be labour intensive and a job where I'd be expected to get my hands dirty.

As Jack took me on a quick tour of the pub, he kept apologising for talking too much as he filled me in on a bit of the pub's history. I learnt that the staff room was once the lady's toilet before it became a kitchen. It was truly riveting stuff, although I did find some of what he shared of interest.

We went through paperwork, and he kept apologising for how much paperwork had to be done and again apologising for talking too much. His constant apologising was more annoying than the mountain of paperwork, but I just went along with it. Jack mentioned he was currently training to be a vaccinator for the covid-19 vaccination roll out which sounded interesting. I also got the low down on his career history and how he first started working in retail for a famous catalogue store before sharing he had trained in alternative medicine. He seemed to be on a spiritual journey which I must admit started to bore me ever so slightly given it was my first day.

As I sat attentively listening, or so it seemed to Jack. I giggled to myself as I thought how Jack reminded me of the character Christine form Victoria Wood's comedy Dinnerladies. The character only appeared in one episode, aptly titled 'Christine'. Like the character 'Christine' who was needy and neurotic Jack too portrayed the same characteristics and mannerisms as the fictional character. He would share stories in a chaotic and sometimes random manner and occasionally the 'spiritual façade' would slip, and you got a glimpse of the 'real' Jack who I thought was quite mesmerizingly fun if not thrilling.

As I completed my part of the paperwork, Jack disappeared only to return with four work t-shifts and asked me to try them on. As I took them from him, they felt damp and I hoped he wasn't expecting me to put them on in that state. I giggled to myself as I was interested as to what size he'd pulled out. He insisted I try them on there and then and I was directed to the gents' toilets, not that I needed any direction as I had been a customer of the pub on many occasions over countless years.

As I walked into the gents I was greeted by the usual warm, musty smell of urine that first hit the back of my throat before it managed to penetrate my sinuses despite suffering from chronic sinusitis. I was petrified to see what sizes Jack had picked for me. I opened the screwed-up t-shirts to check the size tag, "Medium", bless, am flattered. The other two were "Large" phew! Something that'll fit but thank God not an 'x' in sight! I stood in the men's toilets checking in the mirror that 'large' was the right fit without even bothering with the medium. Catching the sight of the urinal in the reflection of the mirror and thinking 'if that urinal could talk! The cruising, the cocks, the stories she could tell'! Reality hit home where it was, I would be working. It was quite the come down career wise, but I felt quite mischievous, and it was quite an exciting if not thrilling prospect to call this, 'not so new' place, my new home.

When I returned clutching the t-shirts Jack asked if either of them fitted, which I thought 'cheeky bitch'! So, I jokingly replied "no! Have you not got a size small"? Jack looking stunned, rude again, he said "we don't have any small left" whilst looking me up and down. "I'll take the large then" I said to which Jack said "ok" taking the other t-shirts from my hand. Then he had a slight look of confusion on his face as he either realised I was taking the piss or perhaps thought I was slightly peculiar.

I wasn't sure if my attempt at a little light-hearted banter had perhaps gone way over Jack's head or was perhaps just not funny at all. Jack then shared he'd be handing me over to the other Deputy Adam who I had my interview with when he arrived shortly. Simultaneously Jack shared while reading from his mobile phone that Adam had just had a punch up with a van driver in a nearby car park.

I was briefly introduced to Carl, the pubs General Manger who said he wouldn't shake my hand given covid-19 but then quickly said he just didn't like shaking hands with people anyway. Jack objected and said you could gauge so much from someone's handshake. But I was quick to agree with the boss, not to kiss his arse but because I had always hated shaking hands with people throughout my career, especially strangers. I also met Johnnie who arrived with a spring in his step in a black vest carrying a vintage gym holdall.

He reminded me instantly of the fictional character 'Elastigirl' from the animated film 'The Incredibles'. He was very slim and around 6 foot 2 inches tall, from Liverpool and had a strong accent to match which was hard not to mimic. He seemed to move and contort his body to get to his chosen destination with minimal effort. He was very confident and direct when he spoke and seemed to have a fun and witty sense of humour with a habit of speaking in quotes, mainly from the Wood & Walters series by Victoria Wood and Julie Walters.

When Adam arrived, he seemed somewhat flustered and although I think this was a little bit of camp theatrics on Adam's part. It seemed there was a bit of banter going back and forth between him and Jack with Johnnie occasionally offering a comedic narration in the background as he swished around the pub.

It was the usual as you stand and observe and say to yourself 'that must be a private joke' as they spoke in code in a bid not to share detail in the presence of the new guy, me. They then both stood either side of me and I felt like I was the referee and after a few exchanges Adam called Jack a "cunt" and minced off through the fire exit. I said to Jack "Oh! She's good"! in reference to Adams acting ability in playing the stroppy Queen. But Jack didn't catch the sentiment of my remark and said, "I'll talk you through the bar until she sorts herself out".

Jack had shared he had worked at the pub for over fifteen years but as he tried to show me around, he seemed a little lost and confused. He continually questioned himself what stock they sold and where to find certain things such as glasses and ice scoops. When he tried to show me the till system, he kept saying he couldn't find a certain button that he was about to show me which meant I lost interest quickly. Jack just kept saying "Adam will show you later" and I couldn't wait for Adam to return.

When Adam returned, he ran through elements that Jack couldn't show me. I was introduced to Emilio who had come on shift as the pub opened for the day. He didn't say anything on being introduced, it seemed he couldn't even bring himself to look at me. I thought this was bizarre for a hospitality worker. Over the course of my first shift, I tried four times to engage with Emilio and got nothing in return. On one occasion he just turned and walked away when I asked him a question about the job. He was wearing a vest, had a shaved head and was more gristle than muscle. Customers were only allowed to sit outside and not inside due to covid-19 restrictions. So, there were times when me and Adam who were working inside preparing orders to be collected, stood, and chatted.

We had a few friends in common, mainly drag queens from my 10 years on the circuit as a 'drag artiste'. Emilio came behind the bar and Adam shared that Emilio was nervous about having the covid-19 vaccine despite having recently been called for the jab. I'd already shared with Adam that I had, had my second vaccine and I believe Adam was trying to encourage Emilio to engage in conversation with me. I shared my experience with the AstraZeneca vaccine for Covid-19 and how I had absolutely no side effects from the jab. I even wondered if it had been administered properly as many seem to have some adverse reaction or another. Emilio, again, refused to look at me and Adam and he just walked off.

Jack passing the bar with a plastic carrier bag and a rucksack on his back said he had finished for the day and was going on to do some more vaccination training. There seemed to be some tension between him and Adam, although Jack walked back to the bar to say "Will, I am so sorry if I went on and on today. I don't like the sound of my own voice and I just want to apologise if I bored you"! I said sarcastically "apology accepted" to which I quickly followed up with "I'm joking, don't be silly, it's the same with any new starter. I've been in your shoes myself so don't worry".

As Jack left and I stood back, Adam said "she does" to which I enquired "does what"? "Like the sound of her own voice" Adam said. Johnnie then piped up "did she tell you when she worked for the catalogue shop? Oh, what she doesn't know about a 4-slot toaster is unreal, she can even give you the 6-digit catalogue number for it"! I thought this was incredibly mean and while I could sense some tension, I told myself this was the usual 'shade' that my community would throw at each other and where it was always meant with love and affection, well, sometimes.

As customers could only sit outside all drinks were being served in plastic pint glasses. I did ask Adam to clarify at the start how high to go with the ice for a single spirit and mixer. Common sense dictated that some customers wouldn't like too much ice to water down their drink and perhaps not enough ice made the drink look short in such a large glass.

I took ice to the line on the glass as advised by Adam. I did catch Emilio refusing to deliver two gin and tonics I had prepared and placed on the tray. Adam intervened and Emilio complained there was not enough ice in the glass. Adam said to Emilio "there's nothing wrong with it, don't be a twat"! Emilio still protested holding up the glass in front of Adam to gauge the level of ice floating in the gin and tonic "calm down, leave him alone, it's his first day" Adam stated sternly.

Johnnie came over to me as he backed up Adam and sent Emilio on his way to deliver the drink. "Emilio takes a little time to warm to people" Johnnie said to me. Emilio seemed an odd character and this was seemingly odd behaviour and I then started to clock watch and couldn't wait to finish at 8pm.

Whenever I have started a new job the first thing new colleagues wanted to know was where I'd come from to establish if I had the right experience and skill set for the role in which I had just been hired. Here 'everybody' asked, 'are you single? Top or bottom?' and 'where do you live'? Towards the end of my shift, I was asked how I was getting home after establishing earlier that I only lived a 20-minute walk away, sharing that I would walk home.

Johnnie chipped in "oh be careful! Walking along Rosebery Avenue you don't want to…" to which I interjected "…get raped". Johnnie as he became characteristically known, wiped the corners of his mouth with his thumb and forefinger while theatrically exhaling a couple of times said, "well dear, beggars can't be choosers! But thank God for PrEP (Pre-exposure prophylaxis) to keep the AIDS at bay! Actually, you just reminded me…"!

And Elastigirl was off as Johnnie shot across the pub floor and to the office seemingly to take his PrEP pill. Adam was nervously laughing, I guess not sure where my humour threshold was at, although I thought 'it'll be a right laugh here'!

On the walk home as I digested my first day, I did ponder on the AIDS comment made by Johnnie. I'll let you into a little secret, I have been living with HIV (Human Immunodeficiency Virus) for 14 months now. I was knocked unconscious and assaulted back in March 2020 and this is how I had contracted the virus. I found the comment funny and wasn't offended at all. I guess this was the first time where along with Johnnie's comment about PrEP highlighted that I was in some part different to others in that I was living with a virus that they were quite rightly protecting themselves from.

I very quickly disregarded my thoughts on it and suspected I'd hear more abouts HIV/AIDS the longer I work here. This is something I will get more comfortable with the more I hear it. Although that said, I have absolutely no intention of sharing my status given I am not legally bound to do so in my line of work. I am not a danger to anybody as I became undetectable within 4 weeks of infection and HIV has not defined me as an individual. Anyway, its such old news, I mean with Covid-19 on the scene HIV is no longer trendy. Plus I wouldn't want people being on tip toes around me when there is some good banter to be had!

COLLECT GLASSES
& WIPE TABLES

For my second shift the next day I was buddied with Blair in the upstairs bar where it was table service only. Customers could now sit inside the pub given a slight change in government guidelines to kick start the economy. Blair had only been in London for a year and half and is originally from Aberdeen, Scotland. He had a soft Scottish accent, was around 6ft tall, slim, and in his mid-thirties. Blair said his only hobby was running his knitting group which had gone online during the pandemic.

I tried to look past the knitting, and initially Blair seemed fun, but I soon realised he was quite naïve and uptight given he'd say, "do you want to serve that table"? and I'd reply, "no not really"! Just because it would be an unexpected answer to his question. Given his lack of a personality I soon gave up trying to have a laugh to save us both any awkward embarrassment.

Conversation soon turned to knitting and Blair shared that he had the week prior held the first face to face knitting group at one of the participants homes. However, it was his turn this week and he had gone to great lengths getting in snacks and nibbles. I genuinely enquired as to what kind of nibbles he'd purchased. I could imagine nibbles such as mini cheddars or cheesy Wotsit's not being compatible with knitwear? But I think he thought I was taking the piss and with a roll of the eyes he didn't answer.

Early evening, we were joined by Kenzie who had been working in the downstairs bar during the day and had now finished his shift and was having a drink. He has just turned twenty, is short and dumpy with jet black hair and potholed skin. And more noticeably, dirt behind his fingernails which I thought was shocking for a gay man. His first words to me as he climbed onto a bar stool was "Hey! I'm Kenzie and I'm a complete slut looking for a rich daddy"! Having no idea who he was, although I understood he worked here I just replied "nice"!

He had seemingly come up to see Blair given he was also from Scotland. Govan in Glasgow to be precise. Kenzie said he'd come to introduce himself and ordered a cider and blackcurrant before proceeding to grill me. He bombarded me with question after question which I was reluctant to answer given it was all way too personal and familiar for me. So, I fired each question back to him given he was more than happy to talk about himself and that he did.

He said he had, had every sexually transmitted infection going, even pubic lice that were deemed "rare"! Who knew! Kenzie shared these crabs were infected and in turn infecting him with another STI. He also proudly declared that a customer of the pub gave him scabies. He said, "I suspect the others have told you about that, because they all know"! In all his boasting of sexual transmitted diseases the twisted part of me was dying to ask while declaring, 'ah! I'll raise you your STI's and rare breed of pubic crabs for my HIV'! But of course, I didn't, but it'd been a laugh to see his face.

As I came back to the bar after taking an order from a table he asked, "how's my advertisement"? I asked him to clarify, and he said, "how do I look to them, from the back? Now be honest"? I said, "are you sure, be honest"? Kenzie encouragingly said yes. So honest I was, I said "if you're brave enough to sit on a bar stool, you really must master the art of breathing in". He took it in the good humour it was intended, and he replied while laughing "you're a shady bitch" to which I gave him a shrug of the shoulders and said, "I'll take that"!

He stayed for an hour or so and seemed like he was energetic and fun. Although had far too much self-confidence, and absolutely no filter in sharing elements of his personal life. But I guess that's not a bad thing entirely especially given individuals like Kenzie refer to themselves as "Gen Z" (generation Z, born 1997-2012). Who are predominantly known for having no social skills, full of anxiety and think they invented being 'gay'.

It was now my first Friday in the pub and I was working on the ground floor in the main bar doing table service. Kenzie was working behind the bar receiving our orders and preparing the drinks for us to collect and deliver.

I delivered an order to a table who queried where their glass of tap water was. Apologising I thought preparing a glass of tap water was not at all beyond my capacity. So I went behind the bar, collected a glass, chucked in some ice and a slice of lime. Kenzie turned and barked "Will! Remember your only here to collect glasses and wipe tables"!

Kenzie gestured to put the glass down and wait for him to finish pouring an order to then be able to deliver the rather sad looking glass of tap water he presented to me. It was clearly not a joke, and I assumed there must be a strict rule for going behind the bar when someone else is working it, so didn't particularly take offence to his comments.

The next day I was doing the same task and an order I delivered was missing a pint of Pravha. Despite being told roles would be rotated to keep the team engaged Kenzie was for the third day in a row preparing orders behind the bar. I stood patiently observing Kenzie's instructions the day before when I asked Kenzie when he'd finished pouring an order if he could prepare the missing Pravha larger. Overhearing my request, Johnnie who was passing barked "don't your legs work dear, get it yourself"!

Kenzie looked stunned and quickly said "No, it's ok, it's not a problem, I don't mind, really". I suspect in fear of me revealing to Johnnie what Kenzie had said to me the day before. I really had to bite my tongue and just take it on the chin as I naturally didn't want to get Kenzie into some sort of trouble. And Kenzie's reaction intimated that he would. But I didn't want Johnnie reporting back to management that I was perhaps being demanding or unwilling to get the drink myself.

The customers on a whole have been well behaved and adhered to the government guidelines on mask wearing and table service. Most have expressed they are just glad to be back in the pub having a pint with up to 6 of their friends. The obnoxious customers have been the old timers, the single guys who are trying to 'cruise' as they did pre-pandemic. Given we have been full every day from open to close they sometimes get located on the only available table which can be out of view of any potential 'fresh meat'. Although the pub is not known for its 'fresh meat', instead it is more famously known for its decaying old carcasses.

One is a rancid old Queen called Ron who the team call "Randy Ron"! He must be well into his sixties and has a skin condition that looks as though he's been rolled in porridge oats. He speaks to you with such contempt, especially if your new as he is more civil with colleagues who have perhaps worked here longer. "I want to sit in the window! Nobody can see me here, move me to the window now" he demands! And you'd have to explain people are sat in the window and have either booked or secured that seat on a 'first come first served basis'. You'd reassure him as soon as something became available that you knew he would prefer, you'd hold the seat for him to move, but that was never enough.

He'd perhaps like the other cruisers misjudged the mood as the hospitality sector was reopening in Soho. Soho had become a hub for people across London to come and socialise and this meant the demographic had changed dramatically. The gay community is very much now a minority in Soho and in our pub the crowd was predominantly heterosexual. Therefore, the pub had become less 'cruisy' as it was most famously known pre-pandemic.

During my second week, I was designated 'door bitch' or more formally known as the door 'host'. Greeting customers either looking on the off chance that we had available space or with a confirmed table booking. Either way the role was to ensure the business complied with the government covid-19 regulations. Blair joined me for a chat as he oversaw the tables on the street outside when we were interrupted by Simon. Simon introduced himself sharing he was from France, so his name was pronounced 'See-mon' which I thought was hilarious working in a gay pub.

Simon grabbed Blair firmly by the shoulders, his knuckles turning white he declared "thank god I'm HIV negative"! Still the newbie to the team and not really knowing Simon this was clearly a private conversation. I stayed in my post and of course listened in; well, it be rude not to. Simon gave Blair some of the back story, mainly that Simon is not taking PrEP nor practicing safe sex, that's it really.

Blair tried to hammer home how all his worry of being tested for HIV could be reduced if he practiced safe sex. Or perhaps if Simon looked into the benefits of PrEP which was now being provided free by the NHS (National Health Service). And could be prescribed by the sexual health clinic around the corner from the pub. Simon shared when scrolling mobile gay dating apps like Grindr, he judges a guy he intends to hook up with by the image alone. He determines by the image if they look clean and free of STI's. This was also the case to their HIV status as Simon said, "you can clearly see if they have HIV or not" and this seemed to be his assumption that people living with HIV (PLWHIV) resemble the images we saw when individuals were succumbing to the AIDS virus at the height of the AIDS pandemic. Individuals that looked tired and somewhat emaciated.

I couldn't believe my ears and I really wanted to interject and share my thoughts and opinions specifically on HIV as a PLWHIV. I was living proof, although not particularly overweight for my height, more average build that you don't have to look like the image from the late 1980's, 90's when HIV/AIDS was a death sentence. When the Soho clinic I attended on being told my home test for HIV was "reactive" to have a confirmatory HIV test which was positive. My first words were those of NYC's iconic drag queen Lady Bunny "I'm way too fat to have AIDS"! The nurse who did my test laughed as I laughed. Through my tears of course.

But I asked myself if a quick chat would suffice for someone who 'screens' their sexual encounters by their Grindr profile picture. Plus, I had a couple of days earlier been warned to be careful around Simon as he is prone to mood swings. Simon has shared with his colleagues that he is bipolar. I have noticed he can be nice and chatty one minute and then completely ignore you the next, which I don't have much time for if I am honest. We can all have bad days, but I live by the adage 'don't bring your shit to work'!

Ultimately, I found it bizarre for someone who says they are bipolar and perhaps suffers from anxiety. Why would you subject yourself to a situation like this if you're going to get so anxious about your HIV test?

But all I could commend Simon on was despite not agreeing with is strategy nor his sexual promiscuity was the fact he was ensuring he knew his HIV status by getting tested. Which is half the problem with the spread of HIV. But if Simon is mentally fragile as I am told, then I would worry the day that he perhaps gets the result he doesn't want although I truly hope that day never comes.

"LEMON'AIDS"

With the lifting of restrictions by the government as the economy was now attempting to recover from the covid-19 pandemic. The punters were having to adjust to an alternative pub experience, and so were we, the staff.

Several of the team would be assigned to work the floor which involved, taking orders, delivering drinks, and then clearing tables and sanitising them ready for the next customer. When we would take the order, the receipt would be spat out of the till and the designated person behind the bar would make the drinks and plonk them on a tray. With the receipt slipped under a drink to stop it blowing away as you glided to the table of delivery. The receipt served to know what the drinks were and which table to deliver them to.

Customers were always impressed with how fast we would deliver drinks from only just placing their order. Sometimes you never knew when they placed their order as it could have been placed with Johnnie. Prepared by Adam and delivered by me given I merely picked them up at the bar as the next order that needed delivering. But it was always nice to hear positive feedback collectively as a team effort.

So, I was working behind the main bar having to prepare drinks. Kenzie was off so not sure if that's why I was put there or if the manager on duty was enforcing the rotation of tasks as they stated they would. Either way, I pulled the ticket from the machine that read "2 Lemonaids in pint glass". I looked at the name of the cashier and it was Bobby, who had typed in the request as he didn't know how to enter two pints of lemonade on the system.

Bobby started a couple of days after me and like my training it was vague although the system was easy to use. I suspect Bobby just forgot where the pint glass button was but seemingly remembered how to make a written note.

Bobby is from the West Country and has the accent to boot. He is another that is sickly thin and pale and says this is contributed by several health conditions. Many originating around food intolerance and in his own words his addiction to "smoking weed". I liked Bobby from the start as he seemed to live in his own world and would come out with some random crap, some of which made no sense at all. And when I met him on his first shift, he was left stood alone like a lost boy in the school playground on his first day while a group of colleagues stood in a huddle gossiping which I thought was intentional and mean.

As I read the receipt it tickled me as I had never seen Lemonade spelt like that before. As the punters were sitting inside, they had the luxury of a water marked pint glass which I tried to dress up with some fresh ice, lemon slices and a straw. I placed the two pints of lemonade on the tray and laid the ticket beside it. Johnnie came to collect and deliver the order and upon reading the ticket to establish the drinks and table number he screamed, in that scouse accent of his "since when did we start giving the punters AIDS"?

A hush fell over that area of the bar as punters turned and looked on bewildered at the sight of Johnnie stood with the receipt in the air as though he was waiting for his bingo ticket to be checked. I fell about laughing although it wasn't that funny it was just the way he announced it to the whole pub in that manky accent of his. As we all had to continue wearing a face mask I quickly started to choke as I inhaled my mask as I gasped for air in my fit of laughter, and I thought if Johnnie makes a quip about me dropping down dead with AIDS I'll literally die. But thankfully he didn't, and I composed myself although I was waiting for a punter to come and share how the event was somewhat insensitive if not inappropriate.

Johnnie took the opportunity to pull Bobby on it who was mortified at his spelling error. And of course, Johnnie getting a lot of attention and pleasure sharing with enquiring punters what the joke was. The 'joke' soon became exhausted to the point where Johnnie found it hilarious but no longer did the team, including me.

No matter what role you are doing in the pub you are never far away from a conversation and sometimes a debate about Covid-19. You'd have thought people after lockdown, declaring they missed the good old pub, would come to enjoy each other's company. And would have much more to talk about than covid-19. But I guess in one way or another and perhaps even ways you didn't realise covid-19 was dominating our lives.

If the customers were regular or from the LGBT+ community then covid-19 would almost always move onto HIV/AIDS. This was predominantly with the older crowd and there was anger and rage at how the UK government and the world had come together to find a vaccine for the Covid-19 virus but, in their opinion did next to nothing during the AIDS pandemic.

It was clear emotions were still incredibly raw almost 40 years since the first case of AIDS hit the UK. But their strong words and passion were incredibly heart-warming to witness although tinged with sadness. These still raw emotions resurfacing as a result of losing someone close to them whether it be a partner, friend, family member or member of the gay community that they'd lost to AIDS. And while I was living with the HIV virus, albeit with the benefit of amazing advances in science and medication. It was so warming to think they will no doubt continue to be allies of the HIV/AIDS community while they still have breath in their bodies. I could feel myself welling up as I thought these guys don't know me, but they've clearly 'got my back'.

Russell T Davies 'It's a Sin' which hit the screens at the start of this year is such a hot topic too. And again, it seemed appropriately timed given it hit the screens just as covid-19 vaccine was starting to be rolled out nationally. It was interesting to hear the correlation customers made of the two viruses, HIV/AIDS and Covid-19. But simultaneously scary that despite their anger at claims not enough was done to find vaccines nor a cure for HIV/AIDS at the height of the AIDS pandemic. Meant they openly stated they were refusing to take a covid-19 vaccine, citing they didn't trust the government. And given they lived through and survived the AIDS pandemic meant they were of an age where they were perhaps vulnerable to covid-19.

The following day I came on shift, and it was a glorious day outside and I was working the upstairs bar which was quite given everybody was opting to sit outside in the sunshine.

A well-spoken chap in a cream Panama hat, brown deck shoes and shorts came and sat by the window overlooking a bustling Old Compton Street. He initiated a conversation with me by sharing how glad he was to be out of the house for the first time since the end of lockdown. I prepared his double G&T and delivered it to his table. I asked how he was enjoying his newfound freedom given he shared he was reluctant to come out given his advancing years and being a "shielder".

I slipped into hotel mode speaking the Queens English. Although with a northern accent I have often been dubbed Mollie Sugden's, Mrs Slocombe as I fall in and out of speaking posh and then common. He said he'd been to an art exhibition in Knightsbridge, confirming it was all safely organised and covid secure.

He asked what he could do for the remainder of the afternoon, given the pub wasn't busy and he couldn't see any "old faces" downstairs. I said perhaps he could grab an Antipasto box from the deli just down the way and perhaps find a bench in Soho square or a nice spot on the grass and have a picnic and people watch whilst enjoying the sunshine. He said that sounded "a charming idea".

The conversation quickly turned sombre as he noted that coming to the pub today reminded him of the late 1980's and the AIDS pandemic. He recounted how he would regularly walk into the pub during the AIDS pandemic and either see people "I only knew to say hello to, you know, regular faces" or "friends and acquaintances for a convivial drink or two". He continued "they would look incredibly ill. Thin and withdrawn, eyes sunken in and then a couple of days later you didn't seem again. It took a week or two to realise they'd vanished. You made enquiries, either with the bar man like yourself or another regular who would confirm whomever you were enquiring about had died of AIDS".

He spoke in exceptional detail, sharing the layout of the pub as it was back then. "It was dimly lit you know, with clouds of cigarette smoke lingering in the air. We had proper music in the 1980's not this rubbish you listen to today. Played from a tape deck that needed turning when it ended by the bar man". He shared "I used to sit, in that very spot just there when I was 19 or 20 years old" pointing at a seat behind me which made the hairs on my neck stand on end. He went on to share how he and the gay community became to know individual faces and you didn't always, need to know their names given the real sense of community spirit.

"Pete used to sit in the same seat every night at the end of the bar nursing his pint with a packet of Silk Cut on the bar. He didn't like smoking, but it was a low tar cigarette and like most, found it was always easy to engage with guys over a cigarette. He was quite a shy guy really. Like me he was in his twenties and always wore denim jeans and a jacket. He had gorgeous brown eyes with smooth olive skin. He was incredibly handsome; he had no need to be so shy really as he grabbed the attention of all the guys"!

I felt I had been transported to the 1980's as he shared this intimate memory. As he paused to compose himself, I noticed tears rolling down his cheeks as he stared at the end of the bar. I felt so privileged yet saddened to hear a first-hand account within the walls that bore witness to the pain and suffering of a community I was a part of. Men that came to the pub as a safe space to socialise only to be taken by an invisible, vicious, and deadly virus.

"I noticed quite quickly the change in Pete, he looked seriously unwell in a relatively short pace of time. Most noticeable was his weight loss. The next I saw him I hardly recognised him at all, only for the denim and twenty Silk Cut sat in his usual spot at the bar. While he looked unwell, you didn't quite know it was AIDS, but it clearly was. I was going to ask him how he was doing but I got distracted and by the time I turned around, he'd gone. I never saw him again and for a time nobody knew what happened to him until a regular found out from another old haunt he visited that he had died of AIDS. Although by all accounts his sister refused to confirm it as she didn't agree with his lifestyle, but we all knew. But he was not the only one, they were vanishing week on week"!

He was clearly upset while sharing this very intimate memory with me and I found myself crying too and as we didn't have serviettes or the like, I had to offer up some blue kitchen roll to dry our eyes. "Very five stars" I said as I handed him a ball of blue roll. I thanked him for sharing this with me and said it must have been absolutely devastating to which he said, "you'll never understand"! He seemed to have survivors' guilt sharing "I am not sure how I survived, why it didn't take me too? But you will never understand young man"!

What I did understand was the Covid-19 pandemic we are currently living through didn't even come close to the AIDS pandemic. For Covid-19 there are effective treatments that give those infected with Covid-19 a chance of survival. Whereas AIDS, there was no effective treatment, and it was very much a death sentence. Although I read some believed overdosing on Oranges for its Vitamin C and drinking battery acid were effective treatments no doubt, out of sheer desperation.

I was on the other end of the spectrum, I wasn't old enough to fully understand the AIDS pandemic, although was aware of it from age 10. But I was now living with HIV and given the amazing advances in science I was on effective treatment and have a normal life expectancy. Like this gentleman, I too often ponder and perhaps feel guilty that such treatment wasn't available for those before me. Men who were only living their best life, being true to their sexuality only to be taken away so cruelly and for many, at such a young age.

So, while I perhaps couldn't begin to comprehend the fear he lived through and the pain that he still feels. We have perhaps experienced the same emotions and fears albeit with very different outcomes.

He mentioned he watched 'It's a Sin' the drama that portrayed London in the late 80's during the AIDS pandemic. He said the show was an accurate portrayal and was incredibly poignant which I completely agreed even if I was watching it from another perspective. He had a good understanding of advances in medication for HIV and that HIV is no longer a death sentence. Given I did too, prior to being infected, had a partner of two years living with HIV meaning I could share my knowledge on medication and how a PLWHIV can live a full and normal life. My only regret that as he looked somewhat sceptical to my in-depth knowledge on living with HIV in 2021, that I didn't share I was a PLWHIV.

I did however offer him a hug despite covid-19 advice on close contact given he truly seemed he needed one. He swigged the last of his G&T and said "it has been lovely chatting to you, young man. I'll have the same again please, this time 'for Pete'"!

I HAVEN'T GOT COVID!

As several weeks passed, I enjoyed working in the pub given the high turnover of customers kept us busy. It was not always the same old faces except for the diehard cruisers.

I had established a good working relationship with Elias who has worked at the pub for over half a decade and was pretty much part of the furniture. Elias had lived and worked in NYC for around fifteen years throughout the 1990's before coming to London. He portrayed himself as a bitter old queen with no regard for the PC (politically correct) brigade and referred to himself as 'the tranny' [transvestite]. He showed me old grainy snaps, way before digital cameras, documenting his time in NYC living and working on the gay scene which looked absolutely amazing.

I saw videos of his time as a bartender in an established cabaret bar in central NYC. He shared the culture where he and his colleagues formed drag groups and duos. Put on nightly performances in front of a fully attentive crowd swigging pints with the disco ball beaming through the cigarette smoke that hung in the air! I was so envious as in some respects, this is what I wanted to experience in this pub.

Elias was the one who took time to truly show me the ropes at the pub and was the pubs 'mother', because he was the eldest who demanded I call her "T"! I enquired what was the meaning behind the name 'T' and was taken to one side out of earshot of 'generation Z'. It transpired, an endearing and affectionate term used by both Elias and even me on the gay scene in the late 90's and 00's. Was now considered 'hate speech'! So, this was Elias's way of dodging the PC brigade allowing him to at least, retain some of his LGBT culture. I'm old enough to remember when there was no 'T' and the community was merely known as LGB (Lesbian, Gay, Bisexual). Elias made the argument of the term 'Queer' being bandied about, as do many of the customers given, they deem it to be a negatively charged homophobic slur. I've never been one for labelling myself nor taking offence to words, after all, they are just words. But I recognise for some, words have a powerful and emotional significance in relation to their identity.

I affectionately referred to Elias as "T" which he loved and would respond by blowing a kiss each time! I would catch the kiss in my hand and hold it to my heart.

I got to work and bumped into Elias and Bobby in the staff room, which was as I said before previously the lady's cubicle. So, space was at a premium especially when there was more than two of you no matter how skinny a bitch was. Bobby said he didn't feel well, and Elias gave me a roll of the eyes as he made a swift exit to start his shift. Bobby had in these first few weeks had a lot of time off sick citing food intolerances as the cause of his sickness.

Bobby followed me to the upstairs bar as I started my shift, and he did look incredibly pale and peaky, more so than he usually does. I like Bobby but, his long list of health concerns ranging from a plethora of food intolerances. Mental health as he so openly shared and his issues around smoking weed, which I am sure contributes to his alleged mental health. And as he declared, occasionally harder drugs become quite trying if not tiring.

I had heard, and Bobby himself shared he was aware that some of the team, were bitching about him behind his back regarding his health issues. But I don't think Bobby was aware that colleagues were picking up on things I had seen for myself. For example, Bobby said he had an intolerance to Avocado and potato. But would eat chips from the chippy down the road and bring in Poke bowls topped with Avocado slices. There were inconsistencies with his intolerances, although he would sometimes say he would have to pay for it in the morning as he'll most likely be unwell. Many of the stories he shared also seemed a little over exaggerated and I would see colleagues' loose interest and even walk away as he was mid-sentence.

Johnnie and Adam were awful to Bobby, like two crows pecking at weak and injured pigeon, it was awful to witness. I often wanted to intervene but felt Bobby needed to learn how to defend himself. Bobby did share with me as we walked home down Old Compton Street how Johnnie and Adam's relentless digs and put downs were impacting his self-esteem and confidence. I stood for about 20 minutes trying to advise him how to not necessarily tackle it but avoid such and he first needed to start by not giving them the ammunition.

As I prepared the bar to open Bobby was shuffling and tiptoeing around the bar. He was coughing every five seconds and seemed to have a fever of some sort. Bobby said he felt weak citing his allergies, intolerances and medication and I advised he maybe should go home as he didn't look in any fit state to work on the bar.

I strongly suspect he had Covid-19 as he had all the symptoms although he said his lateral flow test was negative. He went down to the main bar and shortly came back up having been sent home by Adam.

About forty minutes later, Adam came up the pub stairs and stormed across to me at the bar with his face mask on. Although just by his eyes being visible, I could see Adam had a face like thunder. "Is she still in there"? Adam shouted in a rage referring to Bobby in the staff room. I hadn't seen Bobby leave so checked the hook behind me to see if Bobby had dropped off the staff room key while I was perhaps doing table service. The key wasn't there so I said, "he must be, yeah". Adam stormed off back downstairs and didn't bother to check on Bobby as he passed the staff room door which I thought was peculiar.

But then I gave myself a telling off that I too was guilty of not checking in on Bobby and given it was forty minutes, if not more, something could have happened to him in there. I popped my head in the door of the staff room and he was just putting on his rucksack. Bobby said he had heard Adam's booming voice and that he was struggling to book an Uber. So, he was now leaving to catch the bus instead as he gingerly walked down the stairs to exit the pub.

There was a new starter who started recently called Rudy who is in his mid-twenties and acts like a dumb blonde. I saw through this act straight away as it only served for him to avoid doing what he'd essentially been employed to do, work. He moves slowly around the bar, complains that he has to serve 'peasants' and was constantly applying lip gloss despite wearing a mask as per covid-19 regulations. So maybe the dumb blonde isn't an act!

He wears these heavy platform style boots to which I stated in my usual caustic fashion. If he perhaps wore suitable footwear to work then, he may be able to move around the bar a little quicker? He wears small, tight-fitting shorts to show what he declared was an eight-inch penis when erect and as I could see quite sizeable flaccid. His excessive use of fake tan means he is a vibrant shade of orange if not streaky along with over manicured eyebrows that look like two opposing steep gradient road signs. But the blonde act didn't work on me, and we got on well once I established, I knew he was being smart. He was, however, very dramatic and sought after the attention of others which at times was draining but often amusing as I'd merely push him away and tell him to go "bore someone else".

The next day Rudy came into the changing room as I was getting changed and declared "Will, Will, you know I tested positive for covid-19, twice yesterday and again today". I replied "no shit sherlock" because Rudy displayed all the symptoms for Covid-19 just as Bobby did the day before.

I also noticed Adam, Emilio and Keith also had the same symptoms, this continuous cough which had me believing it had to be Covid-19 although Adam had this sniffle behind his mask also. But regardless, they all had a touch of something whether it was Covid-19 or a common virus, they all had it.

Rudy had the continuous cough mainly, and when I say continuous, I mean continuous! While they couldn't help it, it was as annoying as when someone eats with their mouth open! I counted Bobby was coughing every 5-6 seconds the day before. How nobody else picked up on this had me puzzled, especially management who were ensuring we all observed the company's procedure on keeping ourselves "covid safe". But I suspect as with many businesses having a staff shortage when we are so busy would be more of a hassle and a drop in revenue.

I advised Rudy he should be self-isolating, but Rudy said he could not afford too self-isolate. I said it wasn't about affordability, it was about respect and safety of his colleagues and the vulnerable customers which by that I meant the old boys given elderly people were at a higher risk of serious illness and mortality.

Rudy defended his decision to come to work knowing he was covid-19 positive as he was in the process of having to find a new room to rent. Given he didn't pay a rental deposit on his first room he had to find the substantial deposit this time around. I did advise there was a £500 one off payment to isolate from the government for those on a low income. But Rudy was not in breach of any UK law as I understood it. A positive lateral flow test does not legally obligate the person to isolate, only a positive PCR (polymerase chain reaction test) test bound the person to legally isolate. But there was an onus on Rudy and others, to do the 'right thing' for themselves and the public, but as Rudy highlighted doing the 'right thing' doesn't pay the bills.

I was again working the upstairs bar when Emilio came up to help. Well, I think it was more a case of a change of scene for him as he had now warmed to me over the last few weeks. As we stood leaning against the bar back chatting, he kept slowly caressing my bare arm and being sexually suggestive. Emilio was leaving the pub and going home to Italy for the remainder of the year. He was continuously coughing, and I said Rudy and Bobby had the same cough. Emilio shared without hesitation that he had tested positive for Covid-19 on the lateral flow test.

Given he was due to fly back to his home in Italy in a few days I asked if this hampered his plans. He said he was initially worried but, he found out today that he does not need to test on leaving the UK. He only needs to take and show a covid-19 test when he lands in Italy. And should he still test positive in Italy he will be instructed to isolate at his Italian home. I asked if he was not concerned that should he still be positive that he will infect his family, which naturally consisted of elderly relatives all living under the same roof. But Emilio quite nonchalantly said he was not concerned.

Since starting at the pub I had been doing a lateral flow test every single day, marking it with the date and time. Taking a photo of the test displaying the result, which thus far has been negative every time. I am double vaccinated because I fell into the relevant qualifying group given, I am living with HIV. I cannot say I am worried about catching Covid-19, if I am honest its most likely inevitable, I will catch it at some point. Given I am working in a small building with poor ventilation and hundreds of customers sat without masks on while drinking.

As I wear glasses, I found a homemade facemask with a malleable metal strip across the nose stops my glasses steaming up. Pressing the malleable metal strip into the bridge of my nose has been playing havoc with my chronic sinusitis. I have had the condition on and off since a serious case of the flu in 2015. I am often bunged up and my sense of smell, has I recall on at least four occasions vanished over the years. Repeat prescriptions of Mometasone Furoate a steroid based nasal spray, saltwater rinses and other over the counter medications have not shifted it.

As I wear my mask daily the sinus pressure across my nose and cheeks has flared up meaning I am also feeling under the weather but also without my sense of smell. My test the day before was negative and this morning I decided to take a second test after the first was negative. Just to be sure given these bitches at work are positive for covid-19 and I'd spent hours within close proximity of them and the touch point/surfaces behind the bar. I guess I was being paranoid given I had been in close contact with Rudy & Emilio and Bobby was on my suspicious, but unconfirmed 'super spreader' list.

I took the second lateral flow test nine minutes after the first negative one and the faintest of very faint lines showed the second test was positive. Twelve minutes later I took a third lateral flow test, and this was clearly negative. Having marked the dates and times as I took each test on the lateral flow test itself, I took a photo for my records.

It has recently dominated the news how any test, but especially lateral flow tests can give false positive results on occasion. Exercising common sense, I believe as I took three lateral flow tests in a relative short space of time, conducting the tests as per the instructions. And in my view the second test out of three was a false positive. Having experienced a loss of smell with my sinusitis several times in the past and currently with swollen sinuses and a sinus headache and no other symptoms of covid-19 I again, exercising common sense determined my loss of smell was due to my sinusitis.

When I got into work today, I shared with Jack the three tests I had taken and showed him the photograph of all three tests lined up. He agreed, the positive test sandwiched between two negative tests and the line being faint was most likely a false positive. As Jack was a vaccinator, he was extremely worried that in work he would pick up covid-19 and didn't want to pass this to any individuals he vaccinated. So, for him to agree was reassuring to have that second opinion to ensure I too did the 'right thing'.

I was working a double shift today so had a 2-hour break between 3pm – 5pm and given the warm June weather I went home for a shower and a change of clothes.

While at home I did two more lateral flow tests, and both were negative. On my way back to work I stopped at Boots on Tottenham Court Road to collect two lateral flow kits, one for me and one for my imaginary flat mate as kits are restricted to one per person.

When I got back to work, bizarrely gossip had started that I was "positive" given Simon came and enquired "are you positive because they say you are"? I was blown away as my first thought was 'is Simon referring to my HIV' as the word 'Positive' or 'Poz' is commonly used on the scene as reference to PLWHIV. Realising he most likely meant was I positive for Covid-19 I replied confidently "nope"!

I wondered who "they" were when Simon asked if, I was positive. Jack was the only person I had shown the series of tests I had run this morning so any suspicion that I was positive for covid-19 could only have come from him. But given two colleagues alone, Rudy & Emilio had shared they were covid-19 positive, I felt maybe rumours were flying around and Simon only having started his shift with me at 5pm had got his wires crossed.

So, no surprise, I was again back working in the upstairs bar when I had a slight DeJa'Vu when I saw Adam storming towards me. With a masked face like thunder! He barked "why are you at work"!?

Adam and Jack had earlier remarked how it was unusual that a double shift was split with a 2-hour window, as it is usually only 1 hour. But I was appreciative of it as I was able to go home and shower as I am OCD when it comes to personal hygiene. So, unless Adam had, had a bump to the head he knew I was on a double shift. Therefore, I didn't fully understand his question nor appreciate his tone. "You what"? I said as I stood behind the bar wiping the till screen with a jay cloth and sanitiser. Adam pulled down his face mask, I thought 'oh must be serious' and he again barked "why are you at work"!?

I stood folding the jay cloth in my hand as I pondered wistfully, and Adam snapped "well"? as he stood at the customer side of the bar seemingly waiting for me to respond. "Hang on, hang on, I am trying to reach my spirit guide to rephrase your question as I have no idea what you're on about"!

"You're at work with a loss of smell"! Adam declared. I thought, blimey that got around quick. Within a split-second piecing together what Adam was getting at, he was assuming I have covid-19. Given he has apparently heard or been informed I have no sense of smell which is said to be a possible side effect of Covid-19. When I should be home isolating, although as the law stands, I am urged to do the 'right thing' and not legally bound to isolate unless told to do so by an NHS official or because of a positive PCR test.

I replied, "sinusitis doesn't warrant me to stay at home" to which he said, "loss of smell is covid-19."! I wasn't sure when Adam qualified as a doctor and had to bite my tongue in putting that to him. He seemed intent on being an arse and I didn't want to inflame the situation. I quite calmly said, "anosmia is caused by my chronic sinusitis. I have tested 5 times today and am covid-19 negative. But instead of bothering me, you might want to speak directly to the two bitches who have declared they are covid-19 positive and were in work yesterday and again today"!

Adam quite rightly asked "who are these people"? and I said "it is not my place to disclose their identity" and it wasn't. Just as it was nobodies place to share my personal health information. This got up Adam's nose, pun intended, and he pulled up his mask, the veins now clearly throbbing in his neck. And just like Mrs Trunchbull played by Pam Ferris in the film Matilda, Adam stormed off and bounced down the stairs to the main bar, and I knew what was coming.

I walked several meters to the end of the bar noticing the spirits in the optics crashing about like the waves of the ocean from Adam's vibrations across the wooden floor. I stood by the hatch and as I predicted, Jack came clomping up the stairs and across the floor towards me. The floor at the end of the bar is raised, so Jack leaned on the bar with both his palms looking down at me. "Will! Can you give me the names of those who tested positive"!

I understood what Jack was asking. And it was for the benefit and safety of customers and staff. But as the law stood, the company, nor Adam or Jack had the power to force Rudy or Emilio to isolate. And at the same time, I had no duty to share information regarding their health with anyone else, especially without their consent unless they were committing a crime of which they were not.

"Sorry Jack, it's not my place to say". Jack puffed up his tits and said, "so you're refusing to tell me who these people are"! I thought who does he think he is talking to? I replied "you know what? I really don't need this, I'm done, you can stick your job up your arse"! I walked from behind the bar towards Jack who was in my way, for me to collect my coat and bag from the staff room. "No Will! Wait, this is really selfish of me, but you will leave us in the shit" Jack pleaded.

I couldn't resist a giggle because the guy was being so honest, he wasn't bothered I'd walk out because I was a valued member of the 'team'. But it was a case he or Adam would have to jump in and help if they were a man down and I admired that level of honesty. But what Jack had done, was not to allow me to pass.

"Will, I don't think you understand how serious this is" Jack said as only a neurotic Jack would. And for Jack it was serious for him given he had expressed concern in picking up covid-19 at work and taking it to the vaccination centre. Where vulnerable people were still being called for their vaccination. But if Jack was that worried about taking covid-19 to the vaccination centre, surely, he'd restrict himself from the front line of the pub or reduce his hours if he wanted to be Florence Nightingale.

Jack was waffling on, and he got my attention when I heard him say "I don't think your taking Covid-19 seriously Will"!

I thought, 'you jumped up little shit'! As I have been known to say it as it is, I said, "look! I will tell you there is nobody in this building that takes Covid-19 more seriously than me. I have washed my hands after every customer interaction, every used glass I collect and after every table I wipe. Look, my knuckles are red raw and scabby, my hands are tough, dry, and flaky through excessive hand washing. I take a lateral flow test for Covid-19 every day before work, I have taken 5 today as I have been around others who have said they tested positive"!

Jack stood shuffling from one foot to the other foot, with his hands clasped in the prayer position attentively listening to my rant. His eyebrows occasionally moving as it seemed he was processing everything I was saying as I went on and on.

"And just to confirm that I am taking it all deadly serious, because I am HIV positive after being assaulted at the start of the Pandemic. I had a heart attack 8 months ago said to of been contributed by the HIV infection. And as for my loss of smell now, my swollen nose and cheek bones is as I shared with you earlier today my 'documented' chronic sinusitis. Brought on from excessive pressure when putting on or adjusting my mask by pressing it deep into my face to stop my glasses steaming up. So don't tell me I'm not taking it "seriously""!

I started to feel sorry for Jack, that I was chucking it all at him and to try and make light of my little speech I ended with, "and breath"!

Throughout me sharing the above with Jack, he kept saying "oh Will"! And I suspect not to be sympathetic, but he most likely felt embarrassed I was divulging so much. Which only came about through Adam's interrogation of me and seemingly sending Jack upstairs to further interrogate me for names.

In one way sharing my status to defend myself showed I was not only taking covid-19 seriously for the benefit of my colleagues and customers. I was in effect trying to highlight concerns of my own safety given I would be also putting myself at risk of covid-19 and possibly serious illness. While there is no clear evidence PLWHIV develop severe illness from Covid-19 living with HIV I am understandably a little nervous. Although my immune system is strong with a CD4 of 976 and I am undetectable while on treatment. My one pill a day is a means of getting out the house, being productive and just getting on with life.

A group of six gents came into the bar so I wiped the tears that had begun to well up in my eyes. Blowing up air from my mouth in the vein hope the well of tears would evaporate in a bid to be all butch clearly hadn't worked. I went and took their order "Six pints of Peroni fella" one of the gents said. Jack passing said "I'll come back to see you in a bit" as he clomped downstairs. I thought "yeah, run along and tell Adam to put that in his pipe and smoke it"!

I'M POSITIVE, I'M NEGATIVE

It was a few hours before I saw Jack again and I had been on my lunch break. On break I did another lateral flow test before eating my lunch which immediately turned negative. And the test was still negative at the end of my thirty-minute break.

Jack came upstairs and approached me behind the bar and asked "Will, are you ok"? Being the pragmatic person, I am I said "yeah". Jack seemed to be in 'counsellor mode' as this is an element of his current studies. He asked if I wanted to 'talk' and I suspected he meant about my traumatic event. I just said I was disappointed in how Adam approached me, which was aggressive and incoherent. But what I was really trying to allude to was, how Adam had come to find out I had lost my sense of smell? Jack was the only person I had told when asking him to look over my three tests earlier in the day.

Jack said in Adams defence "he was told that you are positive" to which I replied, "I am 'positive' but undetectable". Jack giggled and said, "no he was told you was Covid-19 positive because you had lost your sense of smell. I am sorry for how Adam handled it; he didn't handle it very well".

As we spoke and I guess Jack trying to be nice, he came across as apologising for Adam in one breath. But in another was defending Adam and how he had to act upon the information he had received. It felt as though I was still under suspicion, so I said "Ok, let's do a lateral flow test on me. I just did my sixth one for today just now on my break and it was negative. Let's do another"!

Jack naturally stated, "no Will! That won't be necessary, I believe you". And

I knew that in the workplace this was morally wrong, and I wouldn't be comfortable in Jacks position. However, I insisted by saying "no, let's do a lateral flow in your presence and then you will see I am covid-19 negative and there can never been any suspicion, accusations nor gossip". Jack asked, "are you sure"? Jack seemed keen to play scientist which I didn't take as Jack appeasing me, but that he knew it would help vindicate me which really showed there was an element of doubt in his mind to my covid status.

Jack went and got cover for me on the bar as I was working alone, and we both went upstairs to the office. I had collected my test kit I had picked up on the way into work and the negative lateral flow I had done on my lunch break marked with the date and time in biro.

Jack opened a lateral flow test kit he had in the office and laid it out. It was all quite clinical, and he asked if it all looked ok to which I agreed I was happy. He handed me the swab to which I asked if he wanted to take the sample and thankfully, he declined. As I went to stick the swab in my mouth, he turned away to give me some privacy. I said "Jack, you have to watch to ensure I take the sample correctly. That's the point and tell me if your happy or not before I proceed" and he agreed. Jack was happy with the throat and nasal swab, and I handed him the sample and he processed it in the solution.

As he did this, leaning over the worktop in front of me as I sat on the chair I said, "is this normal to stick your arse in your clients face"? He turned to look at me clearly shocked and worried. Realising I was taking the piss Jack giggled. Not that I was complaining, he has a nice arse, admired without it being sexually gratifying.

Jack poured the solution onto the test and said, "we need to give it fifteen minutes". This naturally led us to chat, and it started by Jack sharing he has lots of friends that are living with HIV. I thought 'this guy is smooth for a counsellor'! Jack mentioned he also knew the head clinician at my clinic which I confirmed was the doctor who oversees my care. Jack seemed knowledgeable about HIV, treatments, and U=U (Undetectable = Untransmissible) and it wasn't long before I got talking about how I became infected with HIV.

I shared that after splitting with my ex who was living with HIV. I had remained single for five years and had no sexual activity. Given I was working long hours as an operations Manager for a hotel I just didn't have the time, plus casual sex was not really part of my life once I turned twenty. Friends had said I could do with some "fun" as they felt I was overworked and just needed to get laid.

I downloaded the gay dating app, more famously known for casual sex, Grindr. I spoke to a faceless profile for a couple of hours before the guy invited himself over for some "fun". Having sent his face picture saying he had a girlfriend so had to be discreet. I agreed and gave my address and within 10 minutes he was ringing my doorbell and I had already decided I didn't want to go through with it. I contemplated not answering the door in the hope he would go away. I decided I'd be polite and just tell him I didn't want to proceed with anything more than perhaps a drink of which I intended to offer him.

Once I shared this with him, all I remember was falling backwards before waking up on the floor with a sore jaw, and him on top of me. As I was coming to, I saw the clock on my sideboard meaning I could only have been out a few minutes or so. He had penetrated me but seemed to be having trouble with his erection and couldn't get it back in as I was coming around. He said he had not ejaculated and told me I was disgusting, and I should get dressed as he'd pull off my joggers in the process. After he left, I sat up and realised I was laid in a pool of my own blood and my anus was throbbing. I staggered to the bathroom and my mouth was bleeding as he had bust a tooth where he had punched me in the face knocking me unconscious.

I tried to clean myself up as best I could and for some bizarre reason, I grabbed a bottle of silver tequila from my bar and poured this over my anus as I laid in the bathtub. Believing the alcohol element would perhaps clean my wound in the panic of being alone and not knowing what to do. I took myself to bed with a bath towel between my legs where I cried myself to sleep. The next morning, I woke, and I googled 56 dean street and by chance the first page I came to was for PeP (post-exposure prophylaxis for HIV) but I couldn't truly appreciate what PeP was or did. Although I had vaguely heard of a pill you should take after unprotected sex, I didn't fully comprehend that it was for HIV as I had not moved in circles of casual sex since PeP has been around.

I clicked off the website as I felt approaching the clinic would be too shameful. I instead ordered a STI test kit from Sexual Health London which I could do in my home and the results came back a week later as being positive for Gonorrhoea of the anus. I went to a clinic for treatment near Southwark and I explained how I had become infected with Gonorrhoea to the nurse. She was outraged slamming her desk, but when I asked if she could do a HIV test after seeing a HIV poster on the wall of her office. She said no as the result had come back negative on my SHL home test for HIV.

As a week had already passed and being too late for PeP I assume this is why she said come back in three months for a HIV test, it was already too late. She gave me an injection in the arse and said come back in 7 days once I had finished the antibiotics to treat the Gonorrhoea.

When I returned to the clinic the nurse just asked if I had seen any improvement to which I said I had. She said it would be faster given the covid-19 pandemic to order another SHL home test kit to test if the antibiotics had successfully cleared me of Gonorrhoea.

As I walked to the tube station to head home, I ordered another SHL home test kit and sent off the samples which were urine, blood and an oral and anal swab. I got a message saying SHL were processing my samples and then a few days later I got a text message asking me to call them about my results, and from that moment I knew.

I called Sexual Health London and once the representative pulled up my details, she became rude and arrogant, and the conversation went as follows:

SHL: When did you last do a test with us?

ME: About 2 weeks ago.

SHL: Ok, so why have you ordered and taken another? Because you only get financial allowance to do 1 test every 12 months!

ME: Because the nurse at the clinic said due to covid-19 that I should do a home test to check the Gonorrhoea has indeed gone.

SHL: Hmm. But I don't understand why you ordered a new test!

ME: Because the nurse told me to, do you have the result?

SHL: Yes, Gonorrhoea came back negative. But in future can you make sure that you only order the tests you need!

ME: I just ordered a home test kit, that's all that is available on your website.

SHL: Yes, well next time call us and tell us what test you need, and we can send it out. Ok!

She was then trying to terminate the call; the whole time I was thinking she hasn't mentioned HIV yet.

ME: And the HIV test? Do you have a result for that?

SHL: When did you last test for HIV?

ME: About 2 weeks ago, with a SHL test, it was negative.

SHL: Yes, I can see! So why did you do another HIV test?

ME: Because as I have said I just ordered the home test kit from your site as the nurse instructed me to and sent the samples back. The leaflet in the kit says if not all samples are sent then a kit may be rejected.

SHL: It came back reactive!

ME: What's that mean?

SHL: Reactive.

ME: What's that mean?

SHL: (Tuts and Sighs) The test showed antibodies for HIV.

I called Terrence Higgins Trust and spoke to a representative who was working from home. She was amazing, as she searched for a HIV clinic for me to take a confirmatory HIV test. She said HIV was no longer a death sentence and that I will live a long and normal life. From the call it sounded as though no confirmatory test was needed.

I asked if the test could be a false positive and she sympathetically said, "I could tell you that it may be a false positive, but if I am honest with you, it is most likely accurate but let's see". She gave me three clinics around the

Croydon and Bromley area, and I thought no, I am not going to any of them. So, I called 56 Dean Street and they told me to come in immediately.

I was quickly whisked into a room with a male nurse. I recognised him from a date we'd been on in 2012 in the new Stratford Olympic village. He was a lovely chap, but for me there was just no spark although he tried to convince me there was something there, something we could pursue. Fast forward eight years and here he was doing a confirmatory test on me for HIV. I am not sure if he recognised me, but it was all irrelevant.

A quick prick of the finger and no messing he turned and said, "that confirms it, I am sorry William". I said the first thing that came into my head and that was a Lady Bunny quote "I'm too fat to have AIDS". We both laughed, me through my tears. After a chat about medication, I was keen to start ASAP, so he called the head clinician who squeezed me in. I was booked in and started medication the next day which was the day that the first UK lockdown legally came into force. And here I was walking through Trafalgar Square with six months of medications which consisted of two tablets and my backpack suspiciously rattling like a pair of maracas as I walked down Whitehall passing patrolling police officers with firearms.

Jack listened to my story attentively, showing his reaction and emotions through his facial expressions. I said "right, is the test ready"?

Jack got out of his chair and looked at the result of the lateral flow test that was in front of me. "Negative" Jack said. I didn't want to gloat, but I just said, "I knew it would be". There was no question of the result given Jack had overlooked the testing process.

Jack asked, "would you like a hug" and I said, "no thanks" although I was dying to say, "yes please". But I felt I had already divulged so much to someone who was a work colleague, something I have never done in my working career of 23 years. And I was keen to get back to what I was being paid to do, work!

Jack popped out of the office, and I had a peak at the test just to make sure it was negative, and it was. He came back with what looked like a biohazard plastic bin liner for one lateral flow test to which I said jokingly "that's a bit excessive for HIV"! But Jack to the end wanted to ensure it was all very clinical, even the clean-up. I just hoped he showed Adam the result before chucking it away.

Before I went back upstairs Jack said he wanted to apologise on behalf of Adam and how he approached me. I said to Jack "I appreciate the gesture of apologising on behalf of your colleague, but if Adam feels I am due an apology after you share, I am covid-19 negative. Then he should have the balls to come and do it himself".

Jack said he would not share what I had told him, and I said I didn't think he would, oddly. I walked back down the stairs with mixed emotions, I felt vindicated from the whole Covid-19 fiasco, but I had now burdened Jack with keeping my secret of living with HIV.

TO ISOLATE OR NOT TO ISOLATE?

After the whole covid accusation Adam seems to of stopped speaking to me, either entirely or now and again he will choose when to exchange pleasantries. It's no skin off my nose, but I do find it all a little immature. I mean after all, I proved that I was not covid positive so if he was to be upset with someone, let it be with the source of his misleading information.

I had witnessed for myself that Adam had a vindictive streak in the way he either spoke or treated other colleagues. And I was now slowly starting to be treated with the same level of distain. I came on shift on a grey and overcast day and got changed into my work gear and headed downstairs. I greeted Adam and just got a grunt in return before he said, "your down here tonight"! Which meant I was doing table service. Simon was working behind the bar preparing the orders and I got to work delivering them and clearing tables.

Adam had issued earlier in the week a policy of how the pub was going to operate in a covid safe manner. This included having all the air conditioning units on. All four fans behind the bar to blow the customers covid away and all doors, except fire doors to remain open to allow for fresh air to circulate. Dressed in a grey ring spun t-shirt it was not even 10 minutes into my shift when I started to feel cold with the hairs on my arms standing on end as I walked around with goosebumps.

Adam was stood at the door, and I asked, "can I pop upstairs and put my hoodie on because I am frozen"? Without even looking at me he said firmly "no"! I thought maybe it was a joke and stood waiting for him to perhaps say 'course you can' but nothing followed.

It was a plain navy zip front hoodie that I'd often worn into work. Something not to overheat in yet to keep the chill off on the late-night walk home. I took this as Adam being a total bell end because I recall when getting the job looking at the pub's social media. Seeing staff in jumpers and hoodies that didn't show the pubs branding, one image that stuck out in my memory was an image of Blair in a hoodie.

Occasionally I had to venture to the upstairs bar when delivering orders customers placed on the mobile app where the receipt printed in the main downstairs bar. And even taking and delivering orders to customers sitting outside on Old Compton Street it was noticeable warmer upstairs and outside than it was in the main bar where I was spending most of my 8-hour shift.

Blair had just been promoted to team leader, how I wasn't sure. He is a complete wet fish and, in my opinion, hasn't got the skill nor personality to lead a team! Blair himself said he didn't apply for the role and was "just told" and apparently had no say in the matter. Need I say more?

Team leaders were technically 'supervisors' but were classed as part of the 'management team'. Something I had never come across in the hotel sector of hospitality. Where a "team leader" was merely expected to take on more responsibility with no or little extra pay under the guise of 'on the job training'. I shared with Blair "I am freezing! Adam said I am not allowed to put on a hoodie, but can I work upstairs instead where it is warmer"? Blair was reluctant to speak to Adam and said he wasn't sure. I said, "well can you go ask him please". And that he did as I gently placed my arm behind him and gave him a sense of the direction, he needed to head in. Adam glared at me across the floor from the main entrance where he was stood with his clipboard as the door host.

As Blair walked back towards me, I could tell by the way he contorted his face that the answer was no, and he confirmed as much when he said, "sorry Will! I tried".

With every order ready for delivery, I hoped it was for either upstairs or outside to warm myself up. It was bizarre that it was warmer outside, each time crossing the threshold of the pubs main entrance. Was like stepping off a plane in a warm far-flung country and being hit by that wall of heat. While I stood in the bar Blair crept up behind me and said "Will, your shivering" and I turned around and declared "surprise! Surprise! It's Cilla Black"!

As I finished clearing a table and taking the empty glasses to the end of the bar. Simon was working behind the bar preparing the orders and this was always his preferred role. As I returned to the bar with my jaycloth Simon was now stood on the outside of the bar next to Adam with a face like thunder. Simon said, "Will, do you want to work the bar"? He glared with his eyes intimating for me to say 'yes' as Adam stood beside him. I knew Simon had been pulled out from the bar and I knew that I would be colder given the bar had four fans on full speed directly above the bar to keep staff cool when the bar is at full capacity. The fans no doubt a welcome addition during 'normal times' when windows and doors are usually closed.

As Simon had asked me a closed-ended question I responded with "don't you want to work behind the bar Simon"? Simon again gestured with his eyes, intimating for me to get behind the bar and save myself the onslaught. But Adam sternly barked "just get behind the bar Will"! And I did. Within minutes I was shivering so hard it must have looked as though I was having a seizure to customers looking on. The more I tried to stop shivering to avoid it being noticed only made it worse. Behind my mask my nose started to run, and my teeth started to chatter uncontrollably.

It was immediately clear this was an intentional act by Adam, and I guess some would say harassment in the workplace. But this was the least of my worries as I started to feel concerned for my health. As a PLWHIV I was told that while my immune system was stronger than most people not living with HIV. That avoiding 'opportunist infections' was advisable. Infections such as cold and flu along with pneumonia and the like. I had received both the flu and pneumonia vaccines and common sense would dictate that keeping myself wrapped up and warm and not exposed to the elements was advisable if not preferable. But this proved difficult when someone is intent on being vindictive and malicious.

I tried to convince myself that I would be ok and to just get on with it. But I have to say a few times it became so unbearable I thought it was not worth the 'risk'. I should just tell them to stick their job and put my jacket on and go home. Nothing or no one was worth jeopardising my health for.

This brought back flashbacks to me looking up PeP after being sexually assaulted. Which led to me being infected with HIV and failing to listen to myself and subsequently doing more harm than good to my health. Just to clarify what I had said earlier, on the walk home I looked up the pubs social media and saw current team members at work, wearing hoodies, jumpers and jackets while carrying trays of drinks. So, what did Adam get out of denying me to stick on a layer when I said I was "freezing"?

My shift the following day with the weather pretty much the same, I came on shift wearing an open fronted plain hoodie and have worn it since without anybody batting an eye lid!

Last night while I was in the staff room on my lunch break Rudy came in and complained he was 'freezing' and said he was putting his hoodie on. His hoodie had a giant image of an Alsatian dog's head on the front and Adam didn't say a word. I was working the upstairs bar so was nice and snug. On the last orders bell, I turned up the lights and turned down the music to a conversable level. Kenzie was passing by as I started the clean down of the bar which I would have to do alone when the team downstairs would do the same level of work with around six of them to divide the chores.

Kenzie took exception to me turning up the lights and turning down the music slightly and shouted "erm, what do you think you're doing, you can't turn the lights up on the first bell"! I didn't take kindly to his tone and stated, "oh well, never mind".

Kenzie leaning over the bar trying to reach for the light dimmer switch said "you've only been here two minutes; this is not how we do things here! I'll tell Johnnie"! I wasn't afraid of his threat, as an operations manager in a hotel I was used to closing a hotel bar and functions of large numbers and merely remarked "ok cool" and off Kenzie went.

When I woke up this morning after my shift at work last night, I had a notification from the NHS Covid19 App. It was instructing me to self-isolate for 5 days stating I was a contact of someone who had tested positive.

I emailed work with a screenshot of the alert on my Covid-19 App. I also included the last 3 days of negative lateral flow tests and the corresponding NHS log of those tests with their unique identifying number. I also noted my temperature at work last night was ordinary at 34.3 degrees and that I had no symptoms of covid-19. I thought this alert must have been triggered by the Bluetooth element of the app on my mobile phone despite never using the app to check in anywhere as I didn't go anywhere other than work.

Then I got a call on the mobile from NHS test and trace saying they had been given my mobile from someone who tested positive for Covid-19. Nothing out of the ordinary you might think, but this was extremely suspicious.

Whenever I leave one job and search for another, I always use a new, secondary number by buying a cheap pay as you go sim. This second number goes on my CV and job applications. This stops cold callers offering me jobs in Dubai or China and the usual personal injury scammers on my main mobile number. This mobile NHS test and trace were calling me on was on my CV when I applied to the pub who then used it to add me to their WhatsApp group.

I didn't say anything to my boss when he added my secondary mobile to the group chat as this suited me well. That my personal mobile wasn't going to be bombarded with work chat which I absolutely hated. Therefore, the only people with access to this mobile number to pass to the NHS test and trace team, was those in the work group chat. As it could be seen when they looked up the members of the group chat.

So, it is clear it was not a covid positive customer I had been in close contact with, but a member of the team giving this mobile to the NHS. I didn't mind isolating as it was the right thing to do but as I had now been informed and received a letter from NHS test and trace, I was legally obligated to self-isolate.

I got a speedy response from Adam which read:

RE: Self Isolate – Covid App

"Hi Will, On Monday Carl sent a message to the work group chat explaining that you are still able to work in this situation. As you have mentioned, you have done daily lateral covid testing resulting in being negative and have no symptoms, so we are happy for you to work. If you would like me to forward the message again then please let me know. Adam".

There was a group chat message along those lines, so I telephoned the NHS test and trace helpline who confirmed what Adam had shared was not yet in effect until late July. And I was legally bound to stay home and isolate as I had been "instructed" to do so by NHS Test & Trace. Refusal to isolate would be me breaking the law.

The NHS reminded me that the letter they had issued instructing me to isolate at home had a unique reference number. My employer was invited to enter this number on the NHS website along with my full date of birth which would verify the letter was genuine.

I replied to Adam's email above reminding him I was legally obligated to stay home and isolate for five days. Five days was a long time to sit about indoors, but I first wanted to establish in the private group chat, who it was that tested positive for covid-19. By the end of the second day, not a single colleague had called in sick and not a single colleague was off work!

And apparently NHS test and trace had not contacted a single colleague to self-isolate as a contact like I had! None of this made sense! The individual who tested positive must have been instructed to self-isolate and were legally obligated to do so. And the same must be said for others who were 'contacts' as there is never less than 4 working a single shift.

Carl, the General Manager emailed me back and it seemed somewhat of a 'U-turn' compared to Adam's email previously. It was now the company's policy to respect NHS test and trace, which didn't carry much weight as it was 'the law' for me to obey the NHS test and trace instruction to isolate. However, Carl said I would receive statutory sick pay and he wished me well for the duration of my isolation of 5 days.

I wasn't sure if Adam was just ill informed or was somewhat peeved that I was what he perhaps perceived as me taking a holiday.

Being instructed to isolate by NHS Test & Trace they provided me with a unique reference (CTAS) number, and I was able to claim a one-off payment of £500 from my local authority. This was a simple process which saw this payment in my bank the following day. Meaning I was earning more per day than if I had worked, and I was to receive statutory sick pay on top.

I spent a large portion of my 5 days isolation job hunting given the way Adam was behaving. His behaviour didn't affect me too much nor did I spend much time thinking about it, but I just couldn't be bothered dealing with it. I am just way too old for this kind of immature bullshit! But I did conclude over my five days isolation that something dodgy was going on!

While I was away, they introduced a new guy to the group chat called Emre. I saw him interviewing with Adam last week in the upstairs bar as I was preparing to open. He looked incredibly young, a twink by all accounts. He gave Adam a run for his money given he was a very confident speaker albeit a little wet and naïve. Within the first few minutes my toes curled as I thought 'Adam won't like someone as young and confident as that' so I am very surprised he got the job. But then the company and management have expressed they are finding it hard to attract candidates to apply let alone hire.

THE BURNER PHONE

From the start of the covid-19 pandemic I avoided public transport completely. I wasn't scared of covid-19, but I guess it was just one step to mitigate catching the virus. Plus, I liked the exercise, especially on my arse and legs which some describe as my best feature. I had been released from my isolation and as I walked to work it was a lovely summers day and Old Compton Street was filled with the lunchtime hustle. There was a faint waft of salt and vinegar from the chippy, the smell of the Soho drains and cigarette smoke blown in my face as I squeezed past the gormless tourists. Tourists who'd seemingly come to gawp at the gays in their natural habitat as they looked puzzled at their paper maps of London before moving along.

I made my way up the fire escape to the upstairs bar and staff room where upon I opened the door and was hit by the warm musty spell of the beer-soaked carpet. Despite my sinuses still playing up I took a sharp, long inhale of the bar and said, 'by heck cock, it's good to be back'! Channeling Julie Goodyear as Bet obviously, minus the leopard print coat and heels. Instead sporting a baseball cap and flip flops!

Having got changed and tarting myself up I made my way from the staff room to the main bar downstairs. I bumped into Blair and Simon along the way who said it was great to see me back. Having to correct them that I didn't have Covid-19 but was a 'contact' allegedly. By the time I got to the main bar Bobby said he had missed me, and Johnnie screamed while simultaneously scanning the bar to see whose attention he was grabbing "oh here she is! The Covid Queen back from her holidays"!

I retorted "you know what! I had a lovely holiday; I was constantly kept posted that not a single bitch here has tested positive and had to isolate. So which bitch tested positive and told NHS test and trace that I was a 'contact', yet didn't isolate themselves"?

I had shared in the main work group chat that I had been given a payment from the government to isolate and highlighted this made me financially better off, which it did. I shared in a bid to encourage others to isolate if they test positive and for them to do the right thing without having to worry about finances.

Me and Johnnie stood outside on the door enjoying the sunshine like two tarts in an Amsterdam window. Johnnie asked me how I came to this theory, and I shared how the mobile number that NHS test and trace had called me on had only been shared on my CV. That in Carl's haste to add me to the group chat meant I didn't have time to give my main mobile number for work purposes.

Therefore, meaning it could only be a member of the team who had access to this mobile number to pass it to NHS test and trace. And for the NHS to call me instructing me to isolate stating I had been a contact of someone who tested positive. And who gave the NHS my number to call me.

He asked why I had a second mobile number to which I shared I always did this for job applications. To ensure my main, personal mobile was not bombarded with cold callers and spam. Blair came over and joined us, listening in before seeking clarification to which Johnnie quipped "she's got a burner phone"! Giggling, I said "yeah exactly, a burner phone"!

Keith came and joined the conversation where Johnnie shared my theory of being told to isolate as a covid contact as being malicious. Before Keith could comment on my theory, we were interrupted by Jack who was coming on shift. He only lived around the corner and rented a room with the landlady of the flat who was an elderly lady from Spain. Jack anxiously asked me "Will! Do I smell of garlic, sorry, do you mind"? As he leaned towards me pulling the neck of his t-shirt for me to sniff. "Afternoon Jack, nice to see you too, I had a lovely holiday thanks for asking" I said sarcastically.

I went in for a nosedive and he smelt, well, fresh. Jack flustered apologised and went on "oh I'm sorry Will. She is a nightmare; I took my clothes out of the washing machine and left them on the airer in the kitchen. She cooks everything in chilli and garlic and smokes like a train so all my clothes stink of garlic and smoke. I've put them back in the washer, but I needed a shirt for work". I gently took hold of Jack's wrist and said sympathetically "there is a number you can call if you or your washing are experiencing domestic abuse at home you know".

Jack replied sincerely "you know I did my Tarot cards…" to which Johnnie interrupted, "oh Jesus don't get her started on her crystals and tarot cards"! Having been interrupted Jack smiled awkwardly and went inside taking Johnnie's jibe as his cue to shut up. I felt incredibly sorry for Jack and wished he'd have hung around to give as good back. Jack can be just as shady and funny with it but he lacks confidence in his delivery.

Blair looking at me said "wow, do you think she's in danger"? Johnnie, cackling, asked "who? Jack or his landlady"? I interjected "were all in 'danger' now Blair's found his library card"! In reference to this shady side of Blair that I've noticed is slowly emerging since he's been up in the manager's office in his capacity as supervisor.

I went and introduced myself properly to Emre who seemed incredibly quiet and reserved, certainly not the confident guy I saw at the interview. He's been working here for a few days so maybe he is still settling in.

An hour later Adam came on shift and for me it seemed like a dark cloud came over Soho and like the sun, I wanted to hide. He was stood at the end of the bar when I enquired how he was. He didn't reply but instead bounced the question back to me. I was known to be upfront and honest so said I was bamboozled as to why I was the only one contacted by NHS test and trace and similarly the only one having had too self-isolate.

He mentioned he'd seen my message regarding financial support and said it was funny that I was financially better off isolating than working. Highlighting how little the company was paying in terms of my rate of pay. The conversation continued regarding the governments financial support and how it helped him through the national lockdown with the furlough scheme. We were clearly making conversation purely out of courtesy and just before it became awkward, I shiftily looked for a job to do and luckily spotted some empty glasses to collect and a table to sanitise. As I grabbed the sanitiser bottle and a cloth Adam shouted "Will! Get the condom buckets filled"!

We didn't have the usual, loose packets of condoms but I found these boxes that contained two condoms and two sachets of lube with some information on ways to prevent HIV. I topped up the buckets with about 150 of these condom boxes and Adam gave me a thumbs up from across the bar. It was great he was seemingly happy the job was done, and I smiled politely whilst saying "oh fuck off", to myself.

A few minutes later Johnnie and Blair were stood with Adam at the end of the bar and Adam asked me about the 'burner phone' and if what Johnnie had relayed was true. I briefly outlined how NHS test and trace had contacted me to ensure what Johnnie had shared was somewhat accurate. Adam agreed this was suspicious and along with Johnnie and Blair, between them speculated as to who would so something like that. They never did figure it out while I stood there, but then I didn't hang around too long.

Adam sent me upstairs to help Bobby on the bar as we got busy, and I remained with him for the rest of the night. Business did tail off towards closing time, but I knew Adam wouldn't come up as you were generally forgotten about upstairs plus it was an opportunity to stay out of Adam's way and enjoy the shift.

As we waited for the glass washer to drain Bobby took the rubbish downstairs. Once done I went down to see if downstairs needed any help and I set about vigorously wiping down the tables with sanitiser and blue roll. I thought I'd pick up a pack of those condoms to see what was inside. I was interested as they were heavily marketed with HIV prevention and was intrigued what advice people were being given. But both buckets were completely empty, but for a tomato sauce sachet from the chippy down the road. It had been there in the bottom of the bucket ever since I've worked here.

I was just as guilty, but wondered why nobody had removed it? I used to giggle at the prospect of someone drunk enough taking it home believing it was a sachet of lube, only to smoother their encounter with tomato sauce, heaven forbid the scene when the lights came on!

Tables cleaned and dragging my tired old carcass back up to the staff room to change I walked in on Bobby sat on the floor with his legs spread. A large pile of the condom boxes between his legs, he was opening the boxes and chucking the condoms in the bin but keeping the sachets of lube. Oddly my first question wasn't 'why'? But, 'how'? How did Bobby get that many packets upstairs without being seen? He wouldn't have got into trouble, but I reckon someone would have asked if he seriously needed that many boxes that looked more than a hundred. I thought it was a terrible waste of condoms, as we could have put them in the bucket as we usually did but I just grabbed my bag and got changed in the bar area in total darkness.

I cursed Bobby on the way home as it soon transpired as I walked up Charing Cross Road towards Centrepoint, I had put my sweater on back to front when getting changed in the dark. It was now chocking me, and the label was scratching my throat. Then, I'd only just turned onto New Oxford Street at the Centrepoint building when Adam posted a message in the group chat. It said something along the lines of 'when we close the upstairs bar can we make sure we turn off the tills!'

I had closed the upstairs bar and I remember saying to myself 'turn off the tills' of which you needed a special key to do so. I couldn't find the key before I seemingly got distracted and forgot to turn off the tills. I had no issue owning up, not to protect Bobby, but because it only showed how petty Adam was being. He'd obviously discovered the tills still switched on while doing a final sweep of the building. I am certain this task formed part of his duty and was for the purpose of rectifying something that, on this occasion had been forgotten. Plus, as Blair was shadowing Adam as part of his training, this only served as a good example of why they do the sweep of the building on locking up.

I replied in the group chat "sorry, that was me"! When I came on shift the next day, Blair approached me in a flap and said "I am so sorry Will! I told Adam not to post it in the group chat as it wasn't a big deal. But he was furious with you for leaving the tills on"! I knew Blair was being very disingenuous, I knew he didn't have the balls to say something like that to Adam. But I did believe Adam would have lost his shit at the tills being left on, especially because it was me.

In response to Blair I merely said, "I truly don't give a toss Blair, leaving the tills on is hardly a disciplinary matter! It says more about Adam and his management style, neither of which interest me"!

LAST FOUR DIGITS

Since being diagnosed with HIV my alarm has gone off at 9am everyday to serve as reminder to take my one pill a day to remain undetectable with the 'medisafe' app. I use the burner phone, as Johnnie dubbed it, as the alarm so that I can switch off my main mobile in a bid to prolong the life of the battery and general health of that device.

As I took my pill at the kitchen sink with a fresh glass of water, I noticed a message notification on WhatsApp. It could only be work so I opened it to see if it was a change of shift, staff shortage of perhaps Adam being sassy again. I noticed immediately that the sender showed as a UK mobile number meaning they were not in my contact list, and I could see the preview of the message started with "Hi Sweetie". Intrigued I opened the message that read:

"Hi Sweetie,

Just to let you know that I know you have AIDS!!! Don't think you'll be as popular once I tell the others so do us all a favour and fuck off!!! The guys are scared of covid so am sure they won't want to catch AIDS!!! BTW your *[Sic]* videos in the group chat are shit! Do yourself a favour and resign before you embassy *[sic]* yourself more. xxx".

My first thought was 'illiterate'! And from the excessive use of exclamation marks this person clearly felt they were in danger, or perhaps, drunk. As I popped the oranges into the squeezer and slid my glass down the worktop, I said to myself "for the love of Princess Di', we're not in Kensington anymore"!

I had already figured out this message could only be someone from work that had access to this mobile number. I noted the last four digits in my head and went to the work group chat and looked up the 'members' list. Scanning down the list none of the phone numbers on display matched with the last four digits.

During my recent covid 'contact' isolation, I did try remaining open minded that my mobile number could have been mixed up, but this could only have been true if someone had taken my mobile number from my CV from a recent application to pass to the NHS test and trace team. Or someone from work. There was no other rational explanation.

However, the message indicated that the 'sender' was a work colleague as they refer to my videos posted in the work group chat "your videos in the group chat are shit!" Was this message and my recent isolation connected? As I slurped my freshly squeezed orange juice from the glass as I sat tentatively on the edge of my red velvet cinema seat in my boxer shorts, staring at the message, I said to myself 'is this supposed to make me upset'?

The message was so incoherent, although the sender has stated what they wished me to do, "resign"! Well, it will take a bit more than a text message for me to resign, so that isn't going to happen. As for the remark about me having "AIDS", well that didn't affect me either as I don't have AIDS. Aged 38 and having every gay slur thrown at me by bullies since the age of nine this didn't even come close to bothering me at all. I did ask how the person found out about my HIV status and they clearly had because they were kind of on the right tracks in terms of me living with HIV. But what really bothered me was the method of communication. I have always been upfront and honest with people and have mastered the skill in being diplomatic. If only this person had, had the balls to come and share their knowledge or concern with me face to face. As for who the person was, yeah that did intrigue me, but ultimately, I truly couldn't care less. I asked my smart speaker to "play playlist one" and the first song that randomly played from the playlist was Tina Turners 'Goldeneye' which made me chuckle.

One name immediately came to mind as the possible sender although I had never met nor worked with the guy. The others called him 'Bagel Boy' and he works 2 hours a week on the day that I am always off. Colleagues from across the team had shared that he is somewhat irritated by my videos and is generally vile about me which with a roll of the eyes I'd say to colleagues 'oh please'! I didn't have time for either hearsay or the opinions of someone I'd never met! If anything, this message showed the senders own insecurities and disturbed state of mind. Colleagues alleged that Bagel Boy and Adam are extremely close because they both do drugs together, allegedly. I have to say the timing of such a message after Adam's little hissy fit in the group chat about me leaving the till switched on is perhaps an interesting clue.

I haven't asked what Bagel Boy's real name is as I don't really get into much conversation about him as I say, I never work with him. The others always have a lot to share which is always negative. They say he is a struggling actor, although someone did check out his social media. It turns out his alleged qualification in acting is that he spent a few months in NYC. Where he paid to attend an unaccredited 'acting school'. I guess it has become somewhat of a cliché when people with overinflated egos and dreams head to the 'big apple' in search of fame and fortune. Finding themselves slaving away in a restaurant to then hand over their hard earned spondulix to some unaccredited back street acting school.

Back in London he was now working in a bagel shop somewhere close to Soho hence why the others call him 'Bagel Boy' as a pejorative. In the private group chat, he is merely referenced as a bagel emoji when they are bitching about him. All colleagues could find on the internet of his alleged acting career was a single video of Bagel Boy performing in an amateur production of the 1966 musical Cabaret by Joe Masteroff. The boys then posted voice notes of their renditions of Willkommen stating it was hardly vocally challenging, even for them who couldn't sing, while I thought it was all a bit bitchy, I did agree they had a point.

Despite several members of the team sharing Bagel Boy's opinion of me at varying times, they contradicted themselves slightly given they said he didn't speak to them, but they were able to convey his negative opinions of me. They said he would either refuse to even acknowledge them when he came on shift, as they greeted him. Or he would sneer and look down his nose at them in contempt, very Kenneth Williams like by the way they would contort their face as they showed me.

But with all this, I needed proof before I could point the finger so, as you do, I turned to Google. A search in Google didn't yield any results that indicated who the sender was. I was faced with two pages of results where the previews of each result just showed row after row of mobile phone numbers. I didn't have the time to go through them all as I had to get ready for work.

As I walked into work with my cheesy pop paylist playing I had put the message to the back of my mind. After I changed and came down the main stairs of the pub to the main bar Jack was stood at the bottom of the stairs. He turned and upon seeing me put his hands in the prayer position, something he has been doing a lot lately. I thought 'Jesus, here we go again'! "Have a nice day" he said sweetly as he bowed his head, I smiled and said "have a nice day" in reply but didn't do the hand gesture as everyone else felt compelled to do so. Jack would always break out into a giggle which always left me bemused and I'd giggle back before looking at him oddly and continuing my journey. And by 'journey', I mean usually to the other side of the pub and not spiritually.

I found it all a little awkward and insincere as I knew it had some religious meaning although I had seen on the news Prince Charles has been doing it when greeting people as an alternative to a handshake given the pandemic and assumed Jack was doing the same.

Blair collared me and said while laughing, "what did you just say to Jack"? To which I replied jokingly "it's what he says to me, I've got a job to do I haven't got time for this 'have a nice day' bollocks!" Transpired Jack was saying "Namaste" a Hindu custom as a non-contact greeting.

I guess that's why Jack always broke out into giggles when I'd reply, "have a nice day". All these weeks I thought Jack was saying "have a nice day" to which I always, if not awkwardly replied with the same, but he never said anything to correct me. Anyhow I continued replying with "have a nice day" and eventually Jack stopped this customary greeting with all of us, I guess that journey had ended abruptly, or he perhaps just got bored, who knows.

Later in the shift it started to rain and despite the umbrellas out on the tables we had outside on Old Compton Street there were little too few customers. Jack and I stood on the door overlooking the tables that were being battered by the rain and we got onto the subject of HIV treatment, how I don't know.

Jack shared that he had friends living with HIV who, overtime had shared how effective the treatment was. This led onto my viral load (VL) which Jack recalled being in the millions when I shared my status with him a while back. My VL on diagnosis was 2.6 million after being infected with HIV 25 days earlier. As I started medication on day 26 post infection, within 4 weeks my VL dropped to 86 which meant I was undetectable given the power of modern medication. I remember the nurse ringing me and saying, "amazing news, your viral load is 86" and with my pen and paper in hand ready to log the result I replied, "ok cool, 86 thousand". The nurse laughed saying "no, just 86, isn't that amazing"!

When my clinician at Dean Street gave me my initial medication he said, "you're a poster boy for 'when', not 'if' a cure comes along". He was referring to starting treatment so early from being infected meaning the virus had little time to cause havoc with my immune system. But as I have come to learn living with HIV is, you don't spend time wishing or hoping for a cure, you live each day being truly thankfully you can live a normal life.

As me and Jack had this conversation about viral load, we were interrupted by two fellas who took a seat under an umbrella, and I went over and took their order.

I'd put the order in the till, and it printed a ticket behind the bar. I went out with the credit card machine already hitting the 'no' button as I always did when asking the customer "would you like to leave a gratuity"?

After confirming the amount due I left the machine with the customer to tap his card as another table had arrived. In a bid to be productive I went and took their order and went into the bar to enter the order into the till for the bar to prepare. I sent the payment to the same credit card machine I had left outside as my account showed the previous customer had successfully completed payment.

My intention was, as I had done many times before, to thank the previous customer for his payment while picking up the credit card machine, to click 'no' for the gratuity and present the machine to the new customer to pay.

How, I do not know, given it was only a short walk from the outside seating area to the bar inside the pub. But I found Jack outside with the two fellas I had served asking them to essentially pay again. I heard Jack saying, "no it is asking if you want to leave a gratuity, that means you haven't paid yet". The customer said he was sure he just paid but got his phone out to tap again to which I interrupted "No, Jack" to which I got a short shrift "Will"! And the palm of his hand in my face.

I thought 'oh, ok' and stood by as I knew I would be needed to explain. As the customer tapped, he said "oh the price is different" but he had by now tapped and paid. I politely enquired with Jack "may I speak? This customer has already paid, 'that' transaction was for this other table behind me". The customer then with his mobile showed Jack his notifications on his mobile phone of which he had used to pay showing he'd just paid for two rounds, at different prices.

Jack bolted upright and said aggressively "Will! Why would you do that, oh that is so…" and he stopped himself. I thought 'no, please continue don't stop on my account'. Jack apologised to the customer and said he would arrange an immediate refund which he did with the credit card machine before handing it to me to complete payment with the table it was intended for.

I left Jack at the door and instead came and stood inside making myself useful. I had come to learn that Jack had a short fuse and that he was aware of this and was trying to change or at least manage this side of himself. But all too often this side of Jack would manifest, and it wasn't pleasant. But we're all human.

I knew he was only trying to be helpful with collecting the credit card machine. But he seemingly had got into a confrontation with the customer over the machine still asking if the customer wanted to leave a gratuity. But what was disappointing was Jacks masculinity got in the way of allowing me to explain before insisting the customer make the payment again.

Jacks tone or attitude didn't bother me, nor his sly dig about me to the customer about staff knowing better than to be 'multi-tasking' with the credit card machine. But it was why he stopped seemingly berating me in front of the customer that bothered me. Was it because he knew he was overreacting, that to do so in front of the customers was poor management? Was it a working relationship or was it because I was living with HIV and he knew how I acquired it and the rough year I have had and he was taking pity on me?

Either way I thought I'd best stay out of his way and that I did. Not five minutes later he came in from the door of the pub and stood next to me on the floor of the bar. I was laughing to myself because it was like being back in school where if you fell out with a friend in the playground they'd come and stand by you in the hope that you'd speak to them.

"Have you seen Pose Will"? I wanted to say jokingly 'piss off, I'm in a mood' but even though I knew Jack knew my sense of humour I didn't want to offend him. I replied that I had not seen Pose. But had heard others talking about it

Jack was known for recommending TV shows and I'd taken him up on a couple. We would often share our views and opinions over text message. But I have to say either in a message or in person I'd often say to Jack "Jesus that's the last time I watch anything you recommend"!

Jack explained Pose was a drama highlighting the black American ballroom scene and where competing 'houses' compete against each other. With most of the series set during the 80's & 90's against the backdrop of the American AIDS pandemic. It didn't sound like something I would want to watch but after Russell T Davies 'It's a Sin' drama of the AIDS pandemic in London I felt it might be a bit too raw to be taking on another drama and I said maybe I would look it up sometime.

At the end of the shift, I went upstairs to help Rudy who had been working the bar alone and the night had been busy despite the rain. I came downstairs to collect the mop and I came down the pubs main staircase and Jack stopped me with "Will, have you seen 'It's a Sin' the piece by Russell T Davies about the AIDS pandemic during the 1980's"?

Knowing Jack as I do, I should have known better but being polite I said "Yes, I watched it twice" and I continued to pick up the mop that was sat waiting a few meters away. As I passed by again, he said "Will! Do you know the scene where the camera is panning through the nightclub, and it focuses on a few men kissing? Well, you know the part where Olly Alexander [Star of the show] is kissing on the dancefloor with a guy…" to which I replied, with beads of sweat rolling down my forehead, my feet throbbing, looking at the clock it had already gone midnight meaning we were on unpaid time and my colleague upstairs waiting for the mop to do the last job of the night I replied exhaustedly "can't say I do, no"!

"Well, that's him! Sat down there on the floor. What are you doing on the floor dear"? Jack inquisitively enquired.

I looked down and saw a disheveled twink sat on the floor who looked deathly thin and quite clearly out of it. Given the pub had long kicked out and we only swept and mopped behind the bar leaving the pub floor for the cleaner the floor was wet and sticky. As Jack was attending to him on the floor I turned and looked at Elias stood behind me who must have read my mind as he mouthed "that's Bagel Boy".

Considering my earlier suspicion over the malicious WhatsApp message and now having set eyes on 'bagel boy' for the first time I stepped over his legs as Jack was blocking my route back upstairs. I dragged the mop upstairs as it bounced off each step I climbed, glancing down, I whispered to myself "hold on tight bitches, its gunna be a bumpy ride"!

GIN, LIME & SODA

I had worked the upstairs bar and was cleaning clumps of hair and chewing gum from the filter of the glass washer as I closed. Johnnie screamed up the stairs for me to come down to the main bar. This was unprecedented as the upstairs bar was always an afterthought. They'd only remember you'd been on shift at all when you'd closed the bar and dragged your tired old carcass down with your coat and bag. Waiting to be released often met with "Oh Will. I forgot you were upstairs"!

I leant over the banister and shouted "what for? I'm elbow deep in hair extensions and whale fat"! Johnnie yelled back "there's a glass of Prosecco here for you dear"! I wasn't at all interested and politely declined. I didn't drink at work whether it was the end of shift or not. After Twenty-Three years in the hotel sector, which is very regimented. I'd learnt not to partake in such activities as they always had a way of coming back to bite you in the arse! Especially when someone is facing some form of disciplinary.

I heard Johnnie say to the others "she's turning her nose up at a free glass of Prosecco" to which Kenzie shouted up "it's from a regular customer, you won't know them, but they passed away from Covid-19. So, his partner bought all the staff that knew him a bottle of Prosecco to share"!

We only sell one type of Prosecco and five different Champagne, one champagne being a few quid more than the Prosecco. But I chose not to throw shade with a response as I walked back to the glass machine pulling a long hair from my fingers. It was a nice gesture and when I went downstairs with my bag and coat ready to be released home. I did thank Johnnie for inviting me but reminded him I never accept his offers of alcohol at the end of the shift saying I always opt for a Horlicks before bed. Boring I know, it wasn't true of course but was the easiest way to avoid having to join the others in helping themselves to the pubs stock. It always made me giggle on Thursdays when Adam would do stock take and then reprimanded us all in the group chat for spillages and wastage of lager and spirits assuming that's why he was missing stock.

Condescending as Adam is he would offer to show anyone who didn't know how to pour a pint, additional training. When in theory stock wouldn't be 'noticeably' down if managers and supervisors didn't encourage the team to help themselves to stock nightly. An average team would be nine guys a night, each with a pint, that's 63 pints a week on top of drip trays flooding due to fobbing. Not to mention the 'wastage' that goes unrecorded.

Given the nice weather that day I had dug out a pair of deck shoes I'd bought during the 2020 national lockdown and had only worn a handful of times. As I headed home mincing down Old Compton Street, I could feel the pain on my heels where the shoes had rubbed throughout the night. As I approached Foyles book shop on Charing Cross Road I thought I'll get the bus home instead of walking. I jumped on the number 19 Routemaster to Islington. As the driver closed the doors Kenzie knocked on the door and the driver let him on. He was about to head upstairs when he spotted me and did his usual, cringingly camp squeal and wave and sat facing me on the seat opposite at the back of the bus.

The bus had not turned onto New Oxford Street/Centrepoint when Kenzie asked "Will, can I ask? Do you find Jack attractive"? I guess it wasn't an unusual question as others had asked me the same before. But I didn't understand why it was such a pressing question for Kenzie to ask. "In what way attractive"? I asked inquisitively. Kenzie smirked "you know! Do you think he looks 'hot'"?

I have always been known if not admired for my honesty and I replied "Jack is not physically attractive, to me, no! But he is a nice guy and I do find some qualities of his personality attractive". And I was being sincere, Jack is not my type, and I was not attracted to him at all. Yes, he is handsome when he trimmed his beard and did something with his hair but, just wasn't my cup of tea in any physical or sexual sense. I do like elements of his personality; he will only share what he wants to share with you, and I guess he is slightly vulnerable but the more you talk to him he grows in confidence which I think is endearing.

"Oh my god I think he is hot"! Kenzie told the whole of the lower deck. Asking me why I didn't find Jack attractive, I played it down by saying "he just isn't my type". Kenzie's eyes looked sceptical at my response "come on! How can you not find him attractive, are you blind" Kenzie exclaimed! I didn't feel comfortable highlighting someone's flaws, but I could only speak honestly. "Well, for me, he is a handsome chap I can say that. But I just don't find him attractive. His nose is crooked, his facial hair is a mess. And as they say opposites attract, I prefer dark hair and eyes and as they say eyes are the soul of a person. But Jack is a really interesting person to talk to and I can have a decent conversation with him and for me that is a really 'attractive' quality for a 'friendship'".

Kenzie was still processing all that I had said before he said "Oh, I thought he was really hot until you said that. But he is boring, I have never in my life met someone as dull as Jack"!

Kenzie didn't quiz me about any other colleagues, and I did wonder why Kenzie had singled out Jack. I instantly thought perhaps Kenzie had seen me and Jack talking and was perhaps jealous. But I didn't think any more of it and Kenzie wittered on "I have management wrapped around my little finger"! Surprised, I asked "how's that then"?

"I have three daddies that pay me for cuddles and sex or buy me anything that I ask for. It's more profitable than work so when my 'Daddy' calls, I just tell Carl I have to go home because I am having a panic attack" Kenzie said. Intrigued, as I pinched myself given, I am sitting on the number 19 bus with a rent boy I asked how often Kenzie does this. He said excitedly, "all the time, it's easy to fake a panic attack and they can't tell if its real or not".

I was so embarrassed as Kenzie was proudly sharing his manipulative behaviour. With a couple of the passengers in front of us turning to put a face to the voice. Which upon turning they only saw my masked face and the back of Kenzie's head leaving them unsure as to who was making what statements. Thank goodness mask wearing is still mandatory on public transport paired with my baseball cap I was pretty much incognito, still I found it all so fascinating if not somewhat dreary.

I quickly changed the subject to the porn star that the team were drooling over that had apparently been in the bar that night. Kenzie's eyes lit up above his face mask which was covering his lower face. He became tongue tied in his rush to share that this porn star, unknown to me, asked Kenzie to be in one of his videos. I didn't mention that both Bobby and Rudy had stated the same to me, I didn't want to be a total bitch and ruin Kenzie's moment, although I was dying to.

He proceeded to show me photos of this unknown porn star, who apparently while in the pub changed his outfit three times in the gents' toilets. Kenzie fell silent and said he was getting off a stop earlier to walk home which was a great relief for me. I did the same when I approached my stop, just to avoid being recognised by anyone on the bus at a later date. Unlikely, but I wasn't taking any chances!

A few days later I arrived at work and Johnnie said I was working the upstairs bar which wasn't unusual. Afterall that's how I was named Anne [Anne Frank] "always up in the attic". I arrived upstairs and as the first customers arrived, they were all dressed in black suits, and I thought to myself 'who's died'? To which a glum looking regular came to the bar and asked if the 12 bottles of prosecco and 70 glasses were ready? I said, "I have just arrived, let me just follow up with the manager"?

I privately messaged Johnnie who was downstairs, and he confirmed it was the wake of the regular who had passed away recently. My first thought was, given Kenzie's diatribe the other night when they were throwing Prosecco down their throats, 'why is none of the nine, long serving, team members downstairs not working the event if this regular meant so much to them'?

My second thought was 'where are these 12 bottles of Prosecco and, do we even have 70 champagne flutes'? Johnnie was no help. He stated they had pre-ordered 5 bottles of Prosecco but even they were not ready. I rushed around trying to find 12 ice buckets and filling them with ice, 12 bottles of cold Prosecco and 70 champagne flutes. I found the flutes, but I was absolutely embarrassed at how water stained they were and of varying sizes, they looked horrendous! I wanted the ground to swallow me up!

As I dashed around it seemed I was the only person in the pub who cared that this pre-booked event went smoothly. Others seemingly avoiding me to avoid having to assist. I was running between three floors including the cellar, and on my way back up I counted nine members of staff including the general manager, Carl at the main bar. One was serving a customer, the other eight were all stood outside the bar seemingly talking and showing off their dance moves. I thought 'are these arseholes taking the piss'! As I refilled the ice box, I heard the fire exit door open and turned to see Kenzie with a receipt in his hand. "We aren't doing web orders downstairs because we refuse to run up and down the stairs, so you have to do it"!

I glanced down at the ticket Kenzie had slapped on the bar as I held the ice box with ice. The ticket had the following drinks, a Gin, Lime & Soda, a London Pride and Pravha, the latter two were only available on draught from the downstairs bar where Kenzie had just come from. Kenzie had spouted he had worked at the pub for 'years' so to come upstairs with a ticket knowing I'd only have to go downstairs for two of the three drinks while in the midst of managing a large function alone that nobody prepared for! I said, "you have come up without the 2 drinks that are only available downstairs"? To which Kenzie smirked and said "are you deaf? We're not doing web orders downstairs so deal with it" to which I replied "I have just seen 8 of you stood around dancing and talking…" but Kenzie stormed off slamming the fire exit door behind him making some of the funeral party jump.

My twenty-three years in the hotel sector as an operations manager where I had vast banqueting experience, I just cracked on with it. I set up the glasses along the bar, turning off the lamps on the bar to reduce the visibility of the grubby and water-stained glasses. This was an arrival drink, so I didn't have time to put them through the glass washer and for them to cool so I went with it as the toes in my shoes curled.

When the arrival drinks were poured and the Prosecco buckets and glasses were on the individual tables, I dropped a short note in the group chat. Sharing my dismay at the lack of teamwork and maturity shown when I had witnessed eight of the nine colleagues stood around doing nothing downstairs. I wrote

"I have to say while I am serving a funeral party of 74+, that a member of the team slapped a web ticket on the bar and stated, "we don't want to be coming up and down the stairs" and when I came down to get ice buckets and ice for the event, eight of the 9 on shift were stood at the end of the bar chatting and bopping. I have to say I find this so disrespectful, and it needs to be addressed"

Kenzie replied almost instantly, although I didn't see his response until later when I had time to take a breather. Within minutes of me dropping the message in the group chat Johnnie came up to apologise saying "ignore the bullshit in the group chat, you and I know you shouldn't be managing a funeral on your own. Let me know who you want me to send up to help you and believe me the matter will be addressed"! I had not read the "bullshit" Johnnie referred as I cracked on with the function who had now asked for me to pour 80 tequila shots. I said to Johnnie "send Kenzie up to help" to which Johnnie laughed nervously and said, "fuck off, really"? and I said "nah. Bobby if he fancies it"?

Both Rudy and Bobby came up to serve behind the bar as the floor was packed with mourners. Bobby seemed hyped up by Kenzie's response although I had still not seen it. Bobby yelled as he sashayed behind the bar "Oh gurl…. Have you seen the drama in the group chat? Don't open it now, you will hit the roof"!

After I had got the bar straight, and the mourners were all watered I took a snap of Rudy & Boddy serving behind the bar and posted the photo in the group chat with the caption '#Teamwork'. It was perhaps stoking the flames, but I felt it needed to be shared.

Kenzie had retorted to my initial message "so busy you found the time to write a whole paragraph about it, it seems". I merely rolled my eyes, smirking given his response was somewhat of an oxymoron, written by a moron, clearly! Talking of morons, Bagel boy quoted Kenzie's statement by replying "well said girlfriend"!

Rudy & Bobby left me a couple of hours later as some mourners left, and the bar was straight to manage alone. I poured 60 more tequila shots and 60 single Gin, Lime & Soda as the deceased favourite drink to toast his memory and the night was soon over. The regular who organised the event came to pay his tab at the end of the night which just fell short of £700 for drinks.

I went through his tab highlighting I had removed a couple of bottles of unopened Prosecco and after he paid, I printed his receipt and had to dash downstairs to collect it. As you can imagine the receipt was exceptionally long and I found Kenzie holding the receipt looking shocked as it was still spewing out from the machine. He declared "I wondered if the till had crashed" as Rudy half-heartedly pushed the grey mop around Kenzie's feet.

When Kenzie said he realised it was a receipt, he said he was astonished at how long it was and how much they had spent. He handed me the receipt and I said disappointingly, "just short of £700".

As I walked back upstairs folding the receipt to give the customer, I thought I hope Kenzie thinks on, at how busy I had been and for the most part working alone while he and others had the option of standing idle or able to take time out as they covered each other. While I had a funeral party and 'their' regular customers to serve and seemingly web orders to fulfil!

Johnnie came to collect the till cash drawer given we had closed and the regular handed me four £50 notes and said "Will, you have been amazing tonight, that is for you, put that in your pocket"! He was sober but emotional. I was not a fan of 'tips' and I stated it was very generous but far too generous and before I could hand the money back Johnnie snatched it out of my hands. The customer said "Will, make sure that goes in your pocket" before he handed Johnnie a £50 note for himself.

I was so embarrassed; I didn't care for the tip and management knew I had no interest in tips, but the greed of Johnnie was what embarrassed me. As we waited downstairs to be given the usual all clear to go home Kenzie shouted "Will! The customer bought us shots for looking after his event, do you want one" to which I politely declined. I couldn't believe what I was hearing, how did they have the gall, especially Kenzie?

Johnnie then appeared and having collected £250 as a cash tip from the funeral party I was handed a £10 note and all nine of my other colleagues were also given a note. I wasn't sure how this was calculated and was also astounded why it was divided by all 10 colleagues? In my twenty-three years of dishing out tips it is usually for those both front and back of house who assisted in an event.

Given nothing was ready on arrival, nobody had done anything back of house. And as for front of house, this would have been me, Bobby & Rudy as we were the only three that served at the event. Even if Johnnie did not add his £50 and only divided the £200, that I had initially been given, this meant £200 divided by 9 colleagues was £22 each so not sure why I was only handed a £10 note and didn't see what the others received.

It was not the money that stuck in my throat that had been snatched out of my hand. It was the principal that the gesture was that of a grieving customer who was truly happy with 'my' service. As soon as I left work, I handed my £10 to the first homeless person I stumbled across and felt relieved that I had taken no part in something that felt seedy if not underhand.

Johnnie shared that Carl the General Manager had told Kenzie his actions with the web order ticket were "not acceptable" and "he was out of order". I didn't care much for the details, but I did wonder from what Kenzie recently told me about his alleged panic attacks. Would management not query, if you know you've acted like a moron and your manager has pulled you up on it before the end of the shift and you've to face the person you've had a spat with so publicly in the group chat. Would that not bring on one of those spontaneous panic attacks?

"WE CALL HER BUBBLES, EVERYBODY DOES"!

You do get some characters that come into the pub and most noticeably the regulars that, can be somewhat entertaining although the vast majority are just annoying.

The old boys that you'd perhaps expect to be sweet, charming old fellas are anything but! They totter in, in their cream leather jackets, rolled up stonewash denim jeans paired with shiny black moccasin shoes with white socks and a grey pigeon combover.

They are generally just vile bitter old queens who are intent on being rude, belligerent, and plain arrogant. You do wonder if there is perhaps justification for this behaviour, which of course there is not. You can't excuse basic manners and common courtesy towards others just because they state they had to fight for the freedom to be openly gay. There is no escaping LGBT history and for most we are aware of the fight that sadly had to be fought. They often remark that they feel the younger generation take for granted their right to be who they are today. If I, or others try and give balance to their views and opinions you are always shot down in flames. So, we all try engaging as little as possible which is an incredible shame.

It is sad to see time after time that the old boys often spend their time in the pub sat by themselves nursing their drink. You can't help but wonder if they have perhaps alienated themselves by not embracing the evolving principles of gay life, built on the very foundations they laid.

The worst one I encounter daily is Ron, who the team call 'Randy Ron'. You know, the one with the skin condition I said looks as though he's been rolled in porridge oats. A stunty little creature that slithers around the pub holding a Peroni always on the prowl for fresh meat. He was a nightmare when we had to follow covid-19 regulations and customers had to remain seated while we offered table service. Most customers both old and new were sympathetic to the regulations and were just happy to be out of the house and back in the pub. Randy Ron, however, wasn't having any of it and he didn't hold back in letting you know.

Most regulars would book seats to avoid disappointment and others were happy to grab whatever seat was available or wait for one to become vacant. Randy Ron would always turn up and expect to be shown in like some V.I.P. and we'd go out of our way to shuffle a few customers around to make room for him. Although no matter how accommodating we are, he will always complain "nobody can see me here"! It was always on the tip of my tongue to say, "even goldilocks and the three bears wouldn't touch you with a teaspoon you silly old bitch"! But of course, you had to smile through gritted teeth, and he'd still protest "I want to sit over there where I can be seen"!

I recall one time he wasn't happy about me being unable to relocate him from the upstairs bar to downstairs which was a lot cruisier. He ordered another drink, and I went over with his Peroni and the credit card machine. He'd already told me I was boring him when explaining the pub was following UK government regulations on reopening hospitality. He told me for the fourth time that he was bored of sitting upstairs to which I merely replied, "and I am bored of you telling me, your bored"! He then told me to "shut up" when I tried to tell him that tapping his freedom pass would not pay for his drink, nor would inserting his freedom pass into the credit card machine.

I went off to serve other customers waving at me leaving Randy Ron with the credit card machine, now trying to enter his pin. When I returned, he stated "it didn't go through, your machine is broken"! He always asked for a receipt, would look at it and scrunch it up and throw it on the floor. I assume wanting to read the name of the person he had been served by which was displayed on the receipt. I returned with his receipt, and he snatched it out of my hand and said, "I'm off downstairs you're boring me" before he slithered away as I whispered under my breath "mind the stairs, you silly old bitch"!

A few minutes later a lady came up the stairs, looking behind her all concerned as she reached the top. She shouted across the bar "there is a man who appears lost on the stairs". I walked over to have a butchers and as I did I said "dear! They're all lost soles in here, it's like Shady Pines"! Ron was stood on the staircase scanning the main bar for fresh meat, or perhaps somewhere to sit and I left him to it.

Randy Ron was a different person when he was drunk. He would slither around smiling awkwardly at folk including me. When he ordered he was so polite and I wondered if the 'vile old queen' act, was just that? Something he couldn't maintain once drunk, and his inhibitions were out the window. And he seemed to pick up trade the drunker he got. I did once step in when I observed a shady looking guy persistently trying to take Randy Ron out of the pub, seemingly against his will. I suspected he was maybe wanting to get Ron outside to rob him or maybe take him home for something more sinister. I couldn't stand the guy but couldn't see him being taken advantage of or come to any harm so stepped in and asked the guy to leave. Ron never thanked me for it and by the time I walked back behind the bar Randy Ron had spotted fresh meat and slithered past the bar grinning.

One customer I really warmed to is a larger queen in his thirties that comes in wearing a pink gilet and the tiniest of tiny shorts. With tattoos up her legs and usually a pair of casual pumps on she will balance herself precariously on a stool sort of, side saddle. She sits holding a glass of Rosé wine up in the air with her elbow resting on the bar. She will glance at passing customers and often give them a disapproving look in a bid to get their attention. Then rapidly turns her head to look in the opposite direction scanning for a hot-blooded male.

In her other hand she holds her mobile phone, connected via Bluetooth to her headphones as she always listens to her own music. Occasionally skipping and searching for tunes she can lip sync to before she starts screeching after a couple more Rosé's. We always play music at a decent volume, but regardless of it either being our own playlist or a DJ she will always have her headphones on. The more drunk she gets the louder she sings completely out of tune as she looks around to see if anyone has noticed her before she acts all coy.

Her quirkiness didn't end there! When she arrives in the afternoon, she'll spend a couple of hours playing the piano to the amusement of the customers. We haven't got a piano in the pub, it's an invisible one that only she can hear through her headphones. She was once sat in the window looking onto Old Compton Street with customers waiting for available seats during the covid-19 restrictions. As the queue grew longer outside in front of the window, she got my attention when passing. Pulling her headphones off just the one ear she said "darling! Can you find me at seat out of the window as people are looking at me as if I am crazy"!

I could see from her tattoos she was very musical, so she was playing her piano to practice finger movements. It wasn't the fact she was crazy, just a little eccentric maybe.

As I got to see she was a regular at the pub, whenever she was playing the piano and I'd be walking past with a drinks tray, I'd stop and mime turning the page of her invisible sheet music. The first time I did it she paused, scowled at me before turning back the invisible page. Which, I took to mean she liked the attention, so I did it at least once each time she was in and tinkling her ivories.

Jack said to me on the door one day "I see you've met Bubbles" to which I looked at Jack confused and asked "Bubbles"?

"Yeah, on the piano" Jack stated as he nodded in her direction. "We call her Bubbles DeVere, you know from Little Britain. Because of her mannerisms and voice" Jack continued with a cheeky giggle. I said I wondered if she had a musical background given the tattoos and the playing of the invisible piano. Or was it perhaps some sort of coping mechanism until the Rosé wine takes hold and she becomes liberated vying for trade?

One shift when it was table service, Miss DeVere as I now discovered she was affectionately known beckoned me over. "Darling! Can you get me a 'cheeky Vimto'"? So, I went to the bar and said to Johnnie "Bubbles is asking for a cheeky Vimto" and given she was known as a regular I guessed Johnnie would know what that was because I had no idea. Johnnie said, "she knows we don't sell WKD anymore, tell her with have Smirnoff ice left". So, I went back, and Miss DeVere seemed put out I was returning empty handed. She again removed only the one side of her headphones to hear what I had to say. She replied, "yes darling I'll have it with Smirnoff and bring me a large Rosé wine" and as I walked away, she shouted "and darling! Don't turn off the tip, I always give a tip"! It was clear how she got the name Bubbles

DeVere, and she had rumbled me for turning off the tip which I do with everybody.

On returning with the credit card machine and her large Rosé wine I got into general conversation with her. It was a mixture of intrigue and pure nosiness, but I asked if she played the piano and to which she said she has a major in piano and was a piano teacher. She plays the piano in theatreland in and around Soho. She said, "darling! You must think I am crazy playing my piano in the bar but it's good to practice my finger movements". Well, customers did often remark if she was ok when playing her piano. I didn't share this with her and said "no! It's fascinating, but how do you know when you've hit the wrong note when your practicing"? It was a genuine question mixed with a tinge of sarcasm to which she replied "darling! I never hit the wrong note"!

Miss DeVere also has a major in French horn and told me she did cocaine but didn't have any with her today and that I could check her bag to which laughing, I declined. She told me she came from money and that she gets offended when I remove the tip feature to which I said I don't do tips so do it with everyone, not just her. She raised her eyebrow as I'd seemingly insulted her as she slid just the one headphone back up against her ear. My private audience with Bubbles had come to an end.

But most importantly I found out Miss DeVere's real name is JJ [John James] of which I was keen to tell the others because although calling JJ by the pronoun 'she/her' affectionately, as gays of a certain generations did and still do as a way of being affectionately camp. I felt it was only right that we at least acknowledged him as JJ in the first instance.

When I shared with Jack and Blair, this insight into JJ and his background they both said I had taken away the mystique of this fabulously eccentric character although she continually keeps us entertained whenever, she comes in.

Once covid-19 regulations eased in pubs and customers could move and sit where they liked I was working as the host on the door as we still had people booking as we were just so busy all the time. Miss DeVere was sat behind me, well, perched on a stool at the bar in those tiny white tennis shorts that left absolutely nothing to the imagination.

A guy sat outside caught my attention as he was back and forth to the toilet regularly. I thought he is either cruising or possibly dealing drugs so followed him in and he was stood at the urinal having a leak so assume he just had a rather weak bladder or an STD.

Three times he passed me on the door and each time I saw him pinch the protruding derriere of Miss DeVere given she was precariously perched on the edge of the stool as she is accustomed to. The first two times she seemed to enjoy being molested given the cheeky smile she had on her face as she watched him walk on in front of her. The third time he passed and pinched her bum she turned to see who else had noticed no doubt to revel in the attention and she saw me watching as I stood only a few meters away. Her cheeky smile turned into immediate shock and disgust, and as she pulled down only the one headphone off her ear she protested "if he does that to me again…"! I walked over slightly confused but felt perhaps she may have been laughing it off previously and perhaps was genuinely upset by it so thought I'd enquire.

"I saw that, are you ok"? I asked her. "Darling! He keeps pinching my bum every time he walks past, and I don't know why! It's not on, I'm not having it"! She said all in a fluster and seemed genuinely upset. I was concerned and said, "Ok do you want me to have a polite, quite word with him when he comes back outside, because it's not a problem".

All bashful and coy she said "no darling! No, it's ok, I quite like it, I don't mind"! To which I giggled and walked back to my position at the door realising that she perhaps enjoyed the attention, including that I had noticed the attention she was getting. Although, I suspect the chap was doing it as a bit of banter as opposed to intimating any interest beyond that. But I was pleased I double checked Miss DeVere was ok.

Many regulars shared that they either met or at least came on a date with a partner to the Pub. While working in the upstairs bar I was having a general conversation with two customers who had been together in 1997. They'd seen each other in the pub regularly and eventually became a couple. They were asking me if they were still classed as 'ex's' given they both now had new partners after splitting up. Quite a dull conversation really but I had nothing else to be getting on with as it was still early evening. Upstairs only really got busy when there is no space downstairs where customers preferred to hang out. Kenzie was passing by and one of them commented that he had 'rather a lot of flesh' on show. I guess this was either the shorts Kenzie was wearing or maybe that he had customised his t-shirt by cutting it into a crop top which only served to expose his love handles, but I admired his confidence.

I switched off slightly as Kenzie 'acted' all coy while he lapped up the attention which made me cringe. One of the customers asked, "does Andy still work here"? Andy was the previous general manager and had left a few years back although many customers always asked after him. When Kenzie shared that Andy had left a few years ago and we now had a new manager, Carl, the customer said, "hmm Andy had the 'Bumpety Bumps' didn't he"? I looked at Kenzie and he looked at me and I said "oh, what's that"?

The customer replied, "that's what we call HIV in the medical profession, Bumpety Bumps". Kenzie looking puzzled said to the customer "wait! Andy is HIV positive"? When the customer confirmed Andy is living with HIV, Kenzie responded with "eww" before walking off.

I found Kenzie's response to someone else having HIV as bizarre given Kenzie's self-proclaimed sexual health history which only falls short of HIV if were honest, is off the scale. I have only been working at the pub for a short period compared to Kenzie and although I have never met this, Andy. Many customers had enquired after him and had also shared Andy was living with HIV. I felt Kenzie's response to learning that Andy the former manager was living with HIV to be incredibly disingenuous. It seemed Kenzie was using the moment to be malicious, which got me thinking given the recent malicious 'AIDS' messages that I had received.

As I walked back behind the bar, I thought, 'what would Jessica Fletcher do' with this insightful piece of information? Moments later I was welling up with tears as I stood leaning against the back of the bar. A remix version of 'It's a Sin' by the Pet Shop Boys was playing. I have been streaming Russell T Davies 'It's a Sin' soundtrack so the track was ever more poignant as I recalled his recent TV series. Combined with Kenzie's reaction I just witnessed it hit home just how stigma around HIV can easily be used as a weapon. I wasn't 'welling up' with sadness, but motivated and empowered given I clearly had a fight on my hands, not just with this silly message but perhaps for the rest of my life.

IT'S ONLY HIS SECOND SHIFT

Information and treatment for HIV today in 2021 has come a long way. Compared to the understandable fear and panic of the AIDS pandemic of the 1980's & 90's. No longer is a HIV diagnosis a death sentence, but many PLWHIV use the phrase "HIV is a life sentence, not a death sentence". Referring to the medication they must take for the remainder of their life, which for many PLWHIV it is a single tablet or a combination of two or three tablets per day. But taking medication for the rest of your time on earth is nothing compared to those individuals that had no access to effective medication and no hope of a 'life' at all.

I've read stories of those diagnosed with HIV/AIDS back in the 1980's took it upon themselves to go to such extremes as drinking battery acid. Or consuming copious amounts of oranges believing these were beneficial in eliminating the virus. And I am sure we are all aware of the stigma that surrounded those suffering with HIV/AIDS. Princess Diana famously held the hands of patients suffering with AIDS in a bid to dispel fear if not the belief, that you could contract the virus through mere touch alone.

Being part of the 'gay community' and before coming of age being on the London gay scene. I was made aware of the precautions to prevent myself catching HIV which really was education and condoms. I remember charities such as THT (Terrence Higgins Trust) and venues themselves such as G-A-Y Astoria & Heaven handing out bags with their promotional flyers. Inside these bags you'd find condoms and HIV literature.

Guys I always met took precaution before having to insist. It was never a discussion and more routine to protect yourself and the other person. And although I wasn't living with HIV, I don't recall much stigma on the scene, even as a HIV negative person. I didn't witness much talk nor concern of

HIV around the late 1990's and early 00's.

In 2015 I met my boyfriend of two years who was living with HIV and when he shared his status after we had dated a few times, I had some knowledge of HIV from what I had learnt on the scene. And with a little further reading I was able to understand that his medication meant he was U=U (Undetectable = Untransmissible). This meant the amount of virus known as viral load, was so low that he could not pass the virus on through unprotected sex. Undetectable is reached when a viral load is under 200 copies per milliliter. In my ex's case he was and still is below 5 copies per milliliter and me and my clinic measure to below 20.

Then there was PEP (Post-Exposure Prophylaxis) a drug taken up to 72 hours after possible HIV exposure which 'could' stop the virus taking hold. There is now a new kid on the block in the form of PrEP (Pre-Exposure Prophylaxis) which is freely available on the NHS across the UK and highly effective in stopping HIV transmission. 56 Dean Street clinic is running a campaign on PrEP to raise awareness this summer. Carl posted a message in the group chat with a photo of the t-shirts available to promote PrEP.

"We've got some gorgeous fitting shirts that I want you to wear instead of your usual uniform! They are to advertise PrEP".

The t-shirts were black. I wasn't sure if this was an intentional choice of colour by the marketing team. Perhaps believing hospitality staff wore black in a bid to hide a range stains/spills obtained in the line of duty. But for me, the colour choice signalled death and wasn't a wise choice in my opinion. Especially as the boys sucking off customers in the toilets meant it would be inevitable the odd snail track would be accidentally left on their t-shirt! Although black, as it is known is very slimming even on Carl, who has a belly that makes him look like he's in his third trimester.

Carl quickly shared an image of him wearing one of the t-shirts in the group chat and I wasn't sure if this was a genuine sentiment or was just going through the motions. Nothing about the post seemed sincere to me. But then I questioned if I was thinking rationally, and I sat down with a cuppa before I got ready for my shift that afternoon. PrEP really is a game changer in stopping HIV transmission, especially within the gay community which is very promiscuous when it comes to sex. And I did read an article about PrEP just before I was assaulted and how it was hoped it would be available on the NHS in England given it was already available on the NHS in Scotland.

Was I seemingly upset that perhaps PrEP had come too late for me and how could I promote PrEP at work when I was living with HIV? I soon set myself straight given it would be unlikely I'd have been a subscriber of PrEP given I didn't live a lifestyle where I was promiscuous. I had, had no interest in what the gay community term as "fun" for over 6 years. I never took a tablet for a headache so while PrEP sounded amazing, I believe it is not something I would have taken regularly and would have instead used traditional courses of protection should I of fancied some casual "fun". There is also all the other STI's to protect yourself against of which PrEP cannot.

When I got to work colleagues behind the bar had PrEP t-shirt's on. And while it all looked sombre with the choice of colour, they were sharing an important message and colleagues such as Kenzie said, "this is an amazing message, I love what it stands for". This left me slightly confused, given Kenzie's reaction the other day when he allegedly learnt the old manager Andy was living with HIV and his immediate reaction was to go "eww"!

As I wore my usual company shirt in a lovely bright, bold pink. Bobby did ask in front of the others "are you not joining us Will"? To which I was dying to respond, 'its pointless closing the stable door after the horse has bolted'! But of course, I didn't. I did say the message was amazing and that had they been in some more vibrant colours I'd gladly wear one. I did take myself down to the cellar to at least pick one up and was surprised to see they had been slung in a heap on the wet cellar floor having been rummaged through. I did feel guilty I was not playing my part in promoting something, that if only lead to one enquiry by a customer for PrEP. It was one more person not likely to be infected with HIV. But then I quickly told myself there was enough of the team wearing them, so sod it.

I eventually made my way to the upstairs bar to relieve Rudy for his break. There were only two chaps sat on the balcony that looked like they were having a business meeting. Rudy had clearly been busy organising his social life as opposed to doing any work as there were a few abandoned tables littered with crisp packets and empties. As I set about collecting the empty glasses and clearing the abandoned tables one of the guys beckoned me over. He asked, "can I speak with the manager please"? My first thought was perhaps he wants to complain about Rudy who was known to be surly with customers. I asked what his enquiry was regarding in a bid to select the right manger to protect Rudy.

The guy replied, "don't worry, its nothing bad". He explained he was from Terrence Higgins Trust a UK Charity predominantly known for services in HIV & Sexual health. Given how busy we have been he wanted to reserve a space set aside in the upstairs bar for around thirty people given they had held many events with us in the past.

I went down and spoke with Carl who said he didn't want to come upstairs and instead had me relay the enquiry. As soon as I mentioned he was from Terrence Higgins Trust Carl let out an immense sigh and rolled his eyes. Without saying anything, he sauntered off to the next set of beer pumps. He stood with his arm resting on the pumps staring out through the main entrance leaving me behind.

I liked Carl and thought mentioning it was THT that it would hold some weight as a charity that was well known within the gay community. He merely said, "uh them, can't they go somewhere else". I tried to pitch the enquiry another way that necessarily wasn't about revenue but more that this should be of interest as a 'community' duty. I felt like I was on that BBC's Dragons Den but talking to Carl I couldn't work out if I was being faced with a miserable Miss Meaden or a fierce Miss Devey!

Carl just sauntered off and I thought, sod it, I am not running after you if that's your attitude. I walked back upstairs wondering what to say to the guy. Do I just tell him to ask for the manager when he goes downstairs on his way out? Or as a PLWHIV be upfront and make a stand and say, don't waste your time with this place given the attitude of its manager!

I decided I'd go with the former, show a little diplomacy and with that I confidently walked towards the balcony where the two guys were finishing their drinks. While my brain intended to be a little disingenuous, my mouth was having none of it! I openly shared that as a PLWHIV and given the negative response of my general manager, that he should perhaps think about holding his event somewhere else. He looked a little miffed, naturally. But thanked me and left. I felt I had done the right thing although it felt pants, I was working in a venue in the heart of the community that was it seemed, tired of the very people it claimed to be proud to serve and protect.

As I made my way back to the bar, I cleared a few tables and was stopped by two fellas that had walked upstairs while I was talking to Carl. Sat at a table with their dog I'd seemingly been stopped by one holding out his hand who declared, "oh look, I've got cum on my hands". I didn't find it funny, in fact I thought it was quite disgusting. Not that I'm a prude, I just didn't find the prospect of someone having spunk on their hand in a gay bar all that amusing. I just replied "dear! You're definitely doing something wrong if you've got cum on your hands and not in your mouth"! His friend took a sharp intake of breath before laughing loudly as he stroked his jack Russell that was sat on his knees. "He's just been in your toilets wanking off a guy" his friend declared. As I walked behind the bar, both hands full with empty glasses I then saw a sweaty looking guy coming out of the toilets struggling with his zip. As I glanced over the other was wiping his hand down his jumper like Monica Lewinski! They both left shortly after leaving behind their unwanted plastic packaging from their newly purchased dildos from the sex shop down the road.

The shift went on to be a busy night and although restrictions had eased around covid-19. Customers were still encouraged to order on the pubs mobile app. This meant the ticket was printed on the till downstairs and the team would have to make the order and bring it to the upstairs bar if that's where the customers were seated.

This generally wasn't a problem as there was always only ever one person working upstairs, usually me! And always around nine working on the bar downstairs with only five tills available, so more than enough staff to handle web orders.

The largest table in the bar was upstairs, table 10 and it could accommodate six customers. A straight group who had earlier told me they didn't realise they were in a gay bar had been drinking a fair amount but were nice enough. When Rudy had finished his shift and I took over upstairs the straight group were still sat at table 10 and in high, but good spirits. As some were putting away their drink quicker than others they had started to order separately, and this meant I had to keep dashing back and forth with the credit card machine which wasn't exhausting but by the time the last person paid they were almost ready to start another round and there were other customers needing to be served.

As I served other customers, I noticed Jack come up with a tray of drinks for table 10. They had ordered and paid on the mobile app separately as Jack was sifting through the tickets when delivering the drinks.

The second time they ordered on the app, Jack brought up the first tray of drinks and shouted, "can you stop ordering on the app, because the order comes downstairs! We have to bring it up and we are busy"! Half the pub turned to look; he even got my attention over the volume of the loud music. I was so embarrassed, but this was typically Jack. Behind that sweet, innocent exterior there was a short-tempered person lingering inside.

As I froze at the end of the bar, to Jack it must have looked as though I was stood with nothing to do. He screamed "look! He is stood there doing nothing, order off him" before he bounced off down the stairs only pausing to beckon me over. He asked so sweetly for me to come and collect the rest of the order from downstairs declaring "Oh Will! The app is a pain in the arse"!

When I returned with the rest of their drink's orders, the loudest of the group with tattoos across his knuckles asked for me to fetch the manager, which for the shift, Jack was the senior manager as the deputy.

I couldn't be bothered walking downstairs plus I knew Jack would get the hump and just kick them out and I felt having dealt with the group for a few hours now, it could get messy. So, I said "aww I am truly sorry. Its only his second shift today and he's finding it hard". Initially that didn't help the cause so I said, "the company likes to give back to local charities, help local vulnerable people and Jack finds social interaction challenging. He is here to collect glasses and deliver orders, but it looks as though he's finding it all a little overwhelming so, please bear with us".

I didn't think they would buy it, because I struggled to keep a straight face as I delivered my plea. But it shows how pissed they were because they did! They were so understanding, my blatant lies sounded convincing enough for them to sympathise with Jacks alleged situation. They said it was admirable for the pub to help local people "like that". Thankfully Jack didn't appear again until well after this group had left, I'd gotten away with it.

As the night grew busier and it seemed more chaotic with drunks, I heard a loud crash of a glass smashing. I peered over the banister and saw it was on the stairs. I went and grabbed a dustpan and brush and some blue roll. When I got their Jack was trying to clean up what appeared to be a full drink when it smashed hence the loud crash. I picked up the shards of glass as Jack worried, I'd injure myself. Although between us we did the best we could in clearing it up as impatient customers climbed over us.

Shortly after I was collecting glasses when Jack came up to me panic stricken. Jack grabbed me by both my arms while I clutched hold of empty glasses. I humorously recoiled slightly at the fact he was restraining me and I said, "can I help ya"? Jack replied, "Will! You won't believe what's just happened. Bubbles has had her mobile phone stolen"!

In a dry tone I said, "dumb bitch! What does she expect when she sits there playing her invisible piano? She's a pick pockets wet dream"! Jack laughed slightly while trying to keep a straight face saying, "I knew I'd get no sympathy out of you". He let go of me and I asked how she didn't know her phone was stolen when she listens to her own music with her wireless headphones. Jack said that was it, she noticed her phone was gone when her Bluetooth cut off given her phone was by then out of range and her music stopped playing.

It was sad, especially when Bubbles is a regular and such a nice guy for something like that to happen to him. But it was such a nice moment for me and Jack to bounce off each other with a bit of banter, a little like a double act in what was proving to be a manic night. Jack often set up a scenario and I'd deliver the punch line. It was these moments that made Jack and the shift a little more interesting and why I liked working with Jack. But I never told him this.

We had two new guys start Liam who was quickly nicknamed 'Lurch' given his overall appearance and persona. I suspect he had an interest in all thing's 'grunge'. He didn't speak much but was clad with silver rings and pendants with greasy shoulder length hair. He had a habit of always having one hand in his pocket, even when pulling and handing over a pint. Which was fascinating to watch and hysterical when sifting through photos customers posted on social media of the bar. Instead of where's Wally, we played 'Where's Lurch" in the private group chat.

The team instantly complained that he had terrible body odour and asked me to walk on by and have a good sniff. I didn't have the stomach for it so declined, but also on the grounds that it wasn't very welcoming.

The other guy was Alex who told anyone and everyone about how he was exhausted after he spent the entire night before his first shift with us. Being the bottom in a foursome he randomly met on Grindr. He had these tiny white tennis shorts on and these white legs that looked like two cocktail sticks. I thought 'he is going to get right on my nerves if he doesn't calm down' and given it was his first shift, I gave him the benefit of the doubt. Once I did the usual welcome pleasantries, I tried to avoid him as much as possible.

STICKS & STONES

Apart from the usual and unusual shenanigans at work. Things on the whole 'malicious message' front has been quiet. I have had nothing since the initial message and can honestly say despite the threat to 'out' me as having "AIDS" it hasn't really bothered me. I have occasionally wondered who it is as this is more interesting than what the person alleges, they intend to do. I must be working alongside the person that typed out that message, that harbours these feelings or perhaps more sinister emotions.

I have not told anybody my status as it really has no bearing on who I am. Nor does it need to be shared given I am no risk to anyone. Me and Jack have spoken about it now and again and I find that a bit of a shame. Although I don't mind chatting to him about HIV and myself living with it. I just wish we had cause to talk to each other about other mutual interests.

And we do discuss other things, often me throwing it open to Jack and enquiring about his interests which at present are all about alternative therapy, his counselling study, and his job as a covid-19 vaccinator. Which his colleagues from the management office rib him about to his face saving the most vitriolic remarks for when his back is turned. Jack would often ask me how the messages I received had affected me. It came across as though he himself was intrigued but I got a greater sense he was perhaps applying my responses to the knowledge gained through his studies.

I was honest and just kept saying I was keen to learn who it was. And why they didn't have the balls to approach me in person to get their views and opinions off their chest. But, in reality, I had a life to get on with and it didn't bother me a great deal as I had been raised with the adage of "sticks and stones may break my bones, but names will never hurt me"!

In a message on this subject Jack once said, "you inspire me with how you deal with whatever is thrown at you. I could learn a lot from you". I know my approach is not for everyone, it just works for me. It has often been said that most comedy comes from people who have had troubled or traumatic pasts. I believe I had an ordinary childhood given I knew no different. I was sometimes naughty and smacked and sent to my room as punishment. I had excellent attendance at school although in both primary and secondary school was bullied for being a tad camp or effeminate.

What may surprise some, as a white child growing up in Leeds, I was racially abused as most students were Asian. My personality, mannerisms and perceived 'gayness' was subject to verbal and physical assault in light of their own religious beliefs and views. Many shared that because I was white and "non-Muslim" that their parents instructed them not to socialise with me. I was good friends with Rafique, and we used to sit with each other in class and then would have to leave the building by different exits so that his parents wouldn't see us together.

I guess the exception to regular kids and the usual school bullying was that my father died aged 40 when I was five years old. When my mother broke her back shortly after he died, I was taken in by a family friend, but social services would come and transport me places while her friend went to work. Aged 5 this social worker used to take me to an office in Bradford where I would be handed to an Indian woman in a Sari. I was told as I was wetting the bed that what she was about to do would cure me. She would then crouch down and perform oral sex on me. I remember protesting as I knew it was wrong and was continually told that this was to stop me wetting the bed. The bed wetting, I later found out was most likely the trauma of my father passing away of which I remember vividly.

I briefly shared with Jack something I had never shared with anyone, that from the age of eleven to thirteen I was sexually abused by a gay male family friend. Do such events influence the person you are when your older? If I was to analyse my past and who I am today, I think I'd have to say no. These are events that I can't say I put to the back of my mind. Like a computer, I merely deleted them but, if need be, can retrieve them from the recycle bin.

But had these events made me funny? Me and Johnnie seemed to be on a similar wavelength and had a similar sense of humour but with our own unique styles, personalities, and no doubt pasts. I'd often encounter a customer or see something or someone across the pub and Johnnie would say, "don't say anything! I can see the cogs turning" or "I know exactly what you're about to say"! And we were able to bounce off each other, often with one having to admit defeat and end with a good chuckle.

So, the person responsible for sending such messages alleging I had "AIDS" was nothing to worry about in the grand scheme of what I have dealt with and been dealt in life. It perhaps showed that the person themselves was suffering from some form of traumatic, or a series of traumatic events in life to be this malicious and spiteful. Or as I have just said, if this is not a defining factor of an abnormal behavior then surely this is just their personality, and an ugly one at that.

It was a Friday in the middle of summer, and I bumped into Kenzie in the local supermarket in Soho. We were both seemingly browsing for drinks and snacks to get us through our long shift ahead.

Kenzie waited for me to pay, and we walked down Dean Street to work. He asked, "are you excited for tonight's shift"? I said as Friday nights go with the drag queen DJ playing cheesy mash up's that I was in fact excited. Kenzie said he didn't want to work the shift as one of his 'daddies' had just sent him a message asking him to go around to his for sex and cuddles. Kenzie said it would pay more than his shift. I thought it was all a bit seedy, but they were both mutually consenting adults and I guess they weren't harming anyone. I didn't want to know any more so changed the subject to try and cheer Kenzie up given he seemed down beat that he'd given his daddy the elbow.

We started our shift and an hour in, Bobby said that Carl had asked for me to cover Kenzie on the bar given Kenzie had been sent home. Bobby said he had just walked Kenzie to the bus stop. Puzzled I asked, "what for"? Bobby replied, "poor Kenzie had a panic attack and he asked Carl if he could go home and then Carl asked me to walk him to the bus stop".

I nearly wet myself laughing, I couldn't breathe as I pictured a feeble and frail looking Bobby supporting the rather rotund Kenzie to the bus stop! The image in my head was funnier than I retell it. Bobby said, "you're such a bitch"! I told Bobby that Kenzie had told me in detail, that he knows how to fake his panic attacks and how he had management "wrapped around my little finger". And the reason for this alleged panic attack and requesting to go home was so that Kenzie could spend the night with one of his daddies.

I didn't see Kenzie for about a week and when I did, I said "Oi! What happened to you last Friday, disappearing like that"?

Kenzie giggled and said in pathetic childlike voice "I had to go to my daddies, and we had cuddles and snuggles". My toes curling and feeling nauseous I said this was a selfish way to behave as it was his colleagues that had to pick up the slack for being a man down for wholly illegitimate reasons.

Kenzie didn't take kindly to this, and I got the silent treatment again, in fact we never spoke after this.

The morning after, I received a call at 8:04am on my second mobile colleagues dubbed my 'burner phone' from NHS Test & Trace. I was being notified that I had to self-isolate for 11 days as I had yet again, been a close contact of someone who had tested positive for covid-19.

Given this was the second time I had been told to isolate and knowing only my work colleagues had access to this mobile number. I asked the advisor, knowing they couldn't, if they could give me any indication as to who had tested positive and passed them my number. They couldn't tell me if it was a colleague or not, but it was obvious to me! As colleagues were the only people with access to this mobile number to hand it to NHS Test and Trace.

I sent the documentation from NHS Test and Trace to Adam to say I wouldn't be in for 11 days as I was having to isolate for allegedly being a contact of someone who tested positive for covid-19, again!

Adam was not happy and replied to my email followed by a WhatsApp message saying that I was permitted to come into work under new government guidelines. I checked back with NHS test and trace, and they confirmed it was several weeks yet before the new, more relaxed guidelines came into effect. I shared with Adam by email that his advice was not yet effective.

He again was not happy, and I thought perhaps this was because they would be short staffed although Lurch in the group chat said he was available to pick up my shifts. Shortly after I got a message from Rudy saying Adam was 'raging' and was telling junior members of the team, including Rudy that I was lying about having to isolate and was merely doing it to pick up another £500 isolation grant from the government.

I sent an email reminding the company that my NHS test and trace letter came with a unique code which could be entered onto the NHS website to confirm I had legally been instructed to isolate. I also shared in the email that I was "furious" having to isolate for 11 days. I would much rather be at work, and this was a big inconvenience for me given I would be so bored sat idle at home. Carl emailed back agreeing that I was in fact legally bound to isolate and that my notice from the NHS would suffice. That he would ensure I was also paid statutory sick pay for the 11 days. He was much more conciliatory than Adam although I suspect it was not at all sincere, but Carl said he hoped I remained safe and well and didn't come down with Covid-19.

So, I deliberately kept my ear to the ground to find out who else was having to self-isolate. For starters it must be the person who tested positive for covid-19 that I had allegedly been a close contact of. Not to mention several other team members because there was never only 2 people in the pub on any given shift. There were always at least four to nine others who would have worked and been a close contact.

Well, surprise surprise! Not one other single team member was off as a close contact, and nobody was off having been covid-19 positive. This just added to my suspicions on this being a method to solely target me and for a second time. But I had to also consider that perhaps others had been instructed to isolate but were not declaring it in fear of losing pay. Would a few who have been contacted be able to all remain silent, surely someone would let slip that they had been contacted by NHS test and trace too?

I took a PCR [polymerase chain reaction] test which came back as covid negative. I then got an alert from the NHS covid-19 app, stating my isolation period had been reduced and that I only had to isolate a total of 5 days instead of 11. Yay! I was set for early release from the confines of my home. I emailed work but they had already given my shifts to Lurch so in the end I was off for the entire 11 days. I arranged a mini break away first to the Isle of Wight and then on the way back stopping off in Brighton. On the morning I was off on my little jolly after being cooped up I opened WhatsApp to another two cryptic messages from my admirer. They read:

"Not sure why your still on the rota! The guy's wont [sic] think your all that when I tell them about your dirty secret! We got enough to deal with 1 disease we don't need another!!!"

"How is isolation? At least it protects us from catching AIDS!!! xx"

As I read it, I genuinely gave a roll of the eyes and headed to Waterloo train station for the 07:35 to Southampton Central.

I did give it some thought on the train and surprisingly for me, I quickly made a correlation with events at work and the isolations. I recall having that little run in with Kenzie, over me turning up the lights at the last orders bell in the upstairs bar. The day after I found myself being contacted by NHS test and trace having allegedly been a 'covid contact' and legally having to self-isolate for five days.

And recently I had jovially asked Kenzie where he disappeared to last Friday. Seemingly he got upset when I shared that his actions affected us all and were quite selfish to which he seems peeved by my upfront honesty.

I didn't lay into him; it wasn't my place, but as a colleague that had to pick up the slack after he went 'home' with an alleged panic attack. I was merely trying to have him think about his decision and how it impacted his colleagues. I got his usually short shrift and Kenzie didn't speak to me for the rest of the shift.

Then, low and behold, the very next morning, again, I receive a call from NHS test and trace having me legally self-isolate for eleven days. Too much of a coincidence wouldn't you say?

It seemed the MO (Modus Operandi) of the individual was to have me isolate so that I wasn't at work and interacting with colleagues. It had been made clear in the malicious messages that they sought for me to resign so they clearly didn't want me around the workplace. I understand not everybody is universally liked, but what had I done, or not done, to be deemed so offensive to this person?

I have always been popular and often invited to social gatherings. As the person that can engage and maintain conversation in a social setting without being annoying nor overbearing. I have often identified individuals I won't and/or don't get along with perhaps before they know it themselves. But regardless, I always treat people with dignity and respect. Therefore, the only reason I could come up with was that this individual was perhaps jealous of my popularity. Or I had unknowingly done something so offensive to this individual to warrant such abuse.

One thing I felt certain of, this individual had no genuine fear in 2021 of contracting "AIDS" or HIV. A long career of reading guest reviews & complaints, I believe I have a skill that can decipher the bullshit from the facts. For me, these messages were more aimed at 'me' as an individual and my HIV/AIDS was just an excuse to be malicious to perhaps provoke fear in me to meet their demand by offering my resignation.

Having spent three days on the Isle of Wight I was now having an overnight stay in Brighton before returning to work in a couple of days. Carl introduced a new guy in the group chat called Ben. I welcomed him with my usual peculiar flare, by popping in a TikTok video of me bizarrely lip syncing to something random. It was only a pub, but I hoped it demonstrated that at least one of us was available to have a laugh. It made a change than the usual and often insincere "Hi" others posted in the group chat.

Back home, and the night before returning to work, I felt compelled to google search the mobile number once again. There were only 2 pages of results so not much to sift through. The second webpage I stumbled across was a list of mobile phone numbers that filled the screen of my laptop. I clicked CTRL + F and pasted the mobile number in question into the 'find' box and pressed enter. The mobile number was highlighted on the webpage and appeared to be clickable.

Upon clicking the highlighted mobile number, it opened a new webpage which was for a gaming console brand. It was a forum that had been archived regarding a basketball computer game. I went through the 'find' feature again and found the mobile number in a post. The user had stated they were stuck and needed some help and offered a few handles for their social media along with their mobile number. I then set eyes on the username, and I got an instant chill and after a few moments digesting the username which was a forename dot surname (Forename.Surname). I felt sick to my stomach because I work with someone of the exact same name, 'now isn't that an unbelievable coincidence m'lud'!

BATTERED SAUSAGE & CHIPS

I returned to work on a Thursday and at the start of my shift I spotted the new guy Ben stood by the bar looking a little petrified. Nobody ever did introduce new guys, so I took the opportunity to say hello and introduce myself.

My first impression was he looked incredibly unkempt for a gay guy. His shoulder length hair was full of fluff and debris. Clearly, it'd not seen a brush in several weeks. He has dirt behind his fingernails and with his dirty jeans and pumps he looked like he needed a good wash. I know you shouldn't judge by appearances, but I couldn't do anything but! I was getting Buffalo Bill Vibes from the film 'Silence of the Lambs' and I had this irresistible urge to shout, "put the fucking lotion in the basket"!

Every time he speaks, he follows it with the most horrendous nervous cackle which gave me a headache after a few minutes. He said he had already been told off for standing around and when I asked, "by who"? Ben pointed out Johnnie and I thought that explains why he looked a tad shell shocked!

I tried to offer some friendly advice sharing "if you truly have nothing to do, then just sanitise your hands as it makes you look busy or as though you had just been busy".

Given the glorious weather we were having in London and the time I'd had off I'd prepared some of my usual home-made food and stocked my freezer. Today I brought in some homemade Greek souvlaki which I had placed in the staff room fridge. Kenzie arrived for his shift and asked me, "is that your lunch in the fridge"? Given many brought lunch in I sought clarification and asked, "which one"?

"The one with the pitta, cheese and salad, it looks amazing" to which I confirmed it was mine and shared it was Souvlaki. As members of the team who are not in the private group chat, mainly the 'originals' as Kenzie dubs them, came and went off shift. I went about asking as I had before, who else had either been off as a covid-19 contact and who, had tested positive?

They all stated "nobody, just you"! Well, with that I shared I knew something suspicious was going on and it could only be a deliberate and malicious act. Johnnie quipped "oh, we have our very own Jessica Fletcher in the house"!

I was working the upstairs bar once five o'clock came and Ben had been buddied with me to show him the ropes as it was only his third shift. I have always been an effective trainer but immediately noticed Ben wasn't interested at all. He said "I'm not here to learn, I'm not even here for the money. I am only here to make contacts as I am a Drag Queen". I shared it was only a stop gap for me too but that didn't mean you had to be complacent about the job entirely.

He grabbed himself a glass and poured himself a lemonade from the soda gun. Everybody had seemingly been told on their first day that helping yourself to drinks, even soft drinks is a big 'no, no'! The company permitted tap water only or soda water from the gun. To ensure Ben didn't get into trouble, despite him working there for a few days already I said "ah, they don't allow us to take soft drinks, its tap or soda water only".

"Mind your business bitch! I doubt the company will miss a few lemonades" Ben snapped back. I said nothing and thought 'you carry on then'. Given covid-19 restrictions we were still busy and still offered table service in the upstairs bar, and today we were packed with customers. I was dashing around serving tables which meant taking the order, putting it in the till, preparing the order and then delivering the order and taking payment on delivery.

Ben spent at least 15 minutes if not longer with each table that he approached to serve. As I worked the floor, I heard him repeat the same old story. He'd applied for Drag Race UK but was rejected and that he'd spent the last five years in the Philippines as its most famous drag queen. He sounded quite bitter about the whole experience with drag race and laid into the queens that had been successful on the forthcoming UK series. Some of which were known locally around Soho and London. Each time I looked over to try and catch Ben's eye to gesture for him to do some work the look on the customers faces was of pure boredom. Ben was clearly outstaying his welcome to promote himself while flicking through his social media on the customers phones.

I was relieved when my lunch break came just to get away from Ben's voice and that fucking cackle which a few hours in was getting on my tits. I took my lunch from the fridge and removed the greaseproof paper from the top of my lunch box to find a single use face mask had been wedged into my lunch. I wasn't sure what I was looking at, and it took some time for me to process that someone had obviously done this deliberately. I slung my lunch in the bin and put the box back in my bag. I went down the road to the fish and chip shop and ordered battered sausage and chips, and as a regular the owner knew that was to be accompanied with a pot of curry sauce.

The staff room was upstairs above the bar, so it was usual to hear noise from the bar or customers walking into the staff room looking for the toilets. I shut the door and all I could hear was Ben's voice! I locked the door and popped in my headphones in a bid to drown him out. As I munched my battered sausage, dunking it in the curry sauce I began to ponder who'd tampered with my lunch box.

I was surprised how I seemed to be somewhat unphased by it and asked if that was normal. Although I had never experienced anything like this in a workplace in my 23 years. I think I had come to believe that such behaviour here was normal. Kenzie asked about my lunch earlier, but would he be stupid enough to tamper with it? And for what reason? And wouldn't it be too obvious given he'd asked me to confirm which lunch was mine after he arrived at work? If it wasn't Kenzie, who else would it be? So many questions but no way of knowing the answer unless I send the mask and my lunch box off for DNA analysis.

After my battered sausage and chips, I brushed my teeth and returned to the bar. I was granted a further twenty minutes peace and quiet as Ben went on his break, shutting himself in the staff room I was tempted to lock the door from the outside until closing time. Customers I went on to serve stated Ben "likes the sound of his own voice"! To which I could only agree. They shared they'd been subjected to Ben's photos of his drag, and all said they could see why he didn't make it into Drag Race UK. Asking if I'd seen them, I said, "no, I only met him today". The customers then showed me Ben's social media pages he'd forced them to join. The customers so eager to throw shade saying, "wait until you see these"!

It seemed Ben was perhaps somewhat delusional about his talent and particularly over-egged his makeup skills. One customer saying, "it looks like a 2-year-old has done her make up with Crayola"! I bit my lip as if to say 'you're naughty' but, the customer was right! I felt awful that having overheard Ben promoting his makeup skills that the several tables he told were now slagging him off behind his back.

After finishing what was a torturous shift, and the lunchbox incident. I had a couple of days off. So, thinking this and the malicious messages over and getting advice from a charity and speaking with other PLWHIV. I concluded I should let the individual know that I knew they were behind the messages. I thought I'd pull on my diplomacy skills gained from my 23 years in hotel management. Much of that being in Guest Relations. I'd tackle this scenario as though it was a guest issue, I'd be sensitive and sympathetic yet diplomatic and to the point.

In my head I went over and over what I would say and how I would say it. I thought I'd do it publicly, as in with other team members around as given the strength of the evidence, I felt he wouldn't be able to deny it and most likely wouldn't with others around. And by that I don't mean others would hear or be involved, we just wouldn't do it in a quiet room with just the two of us.

I had also informed Carl the manager by email what had been happening and that I had discovered who the person was. I only did so as I had also informed the police, who said for the time being it was not a workplace matter unless it involved a workplace device. I shared as bar staff we didn't have access to computers or devices, except our own personal devices. I felt Carl should be in the loop should they go to my place of work to make enquiries.

Carl replied that he was sorry to hear this and sent me a link for a gay charity, should I need any support. I didn't recognise the charity so didn't click the link. Plus, I had already been speaking with PLWHIV and a platform for PLWHIV with Terrence Higgins Trust.

I did, however, thank Carl for his response and concluded my email with "I just wish their demands had been a bit more extravagant, at least it would have made it all a little more exciting"! If it had been more Jeremy Irons in 'Die Hard with a Vengeance' to really make my knickers moist, it would have been worth playing along. Instead, what did I get? A spotty oik with daddy issues who spends most of his time in a petri dish down the clinic!

It was Friday and I was starting my usual shift at 3pm. As I came down the stairs from the staff room, I saw the individual at the main bar taking his temperature as part of covid-19 regulations. As I walked across the pub to register my temperature, I said to myself 'this is it, this is the moment' to inform him that I know he is behind the messages. I had it all planned out in my head and had gone over it several times over the last few days. As I got closer, I said:

"Just to let you know, 'I know' you're behind the messages! Although I am not sure where you got your information, but it is news to me that I have "AIDS""!

As Kenzie put down the thermometer gun and stepped back, I picked it up and pointing it at my forehead I continued:

"Anyhow, just a heads up, I have informed the Police after I found your mobile number on a gaming support forum, so expect a visit. In the meantime, continue to talk shit about me you'll leave me no choice but to break both your legs, understood! Oh, and if you wish to go tell management about this conversation, please do, am sure they'll be as disappointed to learn you were behind the messages as much as I am"!

Well, that didn't quite go to plan or how I had rehearsed it. Once I started, the adrenaline just took over and there I was portraying myself as an old-time east end hard man. I wouldn't harm Kenzie, it isn't my style, as I believe the power of word is much more effective. But I have to say, it felt good! Kenzie looked stunned and said absolutely nothing, I want to say he looked shocked, but he didn't which said it all. He stood looking gormless, perhaps trying to process how I'd found out!

And while I was confident in the evidence I had uncovered. I must admit as I was delivering my little speech, I kept getting flashes of doubt, 'what if I've got this wrong'? But unlike any rational person Kenzie didn't deny it, he didn't ask what I was going on about? He knew he'd been caught out and the game was up!

At the same time as deciding to approach Kenzie directly. I simultaneously thought about the possibility of having to share my status with my colleagues. I still didn't feel my colleagues needed to know and I didn't want to tell them. But at the same time, I didn't really care if they knew, but if they were going to find out then I would rather it be from me.

In essence it was about taking back control of 'my' HIV. Although Kenzie's actions were the only reason, I now found myself even considering sharing my status with my colleagues. If me sharing my status demonstrated one thing to Kenzie and others, that PLWHIV are not afraid nor ashamed to hide behind, nor have their status used against them. Then it was all for the good.

When I had my first shift managed by Johnnie after isolation, he came and asked how I was. But the way he asked me seemed more sympathetic than his usual self and that seemed odd. I suspected Carl had either shared what was going on regarding the malicious messages. Or that Johnnie had stumbled across the email in the manager's office given they all accessed the pubs only email address.

I said I was good and taking the piss that I had, had a nice 'holiday'. "Are you sure you're ok"? Johnnie enquired with such empathy. Something wasn't right here so I just blurted out "you know what! I'll tell you straight! I am living with HIV..." to which Johnnie interrupted in his finest scouse accent and screamed "and so what! Do you want a medal dear"! I continued "I was assaulted in March 2020 and some little shit here has somehow found out and is asking me to quit the job or be exposed as having AIDS".

Johnnie didn't seem surprised, so I think my suspicions were right, he already knew. We both chatted between serving customers about how I had become infected and my treatment which he seemed to know quite a lot about. He shared that his friend was living with HIV and although he himself didn't want the virus he was not scared of it given the advances in science and medicine that exists today.

Johnnie has a similar sense of humour to me, sometimes caustic so I kept referring to my condition as "me having the AIDS". Johnnie shared he isn't one for talking things through or being someone's shoulder to cry on. But if I ever needed to speak to someone then his door was always open. I've only known Johnnie for a few months, and I thought this was a very kind and thoughtful gesture. But decided in the spirit of things to break the seriousness with "alright Princess Diana"! To which Johnnie walking away turned back and mouthed "cunt"!

Just as I finished talking with Johnnie, Jack arrived seemingly starting his shift. I'd not seen Jack for a while given he had been on annual leave before my isolation period. And his holiday ran over into the time I returned from isolation. It was great to see him and during my isolation I had stitched diamantes onto my work sweater which he found bedazzling.

"Hi, how are you Will"? Jack enquired. I thought if Johnnie knows, then surely Carl will have shared the malicious messages with Jack as his right-hand man, apparently. But if Jack had been kept in the dark, I felt I should share it with Jack having already shared it with Johnnie. Jack was the first one to learn of my status and I felt guilty that Jack wasn't the first to know about this.

"Yeah, good thank you. How was your holiday"? I asked. Jack said he spent most of his time preparing for college and did a few odd jobs. While I was genuinely interested Jack said sincerely "enough about me, you don't seem your usual self. What's wrong"?

I was quite taken aback given I was genuinely interested and don't believe my face gave the game away that I had other matters on my mind. I wondered if Jack and his spirit guide, he often gets ribbed for was sensing all was not well. I thought seen as he has asked, I could just slip my news into general conversation "Yeah I am ok. Although saddened to find out someone I work with has been blackmailing me saying I have AIDS".

Jack stood with his hands clasped together looking shell shocked. I could see the cogs in his head trying to process what I had just said. It seemed an eternity before he said anything. As Jack drew breath, stuttered and stumbled he clarified "What! Someone that works here"?

"Yes" I replied. Jack concerned, reassuringly placing his hand on my forearm sought reassurance by asking again "someone said that that works here in this pub"?

LOST BOY

As me and Jack stood behind the bar by the ice trough, I explained how I'd come to receive the malicious messages and what they said. Jack couldn't comprehend what I was sharing and kept repeating "so let me get this straight"! Seeking clarification in fear he'd misheard given it was all so ludicrous, if not sick and twisted. He naturally seemed shocked and the more I shared the more concerned Jack became so I did try, in part to sugar coat some of it.

It was a busy afternoon and colleagues freely passed between me and Jack as we spoke. Most noticeable was Johnnie who kept catching my eye as he stood behind Jack while pouring drinks. Johnnie highlighting the varying degrees of concern expressed by Jack with an exhausted rolling of his eyes. I thought this was a tad mean as Jack was naturally taking an interest of the care and wellbeing on another colleague.

Jack asked how I knew the sender of the messages was someone from work. I had to explain the whole story of my second mobile that Johnnie dubbed my 'burner phone'. How only work colleagues had access to that mobile number from the group chat members list. How, the messages referenced me at work, even referencing the videos I posted in the group chat itself. Jack said "it's fascinating how you have followed a trail of clues like that. But I cannot believe someone like 'this' works here"!

Jack then said he wondered who it was to which I said, "I found out recently when I google searched the mobile phone number for a second time. A few clicks and my search took me to a forum help page that had been archived. But the username was the first name dot surname, and that person works here. What's the odds of that"?

It was noticeable the more I shared Jacks body language indicated he was becoming more and more agitated. He became fidgety, moving from side to side and couldn't keep still. It was as if he was limbering up for a fight and it was starting to unsettle me. I didn't want Jack to feel that way, I guess because I cared, but ultimately, I didn't want the person responsible for the messages, to impact the lives of others.

I started to play down the whole incident with "it's funny really! The messages are so incoherent and as for the spelling and grammar! The guy needs help"! And I did find it funny, not particularly side splitting funny but laughable. The whole event was a nonstarter, and I didn't lose any sleep over it, purely because it truly was that ridiculous. I truly, only wish it had been a little more exciting.

Jack didn't take kindly to me making light of it "no Will! It's not funny"! He said sternly. Jack shared his thoughts, and it was interesting that his first thought was closely aligned with mine when he said, "this person needs help, I do not want to be working with someone who behaves like this"! Jack reiterated that his venue was a LGBT venue and works hard to stand up for rights and fight stigma across many issues including HIV.

Jacks voice broke when I shared, I'd discovered a used facemask wedged into my lunch box. Jack was so gobsmacked he placed the palms of his hands on his temples saying, "no Will! Please, no. Let me get this straight….". And cue Johnnie in the background with the obligatory eye roll, it was turning into a comedy sketch.

Jack insisted "I want to get this sorted out; we need to go to Human Resources. They need to offer some assistance on this, and we need to get this person removed from the company". It surprised me that he didn't ask who the person was, and I suspect Jack was still trying to digest the sequence of events I had shared.

If it had of been me, the first thing I would want to know is 'who done it'? Which only showed that Jack had taken a keen interest in everything I had just shared with him as opposed to getting to the 'juicy' bit.

I still had the burning question of how Kenzie had come to know of my status because it was in effect still relatively new to me. The only people that know is a close friend who is not within my main circle of friends just because they haven't crossed paths and my clinician at the clinic and of course now Jack. The only theory I can come up with and it is so farfetched I cannot believe it to be accurate. Is that Kenzie somehow has a contact in the clinic, a friend, or an acquaintance who looked me up to perhaps see what STI's I'd been in for. Although I have never been to my clinic for anything other than HIV services circa March 2020.

I cannot even explain how many breaches and laws would be broken here so do not in any way believe this happened and my theory should be treated with the contempt it deserves. But how he found out, I have no idea and to this day remains a mystery.

As soon as I shared my query and then theory with Jack he said, "oh god! I hope you didn't think it was me that told someone"! I gently took hold of Jack's wrist and said, "absolutely not! My only thought of you Jack, was 'I hope Jack doesn't think, I think, he shared my status for this person to of found out". It never even crossed my mind that Jack may have shared my status and what I told him with anybody, let alone Kenzie.

Jack then confessed he did share my status, he put it on "a poster in the staff room", before declaring he was joking. It wasn't side splitting, but I appreciated his effort to make a joke and light of the situation.

About an hour later, Jack then tried to guess who it was, he boldly and confidently took a guess "was it, Kenzie"? I cannot lie to save my life and am known for saying it as it is, and this also goes for my facial expressions that generally come naturally. I shared with Jack "the police have said for now, it is not a work-related incident. I want to see what they propose to do once they conclude their investigation". Although I didn't want my HIV being dragged into the public domain with a long-drawn-out legal process. But I had enquired beforehand and was informed of a variety of options in how the matter could be handled upon the conclusion of a satisfactory investigation. One being the incident did warrant something like the "waggy finger" as the officer put it. But given current legislation for such malicious acts, especially around protected characteristics, such "waggy fingers" now carried a bit more weight.

"But was it Kenzie"? Jack asked again. It was interesting that Jack's first thought for someone behaving like this to be Kenzie. And then persist with this line of inquiry and Jack was spot on. Jack is smart so I merely replied, "I will say this, that the person did tell me they have, and I quote "management wrapped around my little finger". With this Jack, it makes me incredibly apprehensive in allowing the company to take the lead on an investigation. I much prefer, for the moment, a third party with more authority and resources to conduct an 'unbiased' and thorough investigation".

And I suppose I was apprehensive in sharing with management, including Jack that it was Kenzie because he is always treated differently to everybody else. Supervisors and managers would refer to him as 'our baby Kenzie' and would always give in to him if he sulked when he didn't want to do something. The panic attacks Kenzie himself took great pleasure in sharing with me he faked to get his own way. I saw for myself, and others shared in the private group chat, screenshots of Kenzie's social media where both Adam, Johnnie and Kenzie seem to have a relationship that goes beyond 'friendship' in the traditional sense outside of work.

Jack once came storming over to me and Johnnie on the door in my first week of work screaming "he is a prick that guy! A total prick"! Johnnie taken aback asked Jack "who dear"? To which Jack stated "Kenzie, who else". Jack turned to me stating "sorry Will" to which I took to mean I had to make myself scarce. It was clear that there was something between Jack and Kenzie, not just from this one event but the atmosphere when they are both in close proximity to each other and breathing the same air. Although Kenzie had shared with me on the night bus, he didn't get on with Jack I didn't fully understand what had gone on with them both. I did ask Elias as the 'mother' of the pub, but he brushed it off with "ah, the two are as bad as each other"!

Jack asked to see the messages and I said I would on one condition. That he didn't let them infuriate him and that he didn't become agitated. As Jack started to read the malicious messages, I felt this was perhaps unfair of me. Who was I to tell someone how to react to something as bizarre and malicious as these messages? This was confirmed as Jack read out in a whisper the content of the messages. His body went all tense including his face as he merely said "right"! when handing me back my mobile phone.

I thought I should give him an opportunity to share his thoughts and not bottle up what he wants to express and has a right to say. I initiated a response with "work is supposed to be a safe place for the LGBT community and surely that includes people living with HIV and even AIDS? It saddens me to think I work here. But I cannot believe in 2021, that these are the genuine views or concerns relating to PLWHIV. I can only view these messages as a touch of the green-eyed monster given, they are purely malicious".

Jack responded "Will! These messages are absolutely abhorrent, cruel and totally unwarranted. This pub always has been, is, and will continue to be a safe place for the LGBT community no matter which side of the bar they stand. I am just so sorry someone as nice as you have had this experience, this person needs to be removed from the site"!

As we stood at the bar we were then joined by Bobby, Johnnie and Rudy who initiated conversation about a screaming queen from Middlesbrough who has become a regular. He is hilariously annoying! Hilarious because he wears these terrible wigs, and annoying because he says he's an actor and stands at the bar doing high kicks and screeching along to songs that could shatter glass!

It wasn't long before Bobby mentioned how Kenzie had served this guy the previous night and was so bold to ask the customer where he gets his wigs in a bid to take the piss. Johnnie then spoke fondly of Kenzie and Jack too joined in the conversation which left me slightly confused.

As the conversation continued it made me more uneasy about sharing the person behind these malicious messages and I was somewhat relived I have for the time being, kept it to myself at work. I did ask myself if Jack was trying to get me to divulge a name after giving me a false sense of security. I have never been someone who 'cared enough' to mull things over or start considering conspiracy theories but it was bizarre I was suddenly becoming a tad paranoid in this instance.

Kenzie has stopped speaking to me and even avoids eye contact, which is a shame. But I don't really care if he wants to play the victim then so be it, he plays it well.

As we all left the other night at 1am I found myself leaving the pub with Kenzie walking in front of me. He held the gate open for me and out of general courtesy and habit I said, "thanks". Kenzie said with puppy dog eyes, "have a good night" to which I ignored. I am happy to move on and forget it, and I have never been one for people to come and offer me insincere apologies should the occasion arise. It's just words and over time I have developed or rather come to learn that having a pragmatic attitude works best for me.

But to a degree, I did feel it was all too soon to be buddies with Kenzie. Not because what he'd done was 'raw' or that he'd touched my emotions. As my closest friends would testify, I don't do emotions! But I think for me it was all about trust, how can you trust someone who would carry out several malicious acts over a period? There had to be some level of 'thought' and 'intent' that went into preparing and carrying out these kinds of acts. For me this is what was disturbing, these were not adrenaline fuelled, impulsive acts where an apology could be considered.

But I acknowledge it will take one of us to be the bigger person to get the ball rolling. But then it's a working environment in a backstreet pub we don't have to be 'besties' if it remains cordial and professional, and we crack on with our jobs. Well, at least one of us can while the other is busy manipulating management, breathing into a bag having a panic attack.

As I made the regular walk home from Soho to Islington that night my music playlist had come to an end and started to play random songs. A ballad came on that immediately caught my attention called 'Lost Boy' by Canadian singer Ruth B.

I was immediately struck by the lyrics and how relatable it was to each one of my colleagues. Based on the story of Peter Pan and initially a snippet that was a viral hit on the Vine application. Ruth B had a massive hit when she put pen to paper and made the record.

The opening line "There was a time I was alone, nowhere to go and no place to call home…". This was reminiscent of how all the boys had shared they had come to work at the pub. Some were recovering drug addicts. Some ostracized by their own family for being gay and made homeless. Another found working alongside and being dismissed from a predominantly heterosexual workplace damaging to his mental health. Some shared they felt alienated and ridiculed for not being able to speak the English language and fully integrate with the natives.

The pub seemed to be their metaphorical 'Neverland' and allowed them all to escape 'reality'. It was their "home sweet home" where they truly felt a sense of belonging "as we soared above the town that never loved me, I realised I finally had a family".

"Neverland is home to lost boys like me. And lost boys like me are free".

I was so moved by the track I played it on repeat for the entire walk home. With every sentiment and every lyric, I was able to picture each and every one of my colleagues, particularly Kenzie. He is truly a 'Lost Boy'.

And what about me? I guess I am a lost boy too. I found my way to this home for lost boys after being raped and infected with HIV. I made a conscious decision to apply for the job to be around members of my own 'community' respectfully known as 'the gays'. Not necessarily to come to terms with the incident nor the diagnosis as I am very pragmatic and moved on quickly. But perhaps it is a metaphorical hug that allows me to put trust in those within my own community. It was an easing into society and the reality that life goes on, although life is and has been anything but normal given this covid-19 pandemic.

I have always lived in my own world and to a degree follow my own rules. I do not seek acceptance, adoration nor attention. But I guess it is always nice to be around people who share a common interest. Who have most likely faced or encountered similar challenges and battles around sexuality and society as have I?

But what has become clear during my time here so far is, a lack of diversity amongst a group of gay 'lost boys'. Who are all vying to hold the map in a bid to determine a sense of direction which in turn allows them to discover themselves? Which only leaves them going around in circles and not really getting anywhere! Stuck in a daily routine in 'Neverland' believing time has stood still. When reality occasionally hits, weeks, months and before they know it, years have passed them by, and they have achieved absolutely nothing.

Being amongst these 'lost boys' meant that I too was going around in circles. "My only friend was the man in the moon, even sometimes he would go away too".

FETISH SOCIAL

It was a glorious Sunny Friday and there was a noticeable stench in the air as I walked through Soho. I guess with the heat all the water had evaporated from the street drains meaning the waft of sewage was lingering in the warm summer air burning my nostrils.

I made my way down to the main bar and fired that thermometer gun at my forehead to log my temperature for covid-19. Carl the general manager like creeping Jesus suddenly appeared, scaring the life out of me! I turned the thermometer gun at Carl and in my best attempt at an American accent said, "hold it right there! Stick em' up bitch"! To which he threw his hands in the air and giggling said "alright Oscar" in reference to the convicted murderer Oscar Pretorius. Keeping a straight face, I retorted "alright Mr Humphries"! Carl still with his hands in the air looking puzzled said "Mr Humphries"?

I, smirking in a bid to keep a straight face given I was surprised Carl was still playing along. In my best Mr Humphries voice said, "don't worry sir the t-shirt will ride up with wear"! Carl looked down realising throwing his hands up in the had instantly turned his t-shirt into a crop top exposing his beer belly. He quickly threw down his hands pulling down his t-shirt to cover his modesty and had gone beetroot red, "fuck off" he exclaimed while laughing.

Carl asked how I was, and I replied I was good as I put the gun down. I enquired as to how he was although I wasn't really interested but thought as he's the boss I better ask and its nice to be nice. I like Carl, he can be fun when he's around. And as managers go, he is alright, but he's never there to, well, manage. And I guess that's where my respect for him professionally starts to dissipate.

It took me a while to catch on when on the day shift with Carl. That he would always leave me in the pub alone saying, "I'm just popping out to get my hair cut". Of course, it was unreasonable for someone to get their haircut three times in a week! And Carl's hair to still look the same when you'd see him the following day. I only cottoned on when Adam and Johnnie were stood bitching about Carl and how "she's always out the door either getting her "hair cut" or buying "sushi""!

Managers behaving this way didn't set a good example to the team. Yet, shit would hit the fan if a team member was genuinely five minutes late back from their break, especially with Adam who just loved having a confrontation with a 'newbie'.

This was the first-time seeing Carl since I shared with him via email my status and how I was receiving the malicious messages. Carl made no mention of it, and I knew he wouldn't as I had come to understand despite knowing very little about him personally. Carl didn't like or perhaps didn't know how to manoeuvre what may be deemed tricky/sensitive situations or confrontational events. But for me I thought he knows I'm an adult of a decent age and if I needed his support or assistance, I'd have the confidence to approach and ask him for it. But as it stood, I didn't need his nor the companies support nor assistance.

Despite Kenzie saying he had management wrapped around his little finger, I did wonder if Carl was a victim of Kenzie's manipulative side or whether it was easier for Carl to let Kenzie behave this way to retain a member of staff. Although Kenzie didn't bring much to the team, he just offered customers a different form of 'service' than the rest of us that had a little more self-respect. Although saying that, Johnnie shared he was known now and again to suck off a customer in the toilets at work, as was Alex albeit more frequently.

As soon as I arrived Carl said "Will, I'm just popping out I won't be long, if you need me just call". I genuinely, cross my heart, enquired "haircut"? To which Carl replied "no" as he continued to mince towards the entrance of the pub. "Sushi"? I shouted. Carl giggled and said, "no. I'm just checking in on a friend in another pub". I'm not sure where this pub was, but I was alone for over four hours, and I didn't see Carl again that day. The warm summer air was blowing through the main doors of the pub, so I stood in the warm breeze whilst behind the main bar wondering what was worse. Potential covid particles or the scent of the drains. My moment of quite reflection ended abruptly when three screaming queens walked through the door. I heard them on the other side of Old Compton Street before I saw them. I stood chanting to myself 'keep on walking bitches, keep on walking' but that didn't work, and they minced on in.

They all had Cinderella "cast" t-shirts on, and the performance began once they ordered three Peroni's, very butch I know. To be fair they all had a good set of lungs on them as they sang over the pubs music and entertained us all with show tunes complete with high kicks and jazz hands. It did get a little draining after a while to the point where their confidence grew the more attention they received, the more obnoxious they became.

Four rounds later they were on the verge of being wasted given they were all sickly stick thin. Johnnie, Bobby & Simon had arrived to start their shift, so I was no longer alone. Johnnie rolling his eyes complained "I can't be doing with that, how long have they been in"? referring to the three singing queens. We stood at the back of the bar bitching, sorry, I mean observing. Johnnie and I played our usual game where we'd name customers after famous faces. They couldn't just have a mere resemblance, they had to literally be a doppelgänger and we'd both agree who won by naming the closest and best resemblance.

We had named two of them Liza as in Minelli and her sister, Judy Garlands other daughter Lorna Luft. We couldn't quite place a famous name to the face for the third guy, so I went with 'crabstick'.

He'd clearly been out in the sun which had burnt only the left side of his face and arm. He was literally pink on one side and white on the other, like a crabstick (seafood stick) with legs.

We have five sets of beer taps on the main bar and me, Johnnie, Bobby and Simon all waited for each other to finish pouring so that we didn't have to venture close to Liza, Lorna and the Crabstick. We couldn't keep it up and I was the first to have venture to the taps in front of the trio to serve my customer. "Ew you've got HIV"! One of them exclaimed. My heart sank given my initial reaction was they were talking to me directly given I had just stood adjacent to them. As I casually looked up from the pint that I was pouring, I realised they were talking to the crabstick. "You had to have a HIV test"?

The crabstick morphed into a lobster turning red with embarrassment clarifying he didn't have HIV. But had to have a test recently and was worried about the result. The topic seemed to of popped up at a comment crabstick had made about having to "milk my finger like this" as he proceeded to show them how he had to massage his finger to give a sample of blood for the home test kit. Of course, it was all rather juvenile and then Liza and Lorna started to milk their finger before they all turned it into a masturbating action.

Then, Liza was trying to be serious by telling crabstick that he shouldn't be putting himself at risk like that and if he only practiced safe sex, he wouldn't need to worry about HIV tests. Crabstick said he liked "bare sex" but said he didn't want to take PrEP when Lorna suggested it. Had they not been as intoxicated as they were and in a silly mood, I'd of happily shared the benefits of protecting themselves as opposed to living with HIV as I do.

Shortly after Liza, Lorna and Crabstick left I was duly sent to open the upstairs bar for the fortnightly fetish event.

It was rammed with men dressed head to toe in leather, PVC, rubber and even a few that were wearing hardly anything at all. Given it was a super-hot day the stench of warm leather, rubber and body odour was immense. One guy was in a clear PVC body suit that clung to his skin like a supermarket chicken wrapped in plastic. You could see the sweat swilling around as he moved.

It was so busy I couldn't leave the bar to collect glasses given the customers would deliberately refuse to move aside to let you through. I guess playing out their fetish of being domineering or to make you feel subservient. I had no interest in their event other than that they had a good time in a safe environment. It was just a pity that they didn't return that same level of respect and therefore nobody on the team liked working the event with some of the team saying it was "grotesque" and "vulgar".

When the team refused to work at the event, where you would usually be left to work alone. The manager or supervisor on shift would turn and look at me to volunteer. They knew I didn't care and would say "I don't mind, I'll do it". This was now my eighth time working the event and as it was so busy, people were being pushed if not crushed up against the bar. I noticed two guys in front of my till. They both looked like oddballs and were dressed in these cheap polyester vests, one of which had 'Benidorm' written across the front.

I was serving a leather policeman when I turned to input the order into the till as he read it out to me. The guy in the Benidorm vest started to gip like a dog. I saw him pick up an empty pint glass and I spun 180 degrees to grab a bin liner as I knew he wasn't going to make it to the toilet to be sick. Just as I was also sure he wasn't going to fit it all into a pint glass.

I was too late and so was he!

He projectile vomited in my direction and all over the till, down the back and all over the bar top! I stumbled backwards to avoid being hit and ended up exiting the bar for good measure. My customer dressed as the leather policeman laughing said "Jesus, you moved so fast"! I was wearing my diamante encrusted work hoodie and retorted "this is dry clean only dear"!

It transpired how drunk this guy was as he tried to scoop up the vomit with his hands to place into the pint glass. I told him not to worry and to just stay at the bar until I get some cleaning products before he attempted to walk it across the pub. But there was a bit of a crush at the bar, and I thought if he stumbles through the crowd and splats vomit on any of their outfits then a fight could break out.

I had to climb over the glass washer and then over the bar top to get to the door for the main bar downstairs to inform Adam and ask for the 'body fluid clean up kit'. I peered over the bar and Adam looked at me scowling as to why I was downstairs. On telling Adam he rolled his eyes and asked where the vomit was and I repeated "all over the bar" of course over exaggerating with my arms outstretched to give an indication as to the size of the pool of vomit, as you do.

Adam followed me up with the body fluid kit. We both had to enter the bar by climbing over the bar and the glass washer which was by the sink. Emre who had been helping me on the bar and proceeded to warn us to be careful when climbing over. He had emptied the contents of the pint glass in the sink which then became blocked with debris from the glass. This was only made worse as it was now overflowing as Emre thought turning on the tap would clear the blockage.

The guy in the vest stated he was feeling better and felt he didn't need to go outside for some fresh air. Adam wasn't happy and insisted he go out for some air and then he could come back in, although I knew it was a means of getting him outside to refuse re-entry, and quite rightly so.

Adam chucked down the powder all over the bar which sets into a gel allowing for easy clean up. It was much appreciated that Adam took on the task without hesitation, but boy did he milk it. It must have taken him about 40 minutes or so and while he did an amazing job, he told every customer that approached the bar what he was doing, even if they hadn't enquired.

As the gel sets almost instantly and he continued to break it up and using a card to divide it, then scoop it up I said "Wow, you look like Pablo Escobar" to which he giggled. He did do an amazing job though, that I couldn't fault. I asked what was on the menu and he said, "looks like a full English with fried bread". Having seen the debris in the sink I replied, "yes I can see the friend slice floating in the sink like a Lilo"! I also recalled when serving him, he had egg yolk down the front of his vest.

Emre was upset that we'd experienced this, and I said, "welcome to hospitality. Where the customer expects you to do everything for them including wipe their arse and mop up their sick"! He said cleaning up their vomit was not part of our job and I said Adam had been amazing in cleaning it without hesitation. But we could be expected to do it ourselves, if not, who will, because the customer didn't have the capacity to do it. This event and the general attitude of the customers for the 30 or so minutes Emre had been working this event with me, led him to state "these people, are just dirty people"!

Given this was his first time working this event and he is young and naïve I felt maybe his remark was just because he perhaps found it all a little overwhelming if not intimidating. I went out to collect some glasses given there were quite a lot of empties, and we were almost out of glasses behind the bar. I'd almost given up on asking politely to get by and had come up with a new way to pass through the tightly packed crowd.

Given I was the only team member with long sleeves when wearing my hoodie, I'd learnt that I could merely slide through the crowd as the softness of my hoodie allowed for a smooth passage through the colon of leather and PVC. I'd often hear the odd 'ooh' or 'ahh' but I had to pull down my sleeves and cover my diamantes on the front of my top to avoid them scratching their leather/PVC. But it was fun, and I used to break out into a giggle when I'd fall out into an open space like a turb when it hits the water in the toilet bowl.

As I loaded the glass washer, Emre was still going on about how dirty the customers of the event were to which he then said. "You can see most of them have HIV"! I thought 'for fuck's sake, twice in one day'! As I was bent over, loading the glass washer with dirty glasses I wondered how or if I should reply to Emre's statement. "Really, how can you tell"? I asked as I stood up and looked out at the sea of customers to perhaps see what made him make such a statement. I was expecting him to perhaps say it was an immature joke, given his age he is of course very naïve and immature. In a bid to change the subject and on a wind-up, I asked "here, how do you spell 'HIV'"? I got a blank look and despite humming the Countdown clock from the TV show I got no response and continued with the glasses.

Emre continued "you can just tell, look how dirty they are"! I just could not comprehend how a university student could make such an unfounded assertion. I was going to resist temptation, but I thought in for a penny… "do I look dirty"? Emre looked at me puzzled before saying, "no! You're really clean and you always smell nice too"!

"In that case your HIV radar is seriously fucked" I said before continuing to load dirty glasses into the glass washer. I heard nothing more and as loaded the next handful of dirty glasses I looked through the gap in my legs to see where Emre was. He was at the end of the bar serving a customer and wasn't going to question my revelation further.

The last couple of hours of the event saw a small group of men form a huddle at the end of the bar. You'd hear the spanking of bare flesh and the occasional yelp from somewhere in the bar. The click clacks of handcuffs or restraints being applied and then someone handcuffed or restrained walking to a corner looking subdued. It was interesting to observe, and I was of the opinion of 'whatever floats your boat' but it did make me shudder slightly.

The group at the end of the bar started with kissing before they unzipped the guy's rubber jacket and started tweaking and pulling his nipples as though they were elastic bands. Three others of the crowd then joined in where one started to perform oral sex on him, one was fingering his anus and the third French kissing him whist holding his nose closed. It all escalated all so quickly and although not a prude in anyway, this was a little heavier than usual.

I felt uncomfortable, I guess more from a safety perspective in seeing someone having their airway blocked for what I would have deemed an unnatural length of time. The guy would struggle as though he was resisting or in a state of panic, but when he was eventually allowed air, he seemed to of enjoyed it and allowed it to happen again.

My second thought was surely this would have the pub loose or bring into dispute, its licence to operate. I messaged Johnnie on WhatsApp "my poor eyes" given I had heard stories of similar acts so knew he would know to what I was referring. He immediately appeared and seemingly enjoyed having a butcher's and just said "if its discreet then we just turn a blind eye". Slightly bemused I said, "is that discreet"?

Emre eventually went downstairs declaring he'd seen enough. Shortly after Bobby came up to help me as I was swamped for the remainder of the night. When we had 5 minutes for a breather, Bobby asked "are you ok? You've been a bit quite over the last couple of weeks"? I briefly outlined the malicious messages I'd been receiving and allowed him to read them and then I shared I was living with HIV.

Bobby asked, "would you like a hug"? To which I said, "no I want a cure, what use is a hug"! Bobby replied with his usual noise, "Rah! You'll have to make do with a hug; I'm going to hug you anyway". In my usual sarcastic manner, I rolled my eyes and said, "ok, if you must"!

Hugging Bobby was like hugging a bag of bones he is so slender. He said he was upset by the messages to which I thought was a normal reaction to have. But felt awkward as I didn't want anyone who reads them to be impacted by them. Given they had not emotionally impacted me, and I am living with the virus the messages allude to.

But Bobby started to lose me, although I am sure he meant well, when he said, "I have a friend called Ali, who will sort this person out for £20 if you know what I mean"?

I took back my phone and closing WhatsApp where the messages were, I said "will Ali settle for a few bags of crisps and a bottle of pop instead"? I didn't think the messages warranted bumping someone off or roughing someone up and I certainly didn't need someone else to do it for me. But I think deep down Bobby meant well.

Bobby said he'd keep it to himself and he's a good guy so I believe he will. I am working with Rudy tomorrow, and he can't keep nothing to himself, so I guess he will be ideal to share my status with so perhaps when I tell others it won't be a total surprise. Why have a dog and bark yourself, as they say?

Before the night was over one of the customers came to complain that the urinals were backed up and was overflowing with urine. I went into the gents and snapped a photo and posted it into the group chat with the caption "urgent". Jack came running up straight away and on walking into the flooded toilets asked me "are you ok dear"?

As I stood in the wall-to-wall pool of piss I said "yes! As soon as I saw this stream of piss I thought 'I must go for a paddle'"! Jack laughed seemingly trying to catch his breath at my remark. I said in a serious tone "yes, the stench does take your breath away doesn't it" which only intensified his fit of giggles to which he fucked off out the door to compose himself.

I stood in the toilets too afraid to move, in case the level of piss went above the soles of my trainers as it was slowly cascading from the urinals. Imitating Kate Winslet in the movie Titanic I started screaming "Oh what happened to 'I wont ever let go Jack'"! And as I got no response I shouted "Is there anybody out there? Can anybody hear me" to which Jack flung open the door, not realising the force from the bottom of the door forced the piss behind it to drench the bottom of my legs!

Jack looked horrified and safe to say this cured his fit of the giggles. "Don't just stand there, save me" I yelled. Jack outstretched his arm and I tip toed across the sea of urine and made it to safety. It transpired it wasn't my message that alerted Jack to come up, but the fact it had gone through the floor and was dripping on customers from the ceiling in the main bar.

I'M U=U TOO!

Ben, the self-confessed unofficial drag superstar recently dubbed Soho's very own Imelda Marcos. Not for his shoe collection but allegedly as rumours circulate, he has shared tips on how to claim free drinks. And a term I've never heard before, "skim" money from the till.

Allegedly, when you spot a customer holding cash or if you know they prefer to pay cash you only ring in one drink and calculate the rest of the order in your head. Or you use the 'clear' function on the till to remove items once you have told the customer the total amount due. There are five tills on the main bar and the trick apparently is to use the till furthest away from the customer, so they don't query the 'amount due' on the screen.

Then, you take out the amount not declared along with the customers change if they are due any and drop the undeclared amount into your tip glass which sits at the back of the bar.

I was so shocked that people would do this but was fascinated to learn how elaborate the process was. You never took notes over £5 as if management saw these in your tip jar it could arouse suspicion, apparently. So, it was advisable to stick to pound coins with a mixture of loose change.

The other tip that Ben had allegedly shared was claiming your drinks at the end of the night bought for you as a tip by a customer. You merely collected random receipts with more than one drink on. Preferably with your preferred drink to show to management at the end of the night. This somehow clarified that you weren't merely helping yourself, although you were indeed helping yourself.

There was to a degree a great level of trust on this, after all we were all employed on the basis, we had decency and integrity in protecting the company's assets which in turn kept us in a job.

Ben thought he was being smart, but little did he know he had quite early on aroused suspicion. Adam and Johnnie shared with me they were suspicious when night after night Ben would be claiming and trying to down four to five gin and tonics. Customers mainly consisting of long-established regulars weren't known to be that generous and Ben had nothing special nor unique about him to warrant a reward for his service. In fact, customers had and continued to share that he irritated them.

I did notice both Adam and Johnnie had started to subtly tell the team at the end of the night that receiving a credit card or cash tip was better than accepting a drink. Advantages being the entire team didn't have to wait for team members to consume their drinks before being released home. Freshly stocked fridges at the end of the night, especially mixers didn't look to Carl the next day as though we'd forgotten to bottle up. Given as mixers had been taken to pour these alleged 'tips'.

I only became suspicious of Ben and his little drinks hustle when others made me aware of it. But I thought if this is the company's policy and no procedure to verify these 'tips' then really who's to blame? Good luck to him I say! But I had never seen any alleged theft in terms of cash. Although I did always glance down at his tip glass, and it was full of loose change. What I had been told most likely did have some truth to it as I knew others that have been at the pub longer get tips from 'regulars' who are always stand-offish with new starters and defiantly don't tip.

So that answered my question when I asked, "who's Imelda"?

Ben aka Imelda had a gig at a neighbouring pub, and I had to be persuaded to attend with the others. After work we tottered down Old Compton Street to a small little pub up Dean Street. Ben was already on stage as we had all finished work late and I truly wanted to turn around and leave as it was cringing the moment we walked in the door.

I didn't want to appear rude or hurt Ben's feelings so thought I'd stay for one drink and then head off having shown my face. Ben's patter fell flat with the small crowd that remained and the drunks are usually the easiest to make laugh as they'll laugh at anything, so that said it all. His make-up was horrendous! It looked like he'd painted his face as a customer once said to me "with Crayola"! And his wig! On closer inspection when he came to say hello looked as though it was a £7.99 party city wig and he'd tried to make it a lace front wig. You could see his own hair line given the wig wasn't a lace front to be glued down in that manner.

What I did feel was, Ben was not a drag queen/artiste but was perhaps experimenting with his own gender identity. And in that regard Ben would have my full support. But he didn't show qualities of a drag queen with the years' experience he claimed. I wished him well for the remainder of the night although told him off that he'd agreed with the venue to waive any booking fee.

The next day at work I set about sharing my status with colleagues just to bring the 'whole' matter to a close as quickly as possible. I didn't want to share my status but in essence I wasn't arsed. I just feel it has absolutely no bearing on me and who I am.

Blair was on shift, and I threw into general conversation "have you heard about me having the AIDS"? Blair giggled nervously to which I assumed he had, and he casually brushed it off with a shrug of the shoulders as if to say it was no big deal.

"Although I'm sorry to hear that, but you're, ok? And well otherwise"? Blair asked. I explained very briefly how I had become infected and diagnosed along with being on treatment within 25 days of infection. We were interrupted by Rudy who then catching the end of our conversation enquired as to what was wrong with me.

I explained the same to Rudy and answered his questions around diagnosis and treatment. I explained I was 'undetectable' within 4 weeks of starting treatment meaning I was Undetectable=Untransmissible more commonly referred to as 'U=U'. This meant I was not able to pass on the virus during unprotected sex. Although my viral load was well below the undetectable threshold, I first had to remain undetectable for six months before I even considered engaging in unprotected sex.

Although having HIV meant I couldn't be infected by the 'big one' (HIV) but just like a person not living with HIV I was still susceptible to other sexually transmitted infections so being U=U wasn't a licence to have random sexual encounters without protecting myself.

Rudy had many questions around U=U and even declared that he was pleased I was now cured of HIV! Rudy being Rudy, meant that 'U=U' took a bit more explaining. That I was sadly, not cured, but am expected to live a normal life expectancy. And while I remained undetectable, I was unable to transmit the HIV virus.

As I took time to explain what I had learnt around HIV I felt Kenzie's actions were having a positive impact. Given I was raising awareness and educating my colleagues around U=U. What life so far has been like living with HIV along with the amazing emergence and availability of PrEP in protecting themselves from the virus in a bid to end all HIV infections in the UK.

I'm not concerned if colleagues start talking about me negatively behind my back. I feel any conversation around HIV is good conversation. If they are repulsed by my status, then if that makes them think on to practice safe sex with condoms, PEP & PrEP or take necessary precautions during substance abuse to avoid the virus then that's a win in my eyes!

As I told others I got the odd hug or the reassuring rub on the shoulder which made me want to vomit. But if they felt they needed to respond in this way in a bid to perhaps reassure me that it wasn't an issue then I was happy with that. They were all great about it, like they couldn't care less. It couldn't have worked out better, as I can't be doing with a lot of fuss and attention, it's just not my thing.

My seminar was broken up by a guy who walked behind the bar and declared it was his first shift. Nobody knew who he was nor were we expecting him. Anyhow his name was Gavin, and he was originally from Sussex, Brighton to be specific. For someone who nobody was expecting he sure as hell had a lot of confidence as within 10 minutes of arriving, he declared to us all that "I've been hired because of my good looks" before he went on to share "I'm middle class, a tory and studying to be an optician".

This raised a few eyebrows although Rudy took a shining to him instantly and they were inseparable for the entire night. They both stood and did what Rudy does best, nothing.

One customer remarked that the new boy had the look of a "pretty boy" but has "a head the size of a pea" which in his opinion was out of proportion to the rest of his body. A harsh observation I thought, but true all the same. As I took the cash from the customer I said, "but is there a difference between having a pea sized head, compared to a pea sized brain"? The customer laughed, only turning back to scowl when he realised, I was returning the insult.

Later into the shift, around 7pm Ben aka 'Imelda Marcos of Soho' came bouncing down the stairs. Scanning the pub floor with each step he took in the vain hope that at least one customer had eyes on him. He got halfway down and gave up and just stomped down the remainder of the stairs and across the pub floor in a huff. He took his temperature with the thermometer gun and came immediately rushing over to me saying "what's this I hear about you and the police, something about WhatsApp messages"?

Ben was not on my priority list of people to tell but he seemed to know an awful lot already which showed he'd been in the 'tearoom' catching up. Plus, I thought if I play it down given the mood he is in, he'll be prone to have a sulk and I've got to work with him tonight.

I didn't pull out the messages but just briefly referenced what they said and how I'd reported this, and it "was currently being investigated given I am living with HIV".

Quick as a flash Ben said, "yeah! me too, I'm HIV positive, I'm U=U"!

He was quick to remind me "I'm surprised you didn't twig! Remember when we worked upstairs, and we were talking about covid-19 vaccinations? And I said I had been called for mine because I had an "underlying health condition" and you said you'd already had both of your vaccinations…"?

"Yeah" I said inquisitively. "Well, I thought you would have cottoned on that I was referring to HIV. I don't think I could have been more obvious"! Ben said followed by that horrendous cackle.

But to be fair to Ben I did recall vividly the conversation as I was loading the glass washer as he sashayed around the pub floor collecting the last glasses for the last wash. I did wonder if he had or was referring to HIV.

I told myself off for being presumptive and erased the thought entirely. Plus, Ben said he had only been called for his first vaccine when PLWHIV fell into a particular priority group and had been called 7 months earlier for the first dose. So, I assumed his "underlying health condition" was further down the priority list.

Ben asked what the messages said again, and I told him. He raised an eyebrow and said "oh, how dull" as he walked off cackling, leaving me in peace.

What was interesting was everyone I told, seemed to turn it into a 'Guess who has HIV' game amongst the team. And while they stated they didn't suspect me, they started to reel off names of people they did suspect as having HIV. This seemed to be based solely on that person's appearance. For such an old virus, in its 40th year since the first person was diagnosed in the United Kingdom. I couldn't believe it was a now a parlour game amongst my colleagues. Would they play this in a predominantly heterosexual working environment or is it their view that 'AIDS' and 'gays' just merely go together like Thelma & Louise or Wallace & Gromit.

So, who was on their 'HIV list of suspicion'? Jack was at the top of Rudy, Alex and Emre's list. I found the whole conversation odd if not uncomfortable. I could only assume their little past time was based loosely on images and footage they'd seen of AIDS suffers looking emaciated. Or the general perception of living with HIV/AIDS meant you had to look gaunt and frail.

Jack looked anything but thin and was known as 'fat Jack' when I started. Jack himself shared; he'd gone from being a muscle Mary to putting on a few pounds. Although Jack was now working out again and was quite buff up top although he was often imitated as walking like a duck by Johnnie and Adam referring to Jack as a "lard arse" who needs to lay off the left-over bagels given he stomps when he walks.

Johnnie, Bobby and Emre were top of the list for others, who confirmed their loose assumption was based on how incredibly slender and unhealthy they all appeared. Nobody mentioned Kenzie which I thought was odd given he constantly shares the risks and exposure he takes with his sexual promiscuity.

I wasn't offended by their bizarre past time, and I didn't hold back in sharing I found it immature and asked them to stop. What may start out as 'fun' can quickly turn into unfounded allegations. Which have a habit of circulating and can have untold damage on someone's confidence, reputation, and mental health. I asked them to think about their actions and how they'd feel if, what they perceived to be a bit of harmless fun ended up impacting that colleague.

You'd probably imagine Ben living with HIV too would perhaps bring us closer together. But it didn't and I guess it had no cause to. PLWHIV take their meds in the morning and get on with their daily life. Ben did over the next few days share elements of his diagnosis and his experience with accessing treatment in the Philippines where he was diagnosed. He said treatment was much better in the Philippines compared to his experience so far with the NHS in the UK. He shared his CD4 was, and occasionally fell below 200 which he casually shrugged off, but I knew was concerning.

CD4 are white blood cells that play a role in our immune systems and give an indication to the overall strength of the immune system. A CD4 below 200 generally is a diagnosis of AIDS. But HIV medication today is so advanced that I know of people who upon being diagnosed HIV positive and had a CD4 of 3 and another had a CD4 of 5. It took many months but slowly and reassuringly their medication saw their CD4 steadily bounce back to over 300.

An average CD4 of a person not living with HIV is between 500 – 1,400. Upon diagnosis of HIV my CD4 was 973 although now in the UK CD4 is no longer measured routinely. Since 2015 an individual with a HIV diagnosis can start ART (antiretroviral therapy) straight away. Before 2015, a HIV positive individual's CD4 would have to drop to 350 before they'd be offered treatment.

Colleagues often said Ben was a negative energy, vitriolic even. In the private chats the guys would often put the snake emoji in place of Ben's many nicknames. This was said to symbolise Ben's snake like nature as he slithered between the managers and his vitriolic nature being venomous. To say he was new, he had somewhat alienated himself as nobody liked working with him and he would often be seen standing on his own with his legs crossed and his hands clasped in front of him looking lost.

You can be caustic in your humour and still be funny but when Ben tried to be funny, he was the only one who would cackle which echoed over the silence of others. It was said his vile and bitter remarks made people uncomfortable as they came across as sinister as opposed to throwing a little shade.

Ben had a habit of pulling someone up on the smallest thing that he viewed as being discriminative or an outdated term. But bizarrely, he would then himself behave in the same manner.

I wondered if his HIV diagnosis from two years ago had a bearing on his attitude and behaviour. In the end I have stopped making the effort to talk to him as whenever I say anything he replies "no, no, that wouldn't have happened"!

I didn't even question if he was feeling ok, I just genuinely assumed he was not fit for work and avoided him as someone who seemed mentally unstable. I didn't share as much with colleagues, but I overheard several conversations where colleagues had reached the same conclusion.

The other night I came into the bar to get to the staff room to change for the start of my shift. Kenzie was stood behind the bar with his arms crossed and a face like thunder. I approached the bar to get the staff room key which usually hangs on a hook where Kenzie was standing.

Noticing the key was not hanging there meant there was somebody already in the staff room. I gingerly pushed open the door to make sure I didn't hit whoever was stood behind changing.

I got the fright of my life and let out a little squeal! "Hi Will! Don't I look fabulous in full geish [sic] (geisha)"! Ben had dragged up with his Crayola crayons again and had a set of small heels on, a plain black skirt with a black fedora hat. The pièce de resistance, a brown blanket that he had made into a poncho. No word of a lie it looked as though he had swiped it off the local big issue seller's dog. It was filthy, stained and covered in debris.

I did drag for ten years from 2001 to 2011 and was relatively successfully at it, not to blow my own trumpet. I remember starting out I made my own costumes with some of the cheapest fabrics. But you always made sure you took pride in the garments you were making, and you made sure they could withstand being scrutinised especially by 'the gays' who won't hold back in their critique!

I was lost for words as I looked at Ben, but for all the wrong reasons. I think he noticed and started to play down his make-up and outfit by saying "well, it's only half geish [sic] (geisha), I didn't have time to do full geish [sic]"! I felt awful but I could only be honest but managed to delay my constructive feedback by stating "right, I've got to changed, I don't want to be late".

I headed downstairs, passing Kenzie on the way who bizarrely spoke and asked, "did you see Ben in drag"! I replied, looking miffed, "yeah". Well, that confirmed why Kenzie was sulking given a colleague in drag, albeit bad drag, was going to perhaps get more attention than him. Especially as he was working up in the attic.

Shortly after Ben came down and everybody was sneering, including customers and I felt sorry for the guy. Adam and Johnnie were quick to state Ben wasn't on the rota and shouldn't have been on shift. I wasn't sure how true this was because I had seen him on the copy of the rota I had.

Anyhow he dashed back upstairs to get his phone and when he did the whole team were slating his makeup and outfit. I would have usually chipped in and defended someone in that situation, but I couldn't because Ben had really talked himself up since he started working here about how fabulous his makeup is and how flawless his costumes are. And what my colleagues were saying was true, Ben "looks a twat".

By break time Ben had given the dog its blanket back and was back in his regular clothes although with what little had remained on his face makeup wise. He came and said, "so what do you think"? I was still lost for words, well that's a lie! I was struggling how to give someone feedback knowing he wouldn't agree and would most likely have a meltdown.

Ben then said as he stood like Tyra Banks "the others said you did drag for 10 years and was well known. So, I'd love to get some tips from an old pro"! While the others were right, I knew they'd shared as much to take the piss. I said "well, you should always make sure your outfits are impeccable. You could do with some sparkle, where's your earrings, lashes, glitter"?

I saw his hackles come up and he was sticking his tongue into his check, he was pissed! I wasn't fazed, I had nothing to lose, and I was giving constructive feedback, it was up to him what he did with it.

"Well darling! I did say this is only my half geish"! Ben snapped. Exhausted I said "In drag you should 'never' doing anything by half! If you can't give 100% then don't bother at all"!

I walked off and Johnnie from the other side of the bar intercepted me saying he overheard the conversation and said what I said was exceptionally well put but was wasted on Ben. I said, "I couldn't give a toss"!

At the end of the night, Ben did what he usually did, claimed he had more than a handful of drinks bought for him, and he was now redeeming them to consume. As the pub was empty and we were all cleaning Ben stated loudly, for all to hear, "unlike Will! Customers appreciated my ensemble and bought me five gin and tonics to show their appreciation"!

Kenzie who had come from upstairs to collect the mop, along with Johnnie jovially screamed "Oh the shade"! I merely retorted, "dear, the drinks were not intended to be consumed! Gin is ideal for removing crayon from porous surfaces"!

A few minutes later Kenzie came to me all excited saying "Ben is sat in the DJ booth crying because of what you said"! With a roll of my eyes and Johnnie now present telling Kenzie to stop shit stirring. Stood with a jaycloth in one hand and a bottle of sanitiser in the other I'd been wiping tables with, I paused and said, "it's not worth spilling tears for. Crayon can be quite stubborn, but if he keeps at it, it'll come off eventually"! Blair turned, overhearing, and quipped, "you're terrible Muriel"!

'THE ATMOSPHERE CHANGED'

As I was heading into work, I bumped into Jack on Old Compton Street. He said was heading to the vaccination centre, as he used to say, "saving lives one jab at a time". I'm not sure why he was so self-deprecating about his vaccine work. I guess it was a case of him getting the jibe in before someone else did. He didn't need to, not with me anyway. But given he knew Adam and Johnnie constantly ribbed him for it I guess it had become a habit for Jack. But it was something he should be proud of, and I had this conversation with him on many occasions.

Jack asked how I was and said he'd see me later in the evening as he was DJ'ing, and he knew I was working a 12-hour shift. Jack had shared from our conversations that he got nervous when all eyes were on him when DJ'ing. I guess this came about when I shared standing on stage as a drag queen, you get the confidence when you've got a face full of slap on. Jack shared his comfort was chewing on his vape or USB stick. It was kind of sweet that he shared that he had such vulnerabilities with me, given he always held himself so confidently. Well, sometimes masked by the dumb blonde act, but I'm not that gullible.

I was on the day shift with Ben and all we really said to each other was "hey, alright" and then totally avoided each other. Well, I made the effort to say, "hey alright", Ben would just stare into space, and I'd just get on with what needed doing.

He did speak to me briefly to say, "Oh look, you see him over there"? As he pointed to a customer I had regularly served. Tall chap, Scottish accent, ginger hair thrown into a distressed ponytail. Often dressed in a fitted shirt and three-quarter length trackies paired with a clutch bag. "He's the Queens hairdresser" Ben said excitedly! Out of all the famous and not so famous faces that strolled in and out of the pub. That same old phrase, repeated in a giddy voice "He's the Queens hairdresser" was like an echo that had been bouncing off the walls for as long as he'd been coming to the pub. It was the only message that wasn't a Chinese whisper, it never got distorted, every colleague relayed it verbatim.

Mr Carmichael has been teasing the tresses of Her Majesty for over twenty years. He is a nice, down to earth chap and as you'd expect with impeccable manners. It is said he attends the Queen's hair once a week at her various residences. I had to google if he was still doing so during the pandemic as he was casually chatting with his pint, with some unsavoury regulars, the great unwashed! But it turns out like many other nanas around the country Her Majesty was in her protective bubble for the duration of the pandemic.

I only ever heard him mention "Her Majesty" once in conversation when I was at his table collecting glasses, you know, as you do. But what was more pressing for me was, I was always dying to ask him. If he made a bit more of an effort, dress code wise when he visited the Queen? Although he was out socialising, in a grotty back street Soho pub in his casuals, he did always look a little bit like he was on Universal Credit.

As Johnnie, Adam, Rudy and Alex all came on shift later that day I mentioned that Jack was DJ'ing and that I'd not experienced his set before. Collectively they gave me eye rolls and sighs! Adam & Alex were the most critical saying that "it's going to be a long night if Jack is playing". Meaning they found his set boring which I thought was incredibly mean. I am sure there is more to it for a DJ to play tracks but isn't it essentially hitting the 'play' button? It's not like Jack was going to be giving us a three-hour recital on a recorder, tunes are tunes, no?

Well, I was just pleased we got some decent tunes on when Jack arrived. He seemed to fanny about a lot, but once we got some tunes on the place was banging. Well, for about an hour and the place started to empty quick which I thought was bad for a Friday night. Adam and Johnnie kept saying they wanted to bang their heads against the wall because Jack was DJ'ing. Alex surprised me the most as he did nothing but complain constantly. So enraged was Alex to the point where he said to me, "I want to punch Jack square in the face, what is this shit"!

Collectively it went beyond being shady bitches to proper deep and meaningful emotions. Then I couldn't believe it when they would catch Jacks eye and smile and give him a big thumbs up. As I witnessed this, all I could hear was that famous meme of Kim Woodburn "you two faced bunch, you chicken livered shits"! Shortly after I caught Jacks eye and did the same, gave him a smile and a thumbs up and he did the same in return.

At the end of the night as I was walking past with the mixers to bottle up Jack said "that wasn't my best! I need to have a good clear out and organise my catalogue"! I didn't see what the problem was and just said "it's the Friday before payday, the economy and furlough as it is people haven't got the dosh to be splashing about so don't stress it"! He packed up his wires and left pretty quickly, poor guy.

He didn't say goodnight and when I asked, "has Jack left"? Johnnie replied "yeah, thank fuck, I wanted to hang myself"!

The following day I came up the fire escape to get to the staff room. As I opened the fire exit door onto the upstairs bar Jack was sat on a stool by the window "hey Will! I was waiting for you" Jack said smiling. I wasn't sure why, but it was a very nice welcome all the same. I popped on my work hoodie in the staff room and met up with Jack at the bar which he said he'd prepared for opening which was a nice of him. As none of the other managers or supervisors do that.

We got chatting, starting with the police investigation around the malicious messages. Jack wanted to know how I was feeling about it all and naturally he was keen to find out who it was. I said again that I was keen for the police to investigate the evidence I had put forward and allow them to conclude. And see what they advised as an appropriate means of recourse.

"Can I say Will. I think your being too nice to this person and that your making excuses for them. I want to investigate the matter, as it is only an 'allegation' and I want to take it further with the assistance of the company". Jack said.

I said with 23 years in hospitality, most of that time in hotel management I understood the investigatory and disciplinary procedure like the back of my hand. But for the time being I felt, there was no better 'authority' to conduct an unbiased investigation and implement the appropriate level of justice.

Plus given I knew how the company operated with two numbnuts sat in a central office calling themselves "HR". I didn't want my HIV status being scrutinised given it was central to this matter without the individuals knowing what I even looked like.

Jack then asked "Will, would you mind if I share something personal that happened to me? Something traumatic"? I thought 'oh here we go! I'll show you mine if you show me yours'. I suspected this was all part of the counselling training, open up to someone and they'll open up to you. I was genuinely interested to hear what Jack had to share although I was keen for the conversation to be about anything other than 'me'. So, I said "only if you want to".

What Jack told me really touched me considering most say I have a heart of stone. That he felt comfortable to share something so personal with me. Although I was still weary that this was in a bid to draw me into a false sense of security when I truly wanted to stick by my guns for the moment. Although what Jack had shared with me did put me in a position to perhaps see my situation from Jacks perspective.

That Jack had information and wanted to act upon it with an investigation to ensure any appropriate action was taken. Although I didn't feel any action the company would take would compare to any action by the authorities. Jack then kept saying that both he and Carl were keen to investigate and given the evidence I'd shown Jack, the incident was an act of gross misconduct, and the individual would be dismissed.

A very small part of me was suspicious, having witnessed Jack calling Kenzie a prick and seeing they only just tolerated each other. Along with Kenzie himself telling me he didn't get along with Jack. I couldn't help but have thoughts that I was perhaps being played here in order for Jack to get rid of Kenzie by way of dismissal. But while Jack stood in front of me rabbiting on, I was telling myself Jack wouldn't use me like that, he seemed so sincere and kind. But I had only known him a few months.

I was truly listening to my gut on this one and was telling myself to hold out for the authorities to conclude their investigation. They can enforce the law; they can conduct an investigation and gain access to areas that my employer just couldn't.

The fire exit door flew open, which Jack had his back to, and he didn't turn around to see who it was. I was facing Jack and could see it was Kenzie coming through the fire exit. Kenzie looked at Jack and then me as he walked towards me to collect the staff room key which was hanging on the hook behind me. I could have handed Kenzie the key, we didn't need to exchange words for that, and it would save Kenzie the few extra steps. But I didn't, I was frozen on the spot. Jack was asking who the individual was and now here was me, Jack and the number one suspect all in the same room!

Me and Jack remained silent the whole time, although I picked up the ice scoop to look as though we were busy. Jack didn't move, he didn't even turn his head to see Kenzie approaching from behind, although he did clap eyes on Kenzie when he walked behind me to collect the key. As Kenzie walked off with the key and out of earshot, Jack's body jolted like he'd just received a premonition from his spirit guide! Jack said with an enquiring face "Will! Why has the atmosphere just changed"?

I regret it now, but my immediate reaction was to giggle. Jack is constantly ribbed for having an interest in spirituality and mediumship and his reaction just as I described it was comedy gold. He had that vacant look as though he was receiving a fax from the 'other side' but was out of paper, it was all very 'Carry On' film like.

"Will, I'm serious, the atmosphere just changed, just like that". I didn't know how to respond, and he was making me giggle more to which he started laughing too as I was trying to catch my breath while saying "stop it! I'll wet myself"!

I'd already witnessed what a bitchy, backstabbing, and toxic environment the pub was and for me this was not a career move. I was merely passing by, and I wanted to remain relatively anonymous in a bid to retain a quiet life. Jack said "right, ok" in a tone that I took to mean he'd concluded it was Kenzie without me having to say so.

Given Jack had shared something so personal about himself we chatted continuously for almost 2 hours and for his time and patience I naturally thought I should buy him something small as a token of appreciation. Although at times I didn't always agree with his advice, he was an effective listener and offered a valid point of view adding balance to the argument.

I spent a couple of days pondering what I could buy him that was 'appropriate'. I have always been known amongst friends and partners for getting off the wall, quirky yet fitting gifts when the occasion has arisen.

But I had never bought a gift for a work colleague, only secret Santa if I truly couldn't get out of it. Anyhow, I hardly knew Jack nor his personality beyond the boundaries of work so struggled for ideas.

He once asked what aftershave I was wearing and said, "it smells gorgeous". And while it was a risk buying a scent as these too can be deemed 'personal' I knew he liked the scent so thought it was practical. Gays like smellies so I bought him a bottle of Issy Miyake - L'Eau d'Issey Pour Homme. I had to dash from Tottenham Court Road all the way to Selfridges by Marble Arch, popped it into a gift bag with some fuchsia pink tissue paper and a thank you card.

I decided to wait a couple of days instead to present Jack with my small gesture. Given Jack was scheduled to be managing alone and I thought it would save us both any embarrassment by neither being quizzed as to why he was taking a gift bag back to the office. It was all innocent, for me it has always been second nature to bestow a gift on someone that has done something worthy.

I was working the upstairs bar so hid it behind the bar for Jack to arrive and Adam to hand over the shift to Jack. When he came on shift, he came and said he'd come up to see how I was to which I presented him with the bag "this is for you, it is only something small, I had no idea what to get, but just a little thank you for your time, patience and kindness".

He was so sweet, he said thank you and I could see his eyes welling up and he declared "Oh my I want to cry. I know you don't like being touched so…" to which I assumed that was a hug out of the window, but it didn't matter.

I said "I don't mind being touched, but working here, customers do it in a pervy way, they don't just touch you, they grab you. If they remark you smell nice, they drag you towards them or they grab your bum and I find it all inappropriate".

But I still didn't get a hug, but that was fine because it wasn't about that, it was warming that I had shown my appreciation for his time and advice if not the burden of it all.

Jack shot off to get on with his work but shortly came back up through the fire exit with tears in his eyes to say thank you again. I said, "so we've both seen each other cry now, so were equal" and as he wiped his eyes Jack said "you know Will. I never get treated like this; I never get treated like this by men. All men are cunts"!

I didn't know how to reply to that so just said "not all of us"!

Leaving the pub is something I'm always mulling over, but I quite enjoy the job and the hours. Some customers can be a pain but overall, they are quite entertaining.

While I am thick skinned, I must admit the way Adam talks about me behind my back with both customers and colleagues is starting to get to me. If I don't overhear it myself, it then gets fed back to me. Often by more than one person which only verifies the gossip I'm being told to be accurate. I find it not only unprofessional but bad management as it does not promote team cohesiveness and is an incredible waste of time and energy.

But what has been noticed by others and myself, is Adam keeps placing me in the upstairs bar when it is meant to be shared equally amongst the whole team. I can only assume this is some form of sadistic form of punishment. But secretly it only benefits me finically with cash tips that start from £90 upwards per night. And you get to manage yourself without some tweaker barking orders.

While I was working upstairs Jack came to see me. We stood behind the bar leaning against the fridges. A week or so had passed since our last chat in the upstairs bar and he raised the subject of the messages again. It seemed Jack was now playing bad cop after attempting to play good cop. He was a lot more aggressive in his approach which got my back up. I wasn't sure what the 'hurry' was, why Jack was so eager to progress with an internal investigation when the matter was being investigated by the police.

"Will! I don't think you're going about it in the right manner. I have told Carl who the person is that sent the messages and we want to start an investigation"!

I shared with Jack again, that while I had information by knowing where the person who brutally assaulted me infecting me with HIV lived. What I didn't have, was the confidence to inform he police despite several medical professionals 'insisting' I did. I was even made to feel guilty by these professionals whilst trying to process the diagnosis of now being HIV positive. I was being thrust rape leaflets and advice lines into my hands while they verbally groomed me to report the "assault" stating "you wouldn't want this to happen to someone else would you"!

The reason I didn't have the confidence to report the incident to the police was I didn't have the evidence that what he did to me was not consensual. I didn't have the balls to make a stand if I was going to be called a liar, nor asked to somehow prove that he knocked me unconscious before raping me.

However, with this incident of the malicious messages, I had digital tangible evidence that was to a degree undeniable. The authorities had the power to investigate and access information that my employer couldn't. This would allow an investigation to take place and my allegation to be upheld.

As I had shared with Jack last time, two numbnuts in HR for the company I worked didn't have the resources nor the facilities to investigate at the same calibre as the authorities. Would they risk dismissing someone who qualified for an employment tribunal given their length of service. Would any investigation just be a whitewash to protect the business. I felt I was in a better position for the police to deal with the matter and if the company wished to act based on any police action, then so be it. I knew our contracts did state that any legal action outside work could be reason for terminating a contract.

It seemed Jack had not listened to my point on this as he looked vacant the entire time. "I am taking control of the situation" Jack said in an assertive tone. I just shrugged my shoulders and said, "que sera, sera". Jack then walked away. For the remainder of the shift and the walk home I felt really let down and disappointed by Jack's tone and attitude. Although I couldn't fault his determination, but something didn't seem right.

I got into bed and didn't get a wink of sleep. I had only ever tossed and turned so much when I was going through seroconversion, where the HIV virus starts to affect your body. After several hours of lying-in bed staring into darkness and then the ceiling as dawn broke. It dawned on me that I was in those hours starting to resent Jack, who appeared only to be wanting to help me.

I couldn't fault him for wanting to do the right thing and I was happy for him to do the right thing. I just didn't see what the rush was when an investigation was ongoing with the relevant authority that carried more weight.

I truly had not slept a wink and I was exhausted but got up and put the kettle on. I toasted two granary slices and sat at my dining table. I didn't have the appetite to eat, and I sent Jack a text message saying, "if you feel you 'must' inform human resources. Even just to seek advice then I want to be present when you have that conversation".

I felt if the crooks of this investigation would be around 'my HIV' then I should be present while they discuss, probe, and dissect it. Even if I am just to listen in while those conversations took place. As I squeezed some oranges, I got a reply from Jack saying he would arrange a meeting between me, Carl, and himself.

I had been put in the upstairs bar to work yet again, this time by Jack. During the shift, me and Jack hardly spoke given I rarely had reason to go downstairs, and Jack didn't bother coming to check if I was ok work wise or if I needed anything as he usually did.

I came down at the end of the shift extremely tired and exhausted as I had not slept by this time for 39 hours. The boys were still cleaning the main bar, so I plonked myself on a stool struggling to keep my eyes open. Jack came from the office and said, "Will, can I have a word in the office please". I followed him up to the office in silence.

In the office he asked, "how are you"? I could see having looked in the mirror of the bar I looked fucked so thought 'what a stupid question'. I said I was good but tired as I'd been awake all night. Jack had sat himself on the desk with his legs swinging and placing his hands in the prayer position. I thought 'fucking hell, here we go' and while I was miffed and wanting to go home, I had to stop myself from giggling because all I could hear in my head was Johnnie saying something shady, but funny about Jack had he been a fly on the wall.

Jacks face full of empathy said, "I want to apologise for how I acted. It was wrong of me, and I just wanted to say I am handing control back to you". I was confused and given I was so tired I was so pissed off by this U-turn. For me it was a case of, no let's not back off now, let's go ahead now we've started.

Jack was looking at me waiting for my response. The guy looked just as exhausted as me, the whites of his usually sparkly eyes were clouded and bloodshot. His eyelids droopy and I instantly felt guilty that my problem was burdening his already busy life outside work.

I shared that I appreciated his concern and couldn't fault his determination nor resolve in wanting to investigate this matter. To ensure that his venue, my place of work was indeed a safe space for all. "It's you I am concerned about; I want you to feel safe at work" Jack said as he became chocked.

I got chocked and upset because Jack was getting upset and before we knew it, we both became teary but to be fair, we both looked absolutely knackered. I outstretched my arms to gesture a hug and he slid off the desk and we had a long embrace. I wasn't in the habit of hugging people so did the awkward, macho pat on the back at the same time.

"I'll let you know what the Police determine" I said before we both headed downstairs to join the rest of the team who were all sat waiting.

It was clear they'd been speculating why me, and Jack had been in the office. Alex pursed his lips like Kenneth Williams to suggest something else had been going on in the office to which him and Bobby fell about giggling.

They ribbed me in our private group chat and were quite grotesque. But I was sure to tell them we were discussing the "AIDS" messages before any rumours started to circulate which made them take the piss even more. I closed the chat on my phone, smiled because I was young and immature once, before turning onto Charing Cross road on the walk home.

While I am not someone who usually mulls things over, I really did wonder on the walk home why Jack had done a U-turn. I concluded, knowing all those involved that no U-turn was likely to of been made by Jack. I suspect, Jack approached Carl to set up a meeting as we'd discussed in the text messages. Given the relationship between Kenzie, who once told me "I have management wrapped around my little finger", referring to Carl, Adam, and Johnnie. I would bet my life on it that Carl had no interest in pursuing the matter when approached by Jack. Carl is well known for avoiding difficult and confrontational situations although I suspect on this occasion it is Carl's misplaced loyalty towards Kenzie that was the stumbling block in Jacks well-meant intervention.

Although this is me speculating, but I'm generally never wrong when I'm with hunch.

BAGEL BOY

As I popped down the road to the chippy for my dinner break, I noticed they had a sign in the window advertising for staff. I thought I'd enquire to break up the monotony of the people I am currently working with. I'd shovelled chips in my first job at a surrey theme park so knew it wasn't all that taxing.

The owner knew me well and said I could start the following day, working around my current hours at the pub. I said, "well, let me come in and see if it's a decent fit". I'd noticed that during the hours being offered it wasn't that busy and the point of taking a second job wasn't for the money. But just to get out of the house and to be kept busy. It wouldn't work if I spent most of my time stood around not being productive.

I was to go straight into the pub after the trial shift at the chippy, so I messaged Jack and asked for permission to come on site to leave my bag in the staff room. Jack replied "of course" so I set about packing a few toiletries to perhaps wash off the scent of grease and vinegar before starting my shift in the pub. I arrived and got changed in the staff room, I wore navy chinos and a white fitted open shift as per the chippie's uniform policy.

As I left the pub Jack was now out the front with Carl setting up the outdoor seating on Old Compton Street. "Hi darling, how are you? You look nice where you going"? Jack enquired.

"I'm off to the chippy" I replied, having already cleared it with Carl I just assumed Jack may have already known. "Are you getting something to eat"? Jack said looking confused as it was only just approaching 11am. "No, I'm off for a trial shift, well the owner thinks I'm 'onboard' but it is very much a trial" I said while manoeuvring around Jack in order not to be late. "Ok darling, well good luck" Jack said while he threw me a kiss. I read nothing into it other than that he was being supportive and encouraging, in a relaxed and camp manner as us gays do.

But it did throw me a little and I giggled as I walked down the road to the chippy. Wondering if Jack was perhaps questioning himself 'why did I do that'? I know I would given we both maintained a professional outlook in a work environment. And I'd noticed, like me, Jack was very guarded and kept work and personal life, including emotions, separate. But it did make my day and off I went.

The chippy had me put out the outdoor seating after giving me an apron. Jack and Carl were taking the piss from down the road as they spotted me while still putting out the pubs furniture and they seemingly found it amusing. Well, I served one customer and the chap I was buddied with said it is "this boring all the time during the day". Speaking with the owner I said serving one customer in 1 hour and 42 minutes meant regrettably the job just wasn't for me. And with that I headed to the staff room of the pub to change.

Carl said he was surprised I lasted that long and vowed to give me more hours to get me out of the house. I appreciated that, but at the same time he misunderstood I wanted to get out of the house and spend it with some new, more interesting people. Not, spend more time with the lost boys.

While my colleagues all found it hysterical that I'd not only gone to the chippy for a job, but that I had only lasted 1 hour 42 minutes. I got a counselling session with Jack "I'm sorry it didn't work out Will"! I had to remind Jack several times that it was my decision to leave after 1 hour 42 minutes. Given the chippy just wasn't stimulating enough, I'd not been 'let go' by the owner! Jack said concerned "I really don't want you to leave" to which I said I wasn't intending to leave, just fill in some of my spare time. Me and Jack had, had this conversation when I said I wouldn't resign due to the malicious messages as this is what the 'blackmailer' demanded.

But it was inevitable I would resign one day but I wanted this matter cleared up first, although I did want to leave deep down. Just because of Adam's behaviour and the clique between Adam, Johnnie and Kenzie and their vile behaviour to all of us "newbies" which only served to highlight their own insecurities.

That night me and Bobby were working the upstairs bar on a Saturday night and the crowd was predominantly straight. Although I'd only worked in the pub a few months and during a pandemic I was able to gauge the change of the demographic of the crowd. As for years I'd been a customer of the pub, so knew the crowd it traditionally drew. I guess this was inevitable given the regeneration of Soho and the erasure of its seedy history for the benefit of the tourists. Which I saw to be a tremendous shame as it was Soho's seedy and decrepit past that was its charm and made it such a draw for tourists and me when I fell into the gay scene in the late 1990's.

No matter where you partied in London, you always left a club and headed to Soho to satisfy those mid-morning munchies. Old Compton Street itself was lined with small independent cafés and restaurants. Where you were served on 80's dinnerware on Formica tables often by the owner himself. Proudly presenting a cheese omelette accompanied with a bit of limp lettuce and grated carrot as a side garnish. This was a time when Balan's had only the one small café that was reserved exclusively for those with the pink pound.

At least 4 nights a week I'd leave Soho catching the bus outside Foyles bookshop on Charing Cross Road to Madame Tussauds where I worked. I would shower in the changing room before starting my shift and repeating the process again.

The straight crowd are just a pain in the arse! They buy bigger and more expensive rounds often with shots each time meaning they get drunk faster. They guys would want to head off somewhere else but the girls being the somewhat sensible ones of the group. Would highlight how wasted they were already and would most likely not be let into another venue, so would stay put.

Or they'd arrive at our pub seemingly let in by the door team after sharing with me they'd been turned away from another venue for being "too drunk" and didn't realise it was a "gay place". This would often lead to subtle homophobia by the straight men. But would overlook the "gayness" of the pub so long as they could keep chucking drinks down their throats.

With this and a combination of our regulars complaining that their 'safe space' (LGBT) had been hijacked. Me and Bobby spent most of the night absolutely slammed working non-stop. At one point we ran out of glasses as we were turning them over quicker than we could clean them. It was clear the capacity of the bar was well over the legal 140 capacity limit.

Adam had finished at 5pm but was back at the pub and a table was made available for him with me and Bobby upstairs in his capacity as a manager. Adam sent his friend over to place the drinks order for all eight of them. The friend himself was confused as to what mixer went with what spirit. So, as I do with all customers, I took the liberty to read back his drinks order for confirmation. This guy couldn't have cared less but he agreed it all the same before handing me Adam's staff discount card.

The newbies didn't have permission to authorise staff discount on the till, although the 'originals' did which had not gone unnoticed. I gestured to Adam if I could use a supervisor's code to which he rolled his eyes and pouted in dismay. I took this to mean 'no' and that perhaps I should know better.

This meant I had to leave the bar and take his card downstairs for a manager to approve on the system. Well, downstairs was just as rammed, and it took me forever to find someone to approve the discount on the till. I went back up and returned the discount card to Adam and he seemed quite conciliatory "sorry Will. I didn't mean to be a pain". I said he wasn't being a pain, smiled and continued on my way given he knew what the procedure was. How my till ID didn't have authority to enter the discount mode to then enter his staff discount card serial number for the discount to be deducted from his bill.

I had all night, so, his reaction only delayed his order, but if he was willing to wait while I followed the correct procedure that he himself insists we follow then I had no issue at all. And given the size of the order the discount was a decent amount and worth the wait.

I prepared the drinks and popped them on a tray on the bar. I always did this in order of the drinks listed on the receipt in a clockwise direction to make it easy for the customer. On explaining how he could ensure they all each got the correct drink by merely following the drinks on the receipt in a clockwise direction to those on the tray he exclaimed "nah! I don't need any help".

Low and behold as soon as he got to Adams table the guy turned around shouting to get my attention. Holding up a drink from the tray "excuse me, what's this one"? to which I tried to establish where on the tray he picked it up from in accordance with the receipt on the tray. But he had moved drinks around so I couldn't identify them as per the receipt. There were a few different spirits all with coke so I said they would just have to sniff out which was rum and coke and assume the other was the vodka and coke etc.

As I continued to serve other customers, I saw Adam come to the bar and made the effort to get Bobby's attention. "Will has made a mistake, he's put Lemonade in the Belvedere when it should be Soda – change it please"! I'd made the drink as it was ordered, I even read back the order which was confirmed as correct by Adam's friend. So, any mistake wasn't mine, I'd prepared the drinks as they were ordered. I just bit my tongue and thought it was best left unchallenged but didn't understand why Adam emphasised "Will has made a mistake". Difference was I was sobor, both Adam and his friend were not.

A short time later I was emptying the glass washer when I felt a hard and forceful shove on my right shoulder. It was the kind of shove that was hostile and was slightly bruising. As I turned around scowling to see who had the gall to lay their hands on me? I saw a skeletal figure in jeans and a t-shirt walking away from behind the bar.

Bobby was pouring a drink beside me at the taps, "who the fuck is that" I asked Bobby. I couldn't believe that a customer had the nerve to come behind the bar. "That's Bagel Boy"! Bobby said while he also had a look of bewilderment as he said, "he ignored me completely when I said hello"!

Bagel Boy minced across the floor of the bar and joined Adam on his table where he sat on a stool that he'd draped his jacket over. I was miffed, as shoving me in the back served no purpose. Bagel Boy didn't shove me to get my attention for something, it seemed as though it was a malicious act of some sort, and I was not at all impressed.

I had previously mentioned to Jack and Carl that I suspected the malicious messages from Kenzie were not entirely his words alone and that there was someone else involved. I had no evidence and I guess this was smart on the part of anyone else involved. Given Kenzie was desperate enough to do someone else's dirty work as he vied to be favourite with anyone and everyone. A lot of what the others had shared that Bagel Boy was saying about me, seemed to be in those malicious messages and he was therefore my first suspect.

I had never worked nor spoken with Bagel Boy although this is a little disingenuous of me. According to Bagel Boy he had shared with others that in my first week he deliberately asked me when serving him as a customer, not knowing he worked at the pub one day a week. For a brand of tequila that we don't stock and of which he knows, working here, that we don't stock.

Apparently, he found it hilarious that I spent a few moments looking for this tequila in the fridge before returning to him to say we didn't stock it. I can't say I recall the encounter but found it cringing that he found that extremely entertaining. Sad really, but allegedly drugs do have a habit of distorting your grasp on reality and I guess where anything and everything is comically entertaining.

Both original and new team members shared that they did not get on with Bagel Boy. They said he was "troubled" and "constantly being off his tits on 'K' [sic] (Ketamine) doesn't help"!

The Bar was his only stage where he would wear the smallest of smallest shorts and while holding onto the beer taps would bounce from side to side to get the attention of the customers. It all sounded desperate, but the impressions the team did in taking the piss out of him behind his back was highly amusing despite never witnessing this 'dance' by Bagel Boy for myself.

Ben had shared that when he met Bagel Boy for the first time he went up and introduced himself and Bagel boy merely shooed him away and ignored him the entire shift. Johnnie chipped in and asked who we were talking about and said, "this is how she behaves with everybody, then she wonders why nobody likes her"!

Kenzie & Bagel Boy are the same age and apparently both did Drama at school. But others say this is not the only common interest the two share, given the circle this clique moves in at the pub, it's drugs apparently.

During the rest of my shift, I questioned what purpose did coming behind the bar to shove me serve? I kept making a correlation with the malicious messages and the act of being 'touched' which was alluded to in the messages and around the senders unfounded fear of catching "AIDS".

Was Bagel Boy carrying out an action of touching me in relation to the malicious messages? Or was Bagel Boy being egged on by Adam who perhaps knew of the messages and dared him to touch the colleague with 'AIDS'? I was perhaps thinking too much into it, but it was interesting Bagel Boy came behind the bar and ignored Bobby, only to shove me and run off.

Adam and his group including Bagel Boy stayed drinking the entire night right up to closing but thankfully moving downstairs after their first round. Given we had been so busy, on closing Bobby had gone to the cellar to get the stock for the fridges behind the bar. Security on his second sweep of the upstairs toilets said goodnight which indicated the pub was empty of customers.

I could, however, hear Adam's voice booming from downstairs and he sounded wasted. Then Alex came flying up the main staircase and rushed to me behind the bar. He looked flustered and somewhat upset and took hold of my wrist and said, "Adam is downstairs high as a kite screaming and shouting orders and Bagel Boy is doing the same".

I could hear them both clearly but as Alex alluded, they were both incoherent. I felt sorry for Alex as he seemed upset and as a manager in previous roles, I have always said no colleague, subordinate or not, should feel fearful of management in the workplace. So, I said he could stay and "if anybody says anything then I'll tell 'em"! I gave Alex several tasks to do and was confident in telling a supervisor or manager that I needed help should they question it.

Moments later Rudy came sneaking through the fire exit door, first making sure the coast was clear. "Do you need me to do anything"? To which I replied "no, everything is under control". I felt a hand caress my bare calf as I was wearing shorts and looked down to see Alex squatting beside me behind the bar. "What are you doing" I asked confused. "I shit myself, I thought it was Adam or Bagel boy" Alex whispered. "For fucks sake, get up" I said while laughing.

"Will, please don't send me back downstairs, you must have something for me to do" Rudy pleaded. It was unusual to have more than two helping with the clean-up upstairs, if not unheard of! But I had already taken in Alex making us a threesome with me and Bobby. I thought it would be suspicious having four up here. But the more of the team I had upstairs seeking refuge, then who, was cleaning the main bar?

I felt awful turning Rudy away, but I said he needed to go downstairs and help the guys down there clean the bar so we could all go home without any delay. Rudy pleaded "…but Adam and Bagel Boy are tweezered! Shouting at everybody, it's horrendous I can't cope"! Alex interjected "you mean 'tweaking'! Not tweezered" before looking at me rolling his eyes at Rudy's malapropism!

Rudy eventually conceded and made his way back out the fire exit to the main bar. Simultaneously Alex again shot down by my feet and as I turned to look over at the sound of footsteps coming up the main staircase. I saw Bagel Boy heading towards us at the bar.

He shouted while scanning the bar area "Rudy, get your fucking arse downstairs" before glancing over at me, his eyes bulging like car headlights on full beam, and seemingly lost his ability to blink. Our eyes meeting, he flared his nostrils and pursed his lips and I said to myself 'I'd purse my lips too if my teeth were as embarrassing as yours'! Cruel I know, but true.

He then started to skip over towards me at the end of the bar like a ballerina and collected the branded glasses we placed at the end of the bar once washed to go back downstairs. He then skipped across the bar floor to the main staircase before proceeding to skip down it. I said under my breath so Alex could hear "steady dear! It would be terrible waste if we lost more branded glasses when were already short" in a tone that alluded that I had no genuine concern of the glasses!

Alex enquired if Bagel Boy had gone, "yes he's gone, you can get off the floor now"! All three of us got the cleaning done and was undisturbed. We paused now and again to earwig as Adam and Bagel Boy were aggressively shouting orders to the poor bitches that remained downstairs. Not one of us found it funny and all remarked how it was not only embarrassing for Adam and Bagel Boy but incredibly unprofessional. I also queried "where the fuck is Jack? How is he allowing this to happen" given Jack was the manager on duty!

Once we finished cleaning Alex, Rudy & Bobby all collected their bags from the staff room and quickly made their way downstairs to the main bar to be released leaving me behind. I collected the bag of rubbish Alex said he'd take when he left for the night as he was too scared earlier to go down and put it on the street. As he'd first have to encounter these two morons.

I started to descend the stairs with this bag of rubbish, and I could see Alex, Rudy & Bobby just reaching the bottom of the staircase. Alex nervously asked, "all done now, we can go"? We were already on unpaid time so we didn't need to ask, but I heard Bagel Boy in his screechy voice say, "yes you may go now if you've finished the cleaning"!

It was unusual that Jack and Johnnie seemed to be missing and Adam & Bagel boy, clearly off their faces, not on shift that night and had been customers were now effectively closing the shift?

As I graciously approached the last few steps, I glanced over to see who was about and saw Bagel Boy perched cross legged on a stool swaying from left to right. As our eyes met, he scowled, pursed his lips and flared his nostrils again. Adam appeared from the gents' toilets which were directly behind Bagel Boy struggling to zip up his fly. With my sack of rubbish in hand, my jacket on, I walked towards the door to leave with no intention with seeking their permission to leave. I did ask while looking at Adam, who's eyes were also on full beam and eerily looking through me "is Jack or Johnnie not about"? Bagel boy camply screeched "in the office, why"? I didn't respond nor acknowledge him and merely said "goodnight, Adam" as I walked towards the door.

Adam with eyes like saucers and barely able to stand in a booming voice shouted, "Will is this your…". To which I glanced over at the area he was just about to point to seeing a tatty old grey fleece hung over the stained-glass divider. "Nope, not mine"! I interrupted having anticipated his query.

The bitches that had done a runner were waiting for me outside for what seemed like a mini debrief. As I dragged the rubbish bag down the road to the collection point. The others were excitedly discussing how shit faced Adam and Bagel Boy were and this was not purely down to alcohol alone. I said my goodnights and set off on the walk home.

I slept on the entire night's events and by morning decided I would report it to Carl the General Manager to leave a paper trail should anything further occur. I knew I'd be instantly labelled 'trouble' for raising it given I knew how tight their relationships were. Or perhaps how two faced they were with each other, might be a more accurate statement.

But I didn't care, this wasn't a career move for me and why should someone feel so emboldened to feel they have the right to shove someone in the manner I was. UK law states laying your hands on someone, no matter how forceful, is deemed an 'assault'. I didn't mention Adam at all, which really played with my morals, but given he is treating me differently from others I didn't want to be victimised any more than I already was by him.

In my complaint I quoted the staff handbook that states no employee should step into back of house areas when not on duty without permission. Nor should they remain on the premises as a 'customer' after the last customer has left regardless of permission being granted or not. Effectively Adam the deputy and Bagel boy were in breach of the company's policy and no doubt as they were customers all evening and intoxicated, were jeopardising the premises licence by remaining on the premises after closing.

Carl responded quickly by email apologising for the experience and stated he would speak with Bagel Boy.

When I next came on shift Jack approached me and asked me what happened, and I very briefly explained. He asked me to replicate the shove I received to gauge the force of how hard I was shoved by Bagel Boy. Jack was surprised and remarked furiously "who does he think he is! He only works here a couple of hours a week and even then, he wouldn't be missed"!

Jack continued "not to worry, Carl has said he will speak to him. I think he will come in from home and speak with him when he is next on shift".

My whole concern wasn't the act of staying behind during lock up when you've been drinking as a customer. It was heart-warming that perhaps they viewed the place as a second home and felt safe while waiting for others to finish their shift or perhaps wait for a taxi home. But to make a nuisance of yourself and make others doing their job feel uncomfortable if not petrified, I found to be utterly bizarre if not toxic and not a smart representation of the LGBT community.

A few shifts later I guess something must have been said to Bagel Boy. Although I doubt it was serious given it seemed he was taking the piss when he appeared at the main entrance of the pub. Jumping into the air and waving his hands to get Adam's attention whilst waving his bag of left-over Bagels from the shop that nobody really wants. But I suspect he brings them in to keep in favour with those he thinks are his friend. I never touch leftovers, let alone amidst a pandemic with corona floating around in the air.

Adam went rushing over to collect the leftover Bagels and as I glanced to my left Alex was looking on curiously at the commotion. Alex rolling his eyes said to me "oh! It's Bagel Boy"! Alex and I, poignantly, saying nothing further to each other, just a look, acknowledging to each other not to waste our breath on this nonentity and we got on with serving customers.

It all seemed staged, that the self-centred egotistical one-time TV extra. Was making a point that he was not or could not come into the building after having had a chat with Carl. He could have sent Adam a message that he was on his way, was outside or he could have come into the side gate and passed his bastarding bagels to Adam who was stood by the side door to the gate anyway.

Adam came back with his bounty and threw them behind the bar, seemingly in a huff that I dare open my mouth and complain about his little friend.

The following Friday I was working on the main bar and was walking around looking for glasses to collect. As I walked past the DJ booth, I heard a voice "Hi Will" and while I recognised the screechy tone, I still turned around to see Bagel Boy with a regular customer stood with drinks. "I've come into the place I work to have a drink, is that ok with you"! Bagel boy stated. I didn't reply and just continued with my job. I suspect he felt he had somehow scored a point, but then I giggled to myself at how sad it was to come and drink at the place you work on a Friday night when you have the whole of London at your feet.

Surely if you're a 'proper' actor you've got a wide network of friends and places you could be hanging out and networking. Not in a place you work seemingly with only a regular customer three times your age as someone to socialise with. Just an observation!

VAJAZZLED

As I arrived to start my shift Emre, Ben and Rudy were in the staff room. I said "hello" and enquired how they all were. Emre was just starting his shift and Rudy was going on a one-hour break as part of his 12-hour shift. Ben just ignored me while shovelling Sushi into his mouth which suited me as it meant we didn't have to listen to that cackle!

They reverted to what they were bitching about as I entered the staff room, Jack! Emre said "he is just the most boring person on the planet"! Ben unable to resist, interjected with a mouth full of sushi "I'll second that! He is incredibly dull"! I turned and looked at Rudy as I unfolded my work hoodie to see what he had to say but he was, as usual, away with the fairies while smearing lip gloss on his lips. Rudy started to giggle nervously and said "Will, I love you"! Rudy plays the dumb blonde but, he is quite smart and plays the dumb blonde very well. He knew I'd turned to him for his opinion about Jack. But knew I'd defend Jack as Rudy had shared the same opinion as the others with me before.

Rudy's attempt to change the subject didn't work and as I slipped on my hoodie Emre said "Rudy you always say Jack is so dim"! Before I could get my head through the head hole Rudy tried to defend himself "I mean, like, he is so boring. When he speaks to me it is like dead donkey flogging"!

As my head popped through the hole, I looked at Rudy with a raised eyebrow "you mean 'it's like flogging a dead horse'"!

I then said "nobody is interesting unless their being talked about, and you guys never stop talking about Jack. The difference between you guys and Jack, is that Jack has a sense of 'direction'. You guys are so fucking lost, you think life is all about endless, meaningless, sexual encounters with strangers.

Drugs, alcohol, trading phone numbers with customers and the endless swiping of dick pics and the incessant refreshing of Grindr!

You guys are young, enjoy yourselves. But don't compare the responsibilities and priorities of others against your own and deem them to be "boring""!

Ben still shovelling in his Sushi and slapping his lips as he eats with his mouth open. While scrolling through his phone retorted as I opened the door to start my shift "Oh, she's on the blob"! I didn't reply and as the door was closing behind me as I headed down the stairs to the main bar, I heard Rudy innocently ask, "who's Bob"?

Keith works part time hours on an ad-hoc basis and shares a flat with Adam. I have only worked with him a handful of times and he's been a laugh. Since wearing my hoodies to keep myself warm while at work. And to protect myself from customers stroking my hairy arms or grabbing me inappropriately, my diamante hoodies and sweatshirts have been often admired by customers and team members. All I had done was cut out the artwork from the work t-shirts, wonder webbed it to the front of a hoodie and then stitched on a combination of coloured sequins and rows and rows of small diamantes. The sparkle under the pub lights is quite sensational.

As I said "hello" to Keith and Adam as I passed to take and record my temperature with the thermometer gun at the other side of the bar. I heard Adam say to Keith "what's she come as"? I then heard Keith say, "if she turns the hat backwards it'll be PJ & Duncan, Top of the Pops magazine circa 1994"!

Taking my temperature by firing the thermometer gun at my forehead I had pushed up my baseball cap. On hearing this poor attempt at 'throwing shade'. I, instead of pulling my cap back down to rest on my forehead merely spun it 180 so the peak was at the back.

I've never worn a baseball cap backwards; I'd tried in the mirror at home and thought I looked a tit! But given the circumstances I thought I'd give them something to talk about. As I walked over towards them to enquire how the shift was going to pan out. Keith, one of the two-faced duo said "oh Will I love the hoodie, is this white one new"? To which I replied it was, and Adam looking me up and down said "darling, you've been Vajazzled"! I instantly knew this was most likely a backhanded compliment so just replied "That's me! One sparkly cunt"!

They both looked at me aghast, I doubt it was for the use of the 'C-word'! Most likely because I understood what they were saying behind my back. Having spent 10 years as a drag queen my 'library' card was well and truly dog eared!

A short while later chatting with Keith, he said "so why have you gone to such lengths for the company" in reference to my hoodie. I replied, "because I am always freezing given, we have to have the air conditioning on full blast. The fans on full speed to "blow away customers covid" and it's hard to get through an entire shift feeling cold". Keith stood looking puzzled, although he understood clearly what I had said. And surely anybody with common sense would grasp I was saying I was always cold in a t-shirt, so I put on a jumper instead. He was just being a dick; he wasn't usually such a bitch so not sure if he'd had something in his cornflakes or was just genuinely put out by my vajazzled sweater.

So, without hesitation and given I had shared my status with others I added for clarification, "plus given I live with HIV I need to keep myself warm and protected against opportunist infections such as cold, flu and pneumonia". He looked uncomfortable and said "oh, that makes sense then" and he scurried off. I won't lie, I just said to myself 'prick' and got on with serving the next customer.

As the shift went on, I thought when I go on break, I am going to find the gayest of footwear to add to my look. And it didn't take long, as I dug into my battered sausage and chips from the chippy down the road. I found a pair of Converse hi-tops designed in a gay pride theme. They have the pride flag stripes on the rubber soles and the pride rainbow, geometric shapes in pride colours and flowers on a white background. I ordered them there and then, £60 with next day delivery.

A few shifts later I went in looking like the gayest gay on Old Compton Street. The team and customers, even straight customers loved the converse. I wasn't brave enough to wear them on the walk to work as they were so vibrant but kept them solely for work. I wore them home a few times because it was dark.

Keith did share he is too fat to fit into a company shirt, but then I did say he was being unkind to himself. The company only stocked up to a size 'large' and even that was small as they were those muscle hugging t-shirts. But I wondered if this is where his querying of my sweaters came from, who knows.

As I was pouring spirits for an order, I could hear Keith talking with a customer who asked why Keith didn't have a branded work shirt. Keith was confident enough to say the company didn't have his size. But then, quickly stated "unlike Will! Who made his uniform entirely himself, we don't even do sweatshirts, but he thinks he's special"!

I wanted to say 'ere, it's got nowt to do with me thinking I'm special? It's just a case that I'm fed up with being cold' but I didn't! As I finished pouring the drinks for my customer, I walked past Keith and the customer he was talking to. The customer was this big hunk of muscle in a white fitted t-shirt, I know right! And he said "oh my god! Look at that, it is gorgeous"! I knew he was referring to my sparkly sweater but embarrassed I made out I thought he was referring to me so said "aw thanks! Yes, I am single"!

I wasn't sure if he was playing along or being honest when he said "not you! The top. Can I buy one"? I thought cheeky bitch, so as I squeezed past Keith I said "rude! No, it's limited edition, just like me, a one off"! I heard Keith say "that's what I just said, he made it himself. He didn't get permission, just did it off his own back".

I thought 'what is Keith's problem'? It was a bloody sweater; it keeps me warm because I am always cold. Even with an extremely high CD4 count, meaning my immune system was strong to fight infection. Being cold in the t-shirt I was being proactive in wearing a sweater ensuring that I wasn't leaving myself open to opportunist infections such as cold, flu or pneumonia. To me, it seemed like a continued act of bullying by Keith, it couldn't have been anything else.

Keith and Adam stayed behind for drinks after they finished their shifts that night. I briefly heard Keith wittering on to another regular customer about my hoodie. The customer is American, a self-proclaimed regular. And when the covid-19 restrictions existed this customer would tell the door man that he didn't have to queue to wait for a vacant seat/table. Because he was a regular which meant nothing to management nor security, not unless Adam was managing the shift. This customer once pinned Bobby up against a wall by his hip and said, "I am a really tentative top, I have a big cock, I will hold your legs in the air, slowly slide it deep inside you and make you tremble"!

He'd seemingly said this to all the twinks that worked at the pub, and nobody liked him except for Adam, Keith and Kenzie. Johnnie was the only one of that clique that absolutely detested this customer.

I told Bobby at the time to report it, but Bobby was too scared. Saying he knew the customer and Adam were close so suspected he'd be made to feel more uncomfortable whilst working. I'd usually say, 'no you must report it regardless, that kind of behaviour is not acceptable'. But for the first time in my career, I said "yeah, your probably right".

A week or so after Bobby shared this experience, I was working the upstairs bar when this customer was sat drinking with 3 other regulars. As it was table service only at the time given covid-19 restrictions I went over after being beckoned by him. Without pinning me to the wall, this customer started to say the exact same thing to me he'd said to Bobby and the others.

For me, I found this disgusting! I'm by no means a prude and I am not easily offended. But I am here to serve drinks and wipe tables as Kenzie once told me. I don't mind a bit of banter no matter how crude or rude, but I am not here to be sexually harassed. He said, "you've got the most amazing blue eyes. And those legs, wow! Can I just say I am a very tentative top..."!

"You can stop you right there"! I exclaimed. As he looked at me stunned. I continued "if you're going to tell me once you've slid inside me, you'll make my legs tremble, then I'm afraid I am going to have to disappoint you! The only tremble you give me is the one of repulsion at the thought of you coming anywhere near me. In fact, I'd rather sit on the 10ft barge pole that I won't be touching you with"!

His three friends sat around the table seemingly halting their conversation to listen in before breaking into spontaneous laughter and screams as they heckled their friend.

He sat looking dumbfounded. I wasn't sure if he was peeved at my rejecting of his advances or the fact that I knew what he was going to say, practically verbatim given the team have all shared he has said the exact same thing to everybody.

The customer in his American accent said, "your customer service is appalling"! To which I replied, "I am glad you realise I am here to provide customer service and not a sexual service"! To bring this to an immediate end I further stated "and as your familiar with management, you'll know where to find them downstairs if you wish to lodge a complaint. You might want to bear in mind there are two employees', three including me, ready to state how they have found your sexually explicit remarks distressing and act of sexual harassment. Especially the one you pinned up against the wall"! He didn't place his order with me, and my window was now closed as I walked away to another table beckoning me.

He has always avoided me since, until the masks came off when covid-19 restrictions eased and he said to me when wanting to be served at the bar, "hi, are you new I haven't seen you before" to which I said, "Yeah I am new" although I didn't believe him.

And it was this customer that Keith was stood with, slagging off my sweater. I didn't listen in to hear what was being said, I couldn't care less by this point. But what I did overhear as I occasionally passed by, was perhaps best described as drunken jealously on Keith's behalf.

I am starting to become jaded with the place, but love being out of the house. Being productive and most of the team are great to be around, albeit some in short bursts. A portion of the customers make it worthwhile working your arse off. But as for a LGBT+ family/community I was perhaps hoping to stumble across really doesn't exist and it's the "originals" that have made this clear.

It's funny because if there not stitching gay pride flags, switching pronouns like 'she' in place of 'he' thinking they're sashaying through the 1980's and generally thinking their being 'cute & camp'. Then there deluded! If only they were sobor to see that their own insecurities and substance fuelled lifestyles are making for a chaotic and toxic environment. Giving the community they feel they represent a bad representation while inflicting misery amongst their colleagues and peers.

MURDER OF A UNICORN

So, surprise surprise! Guess where I am working tonight? That's right, the upstairs bar dubbed the attic given the team call me 'Anne' as in Anne Frank "she's up in the attic again"!

By now given the upstairs bar was supposed to be allocated 'fairly' amongst the entire team where nobody was exempt. The rota was being published where if you had an arrow next to your name, pointing upwards, it symbolised you were working the upstairs bar. Given the size of the team this meant you would work the upstairs bar every 11 days if everybody was allocated a shift up there. However, quite early on I was being allocated the upstairs bar 2-3 times a week.

I wondered why Adam would create such a paper trail where essentially someone could show they were perhaps being victimised. I didn't mind the upstairs bar, I preferred it. But I knew not to share this with anybody and to keep my cards close to my chest. Almost all the team hated the upstairs bar because they couldn't cruise for sex. You had to literally do everything from taking payment, pouring the drink, and then collecting the glasses and washing them and putting them away. Whereas on the main bar there would be around nine if not more on a shift and you could easily slack off and the workload was evenly distributed.

If I needed 5 mins out from the main bar I would go down to the cellar and given the age of the building. I would sit in this little arched cave area where they stored the tonic waters. As this was a popular mixer there would be large reserves behind the bar so nobody would come to the cellar for tonic. And as the cave was tucked away around this 90-degree corner I would sit on a stack of tonics and hear colleagues come and go and never be discovered. I'd return and nobody would even notice that I'd disappeared.

There was a predominantly straight crowd upstairs too, but they were good tippers and the minimum I earnt in one night was £96. The highest I earnt in one night was £133 which went into my pocket, and I didn't even try for tips. Some customers used to say I was so caustic and funny that I was worth tipping just for being entertaining.

So, Adam putting me upstairs 3 nights a week meant I could take home in cash tips around £220 which got me out the house and was a bit of pin money.

Alex came and said he'd be joining me later in the evening given it was the weekend and set to be busy. Alex asked why I was upstairs "again" and said he had noticed I was being put up here a lot. And that "Adams favourites, Kenzie, Keith and Simon never get put upstairs" and this like me, rattled Alex as being unfair. If you say you're going to do something as a manager, then have some integrity about you and stick to it. Although it seemed a few subordinates were managing Adam, as opposed to Adam managing them, as a deputy manager.

For the last few weeks when me and Alex found ourselves in the staff room. Alex told me he wanted to commit a murder! Kenzie had been given a unicorn inflatable and it had been placed in the staff room. Kenzie himself shared he'd written some statements on the unicorn relevant to him which read 'I'm Kenzie and I'm a slut'. The other read 'I'm Kenzie and I want my daddy'. When it caught my eye when changing or eating lunch, I'd see the self-deprecating statements Kenzie had drawn on the inflatable and think, 'that's a psychiatrist's wet dream'.

Alex was fixated that he wanted to burst it and the first time he mentioned it I said, "that's murder"! It then became a joke between me and Alex over the next couple of weeks. I said I didn't want to be an accessory to murder! And despite what I had learnt about Kenzie, I was not a vengeful person. I did say to Alex that it was rather childish if not vindictive to essentially damage someone else's property. But Alex was intent on bursting the unicorn so I said let's wait for the right moment in the hope that the idea, if not the urge, would pass.

Bagel boy did keep his toothbrush in a glass tumbler in the staff room and I did suggest, not my proudest moment. That we use it to scrub around the rim of the customers toilet and urinal in the pub. However, due to an episode of amnesia brought on by low blood sugar, I can't remember if we did or not.

Alex's murderous intent came about again after our little Italian colleague, Rudy set fire to the microwave in the staff room while trying to reheat his pasta. Turns out Rudy 'forgot' to add water to the dry pasta mix which saw the microwave burst into flames triggering the fire alarm.

This prompted Johnnie to say someone had to go up and scrub the staff room from top to bottom. Bobby put himself forward and spent over 3 hours cleaning the staff room and he did a proper job of it too. I caught Alex in the staff room with the unicorn in his hands and I said to Alex "don't do it! Think of the children, think of poor Bobby, he would get the blame"! As Bobby had shifted everything around in his clean up, I felt Bobby would get the blame for unintentionally puncturing the unicorn and it wasn't worth the bother.

Alex agreed to hold off, the unicorn got to live to see tomorrow, phew!

Alex was now on the bar with me, and trade was steady, so I got talking to a regular who I always had a good chat with. He had previously asked for my number, and he was quite cute and dateable but for me, it was work and not a line I was willing to cross. He did pester and I felt tempted but at the time said, "Kenzie's not had sex in a few hours, see him"!

This customer while chatting observed Adam speaking to me while on the bar. The customer after Adam left said he didn't agree with the way Adam spoke to me, or rather why I let Adam speak to me the way he did. I just said, "I don't really care, I come to work, do my job and go home".

"I can tell you a few things about that muscle Mary" the customer said as he took a sip of his double Laphroaig, no ice. "Honest, I am not remotely interested" I said politely, but that didn't stop him. The customer alleged he had worked with Adam for a prominent airline as cabin crew and that Adam had been dismissed for misuse of drugs. He alleged Adam was known to be a "meth addict" and this is how he lost his job. I said, "tell me something I don't know" given Adam had been open with the other boys about what he said was his 'past'. These were conversations I had overheard while Adam was talking to colleagues behind the bar, although I didn't know what the specific drugs where. If Adam had mentioned 'Tina' in his conversations I would have thought, it was one of his girlie friends as I have never been exposed to nor taken drugs.

Emre said Adam quizzed him on his first day as to whether Emre takes drugs. Emre said he of course said 'no' but then Emre confided with me that he himself takes something called Tea, a concoction of a variety of drugs. I asked if it was served in a teapot, and he looked at me gone out. I thought it was a reasonable question, if it was called Tea because it was a blend of drugs then why not call it a soup as it's a blend of ingredients?

Emre said he also takes 'Tina'. Given this is a guy who is the baby of the team and so naïve and who was adamant that the black sports bra I found in the staff room was a jockstrap. I asked if 'Tina' and 'Tea' were perhaps the same thing, but he assured me they weren't. I told him not to tell me anymore as I'd only become concerned for him.

Adam finished his shift and Jack was in to take over the late shift. Jack came upstairs to check on me and Alex and asked "are you ok working up here again Will? Your always up here"! I didn't mind as I say and I knew it would be a laugh with Alex so there was no need to rock the boat for Jack and so I said, "yeah its cool, as long as I've got Alex".

Me and Alex didn't stop, it was a crazy but enjoyable night as we bounced off each other. I'd anticipated we'd run out of glasses and had additional ones brought up from downstairs in preparation, but we still couldn't turn over glasses fast enough. Between us we just about managed it. I saw Alex taking 5 minutes out talking to a customer he had mentioned earlier he had matched with on Tinder but never got to meet. While I was rushed off my feet, I didn't mind Alex chatting with this guy as he had slogged his guts out earlier. When we both had a five-minute breather Alex said he had kissed and started to wank off the customer in the toilets and was now on a promise. He proposed we got the cleaning done as quickly as possible so he could go back to the customers hotel and finish what they'd started.

After we closed Jack came up to collect the cash draws and said we had worked so hard after reviewing the sales figures. He said we could help ourselves to a bottle of lager each. I had never accepted a drink from work but thought sod it! We have worked hard and me and Alex clinked bottles and took a swig before cracking on with the cleaning. We finished the cleaning with 25 minutes to spare and didn't want to go downstairs as we'd get roped into helping.

I sent Alex to the staff room to collect his things and freshen up. I followed five minutes later once the glass washer had finished draining and shut down the bar. As I walked into the staff room Alex jumped out of his skin as he stood holding the unicorn.

I jokingly said "have you slit its throat" to which Alex replied "no not yet" as he looked around the staff room for something sharp. Kenzie was downstairs and I suggested to Alex "why don't we, not kill the unicorn but hide it! Take a photo, and print a ransom note with a 'tongue in cheek' demand for its safe release"? Alex wasn't up for it and said, "the fucker needs to go, and so does that cunt Kenzie"! I was quite shocked that Alex had such pent-up anger towards Kenzie, and I didn't know why.

I don't know what came over me, but I was about to become the accomplice in the murder of the unicorn. As Alex looked around looking for a sharp object, I went to pull my hoodie over my head when I realised. I was wearing five pin badges so I suggested I take one off for him to puncture the unicorn which would allow it to deflate slowly. This meant it would not create a visible mark which could highlight it as being a malicious act. Although it clearly was a malicious act on the part of Alex, and I guess myself being the accomplice.

The murder weapon was casually placed back on my hoodie, once I wiped any unicorn DNA off and we left like nothing had happened, although giggling like a couple of schoolgirls.

We both made our way downstairs and Jack was stood at the bar as the others were cleaning casually while singing and joking. There seemed to be quite the party atmosphere, and it was nice. Alex was a little tipsy as he'd also knocked back drinks given as tips. In his excitement to get out the door Alex called me Keith to which I didn't appreciate but Jack found funny.

I don't know how Jack got to telling us stories from his past. And although I was interested and could talk to Jack for hours and hours, Alex was giving me the eye glare. I assume for me to say something so that Alex could head off. But as Alex had been vocal about finding Jack dull, I thought I'd be a shit and make him listen and wait.

Jack was telling us about his past relationship and how it came to an end. I felt sorry for Jack as it sounded like he was into this guy, but Jack hadn't been treated well emotionally. Alex to his credit butted in and said "can we go now" which was rude. But Alex wanted to get off as he was on a promise and not stand listening to Jacks life story, which is fair enough. But my heart sank when Jack glumly said "oh sorry. Another boring story. Yes, you can all go home".

By this point everybody was ready to go, and Jack was going to lock up by himself. I wanted to stay behind and let him finish the story as I for one was interested. But I thought it would appear odd in front of the others and as a queue was building behind me, I rubbed his shoulder reassuringly and said, "you're not at all boring" and gave him a wink of the eye. He smiled and replied, "thanks Will".

I came in the next day and found the unicorn was nowhere to be seen. Kenzie started the same time as me so not sure if he had discovered it and tossed it in the bin. Glancing into the bin it was empty. Kenzie was scheduled to work the upstairs bar today when it opened at 5pm but I heard him telling Johnnie "I will point blank refuse to work up there"! Johnnie reminded Kenzie that I had done three nights in a row and Alex had worked up there twice this week and that Kenzie was scheduled on the rota to work the upstairs bar.

I thought 'steady Johnnie, he'll have one of his panic attacks in a moment and have to be sent home' if he doesn't get his own way. Me and Alex looked at each other, facing the punters but listening to the argument that was going on behind us. Johnnie said to Kenzie "you know I have always got your back as my bestie, but it's not fair that Will or Alex go up when they have done more than their fair share". Johnnie passed the buck to Adam by saying "speak to Adam when he comes on shift and see what he says".

I saw Adam arrive and Johnnie followed him I suspect to give Adam a handover as Johnnie's shift was finishing.

When Adam came on the floor, he approached Kenzie. "So, your scheduled for upstairs tonight" and Kenzie just stuck out his bottom lip like a child sulking and rubbed his fists on the corner of his eyes as though he was wiping away tears. I was shocked at what I was witnessing and Alex witnessing the same then looked at me across the ice trough and mouthed "what the fuck"!

I guess this is how Kenzie gets his way by playing the vulnerable child card thinking he is cute. What came next blew my jockstrap off! Adam spun on his feet and looking at me and Alex as we were now stood beside each other, looking on said, "one of you needs to go upstairs"! I had to stop myself from saying 'no, what needs to happen is someone needs to punch that cunt square in the eyes!' Instead, I did the 'in through the nose and out through the mouth' breathing while trying to process where I was and what the fuck was going on?

It was clear either friendship or a 'hold' Kenzie had over Adam was clouding Adams professional integrity. As others had mentioned, Kenzie knew way too much about all the underhand dealings that are allegedly going on that Kenzie at any moment could expose those around him, particularly those at manager level.

"I need a volunteer; I don't care who but one of you, and now"! Adam said aggressively. I was literally still dumfounded, and it was on the tip of my tongue to say, 'nah mate, I was up there last night so, nope not me'.

As Alex was not volunteering, and to save myself any embarrassment given I knew Adam would send me upstairs to be vindictive. I said, "yeah I'll do it then"! Before I drew breath Adam said, "go up now please" to which I, smiled in acknowledgment of his order and made my way upstairs. Walking up the stairs I was fuming! I looked down at the clock which hung behind the main bar to understand why I was being sent up so early and of which Kenzie was stood under, smirking while he watched me ascend the staircase. My only regret as I continued up the stairs was that I didn't take that unicorn and impale it myself!

The only positive that came from witnessing this bizarre episode with Kenzie. Was that it only reaffirmed why I had remained tight lipped in work over Kenzie being responsible for sending the malicious messages. I could imagine Kenzie being approached by Carl, Jack or Adam during an investigation and acting the way I just witnessed. For him to manipulate an investigation by playing the victim and my complaint would not be upheld in order of them 'having Kenzie's back'!

I wanted to share this incident with Jack, to highlight my nervous reluctance to allow an 'in house' investigation to take place over the police. But I couldn't because to share this incident would inadvertently confirm by me that Kenzie was behind the messages. And I am still waiting for the police to conclude their investigation.

The toxicity of the environment I am working in is starting to make me unhappy. And while I could easily walk away with no financial worries, I enjoyed being out of the house and having something to do. Also, why would I let Adam who has no people management skills push me out because for one reason or another he doesn't like me. This for me is not a popularity contest, it is a pub, not a career move. It is very straight forward as there is no career ladder to climb, nor one that would match the experience and qualifications I already hold. Come to work, do your job to the best of your ability, have a laugh and go home, it's as easy at that.

I am not alone on various matters here; others have expressed the same without being prompted by me or my experiences which I generally keep to myself. Difference is the others are too scared to air their grievances as they have rent and bills to pay. Essentially, I work in a team of "chicken livered shits"! *He says in the voice of Kim Woodburn.*

DODGY DEALINGS

A wet and miserable Wednesday and I had been in since 2pm. When Johnnie came on shift at 3pm he said the DJ had cancelled so he was going to serenade us with his playlist for the night. We'd be given soul for the first two hours and then disco dolly for the remainder of the night. I didn't care much although it sounded alright, Alex just looked at me and rolled his eyes with disappointment at Johnnies music choice.

Johnnie remarked I was brave wearing shorts in this weather to which I explained I had to change when I arrived for work. My jeans were soaked all the way through due to the heavy rain as I walked through Soho. It was that heavy rain, with rain droplets the size of PrEP pills. The rain creating a mist along the horizon of the road as it rumbled with thunder overhead. People huddled under canopies and peered out from shop doorways as I seemed to be the only one mincing on by. I had a very important place to be, I had to chuck pints of Pravha lager to gummy yellow 'roll your own' fingered regulars and nothing was going to get in my way!

Liam aka Lurch, the goth joined us at 5pm, he says hello but very much keeps himself to himself. I think he's studying; I only know that as Jack once told me. Jack says he has many intelligent conversations with Lurch about art, history, and politics. It was quite nice to hear that Jack had someone to talk to although I was somewhat sceptical that Jack had any interest in those three subjects. I still hadn't got a whiff of Lurch as the others persistently complain he has the most shocking body odour. But then, with my sinusitis it's hard to smell something that's probably not as bad as those bitches make out.

Rudy, Emre and Alex had also mentioned several times that Lurch is quite "touchy, feely". Even they as very promiscuous gays found it uncomfortable at times as it was more sexual than accidental. When the three of them were once bitching about this I asked, "but like what, what does he do"? Thinking they'd perhaps misinterpreted the odd bit of accidental body contact like a bump or brush. "He grabs my arse, not with one hand but both," said a repulsed Rudy. Emre said "he touches my nipples through my t-shirt in an erotic way". With one eyebrow raised I said "and you let him. You don't immediately brush him off"?

"Well, I quite like it, but it's embarrassing when he does it in front of others" Emre said in a Vicky Pollard 'yeah but, no but' kind of way. Alex mentioned that Lurch just kept brushing past him while pushing his groin into him. This was wrong but they were all old enough if not gobby enough to either raise this with Lurch directly or with a manager. Rudy asked if I would perhaps have a word and ask Lurch to stop, but I said it wasn't my place to do so.

I shared if it made them feel uncomfortable then they should tell a manager. Then as I pondered for a minute, I inquisitively asked "how come he never does any of this to me"? I was being serious although these bitches fell about laughing "Will! Your too much, never change"! Rudy declared. Then Bobby joined us as Johnnie started his playlist and turned down the house lights and switched on the disco lights and strobes.

It wasn't that busy, but Rudy decided to keep us entertained and found it hilarious to ask every customer who asked for a coke, either as a drink or as a mixer. "Diet coke" as he held the soda gun with his thumb on the 'diet' button! In a vain bid to be insulting intimating to the customer that they needed to watch their weight.

What did make us laugh was when we heard Rudy repeat back a customer's order no less than four times, "popcorn and rice"? Turned out the customer was asking for "vodka, no ice". We all had tears streaming down our faces and Bobby looked like he was going into cardiac arrest as he couldn't breathe and was clutching his chest. Rudy didn't understand why we were laughing and got the hump. It was one of those moments where it was more hilarious and infectious seeing others laughing than Rudy trying to sell Popcorn and Rice to a customer, neither of which we sold just to be clear.

This is how tediously boring this shift was. Although we then fell about as Alex kept impersonating Bagel Boy and the side-to-side bopping dance he does whilst clinging to the beer taps. Rudy assured me Alex's impression was spot on despite never seeing it myself found it hilariously funny.

Again, their laughter alone was infectious to the point I then couldn't breathe. Johnnie walked past and scowled as he looked at us as though he'd had enough of the misbehaving children. We then got onto impressions of colleagues, something they said I was "spot on" with. I guess this skill to observe, and mimic came from my drag queen years. As I was always complimented on my lip sync and mannerisms of the well-known personality I was portraying.

The one they always asked me to do was Johnnie. This consisted of wiping the corners of my mouth with my thumb and forefinger in a downward motion, contorting my body to the left and making a few groans and sashaying away. As they say in showbusiness, 'imitation is the biggest form of flattery' and I never did it with malice. I was even put on the spot and asked to do impressions by those I'd be impersonating, Blair, Rudy and Emre to name just a few.

I did wonder why it was so unusually quite as this is the week running up to London Gay Pride of which has just been cancelled due to covid-19. Had this spooked the usual crowds, especially my gay peers or was it just the bad weather that had people staying indoors. Although I have noticed Soho is starting to become less manic as novelty of socialising and 'the pint in the pub' is perhaps, starting to wear off post national lockdown.

Customers that were in did ask if we were doing anything for London pride even though it was cancelled. The answer was "no" although it was rumoured some of the other pubs along Old Compton Street were planning on having mini stage events. I'm not sure how true this is, after hearing Westminster Council moaning that we must keep customers from obstructing the pavements for those that turn up anyway at pride weekend.

We got to about 8pm and was down to only 7 customers and then in walks Bubbles DeVere with her shorts, gilet, and headphones. With her usual panache she ordered a large glass of Rosé and as usual she told me off for turning off the tip on the credit card machine. And she said the same thing "don't turn off the tip, I do tip you know. I do actually have money"!

She took her Rosé wine and floated from table to table exhibiting her goods and wares before she finally returned and settled on a stool in front of us at the bar. She had her headphones on and like Mariah Carey she had her fingertips pressing one side of the headphones. And waving her other hand as she was attempting to whistle like Mariah but in 'our' reality it was like fingernails on a chalkboard.

Red faced and with beads of sweat on her forehead Bubbles indicated in her usual fashion that she wanted another drink. Sliding down just the one headphone "darling! Another large Rosé wine". As we weren't busy, I asked "how are you"? To which she casually slid up her headphone, closing her eyes and started screeching. I quickly realised as she opened her eyes and gave her usual side glance, she was trying to get the attention of the guy in the white blazer.

The four of us had commented earlier on a guy who stood alone in a white blazer and jeans. We all remarked that this guy was very handsome, around 6-foot tall, firm muscles and a cute smile. Alex noted "he's got a massive cock too, look" pointing out the bulge in his jeans!

I gave Bubbles the credit card machine to pay for her wine, again sliding down just the one headphone "darling! Why do you always bloody take off the tip, you deserve a tip"! She screamed. As she slipped her headphones back on, she quickly removed them and said, "excuse me dear, there is a bomb here"! I peered over the bar and could see a navy rucksack unattended.

Against all my 23 years of training, I asked Alex to collect the bag, but he quite rightly refused so I went myself. Bubbles had taken a few steps back from where she was stood, I assume in case it blew up. And so deadpan yet comical she said, "darling! You can't be too careful what with the Taliban takeover" in reference to recent events in Afghanistan. It wasn't particularly what she said, but how she said it. That made me break out into hysterics and couldn't stop laughing. She said, "darling! It's no laughing matter, if it blew up, I'd be catapulted out of that window"! In the same tone I said, "stop it, you're going to make me piss myself" as I tried to catch my breath from laughing hard! Bubbles then said sincerely "darling! I have a very important piano recital to attend tomorrow" to which I retorted "it'd have to be a bigger bag to blow you to the gents, let alone through a window"! She exaggerated a shocked face while smirking but then quickly feel back into her usual persona giving me the dirtiest of looks.

I opened the bag and peered in with the presence of Alex as my witness. There was a flesh-coloured dildo which looked as though it had a bit of dirty business on the end of it. And what looked like a deodorant and a t-shirt. As I zipped it back up Bubbles said, "is it a bomb"? Still trying to catch my breath and with tears in my eyes I replied, "its defiantly a bombsite in there"!

Bubbles continued to act all coy and alluring. Although it was anything but, sad and desperate. And then to our astonishment she seemed to pull it off as the hunk in the white blazer came over and spoke to Bubbles very briefly. Within seconds he lent towards her and stuck his tongue down her throat. The three of us stood in a line with nowhere else to look and with our jaws collectively hitting the floor.

As he came up for air, Bubbles looked as though she was flooded with euphoria and I'm certain that wasn't the only thing 'flooded'! As she struggled to find her words, the hunk gently put his finger on her lips, *(upstairs he added pointlessly)* indicating she need say nothing. He walked to the back of the pub and picked up his pint and stood with his other hand back in his jeans.

Bubbles touching her lips in disbelief as her eyes twinkled, she smiled widely. Alex said softly "who is he"? To which Rudy replied "I don't care now he's been with that" referring to Bubbles. I concluded with my hand on my chest "I think it was really beautiful" and felt myself stupidly feeling emotional having seen how much it meant to Bubbles.

As this shift plodded on, we were still practically empty and there is an air of 'weirdness' about the place. A guy then came in and asked for Johnnie. I asked who he was so I could tell Johnnie who was here to see him. "Tell him its Derek, he's expecting me"! I went and got Johnnie and they went off together, but I didn't see where to, and I didn't think anything of it.

Bobby asked where Johnnie had gone and I said, "some guy called Derek came in to see him". Quick as a flash Bobby said, "apparently it's his dealer"! I did ask how Bobby knew that and as he started to tell me who told him, I interrupted saying "actually don't tell me, I don't want to know".

Three young lads walked in having been screened by security on the door and came up to me at the bar. One of the three said "ere, boss! How much is a single vodka"? I went through the prices of spirits and then at their request the prices of lager noticing one of the three go to the toilets. I wanted to say 'guys, you don't have to give the pretence of buying a drink if your mate just wants to use the toilet'. But I went along with it.

The two remaining bought two shots of Sambuca of which I charged first and then poured. I heard a shot glass drop to the floor as I took the sambuca back to the fridge. He complained to Bobby that his mate had dropped his drink and the pub should pour him another without charge. Bobby called me over and the guys told me another pub down the road always gives them another if they spill one. I told them it wasn't happening here, and they tried to argue that it was a legal requirement if they are still on the premises.

I said "once the invitation to treat has been finalised with a payment, the transaction is complete and forms a legally binding contract. What you decide to do with the product is entirely up to you. I can only compensate you if you can show the product was faulty". By this time, I had walked from behind the bar to look at the floor with the noise of the shot glass still ringing in my ears. It sounded distinctly like an empty shot glass hitting the floor. I know as I have dropped a few in my time when handling them. Indeed, my hunch was correct, I pointed out to the pair "if you dropped your drink, how come the floor is bone dry"?

"Well, it's worth a try, init boss"! I laughed it off with them to keep the peace as they went into the toilets. I quickly compared the two to that 2013 Judge Judy clip I'd seen. Where Judge Judy said it was her quickest legal claim to be dismissed with a pair of defendants she referred to as "dumb and dumber". A plaintiff claimed the pair had stolen her handbag and the plaintiff reeled off its contents, including "an earpiece". One of the pair pipes up "there was no earpiece in their mam", instantly implicating themselves.

Bobby then came rushing out of the gents with the air freshener being chased by the two lads; one was shouting "I'll fuck you up bro next time you talk to me like. I'll slice you in two"! I beckoned security and then cool as a cucumber the lad asked me for a drink to which I said he would not be served and needed to leave. He eerily and calmly asked why, and I stated "you can't speak to my colleague using language like that and then expect to stay for a drink. So, I'm afraid it is time up guys, you need to leave".

And just like the Judge Judy clip I mentioned, one of the pair tried to justify his language by saying "that dick was bothering me while I was doing a line [cocaine], init"! Security swiftly asked all three to leave and they did although they argued for a time outside, but security looked like he had it under control and I asked Bobby and others to stay inside as not to antagonise the situation.

I said to Alex "where the fuck is Johnnie"? Bobby shared what had happened in the toilets and as he did I started to send Johnnie a personal message on my phone as opposed to the group chat. Bobby said the three guys were in the gents and saw them doing lines off the countertop and merely said "guys if you're going to do that, at least be a bit more discreet about it". I said to Bobby "if you were going to say anything at all, it should have been to a manager and for them to deal with given they shouldn't be doing drugs at all, we could lose our licence".

As I was about to send my message, I felt a breeze behind me and it was Johnnie, snorting, wiping his nose and tucking his t-shirt into his shorts. Simultaneously I saw Derek leaving the pub as I started to explain what had happened to Johnnie who dismissively said, "yeah I heard" before walking off sniffling and snorting.

Bobby came over as I was leaning against the back of the bar and leaned up beside me. As we both looked out over the pub Bobby said, "because Johnnie was in the cubicle when it happened". I asked how he knew, and Bobby said, "because the lock is broken, and I walked in on him". I turned and looked Bobby in the eye, and just by the look I got back I said, "I really don't want to know" and assumed Johnnie wasn't in the cubicle taking a dump!

Anyhow, me, Alex, Bobby & Rudy got back to having a giggle and you'd think we'd run out of things to find amusing. But within 20 minutes Johnnie was putting on quite the floor show. He was bouncing all over the place, slurring his words and his body contorting in every direction and his eyes on full beam.

After a few minutes I became concerned that maybe he was having a stroke. The others fell about laughing at my concern and me persistently asking Johnnie if he was "ok". The guys were trying to convince me that he was "high" on drugs.

While I have come across a variety of substance abusers within my hotel career, I even after a hunch, innocently discovered one of the met polices biggest ever finds in one of my hotel rooms, but that's another story. They had always been docile, frothing at the mouth, if not 'dead' in appearance. I'd never seen anyone so hyper.

I guess it shows how naïve I am to this subculture, I mean I'm someone who thought 'chem sex' was having sex on all fours while scrubbing the kitchen floor with Ajax. Never will I refer to a hotel chemical store, usually in the housekeeping office as "the chem's room" ever again!

I think I knew perhaps Johnnie participated in this kind of activity in his private life, but never gave it much thought as it was none of my business. But I think what shocked me is Johnnie is so good, if not dedicated to his job. That I just wouldn't have thought he would do something that incapacitated him at work and made him completely incoherent. A concerned Alex asked "Will. Do you feel vulnerable"? I asked, "about what"? Alex nodded at Johnnie trying to stand up straight at the bar whilst trying to serve a customer with a half-filled pint glass spilling all over. The customer he was serving pointing at me and Alex as if to say, 'can you come and sort this out', the customer seemingly more concerned at his badly poured pint than Johnnie's welfare. As I watched this unfold, I said to Alex "nah, fuck it! We'll be ok, I can always step in if need be".

I didn't foresee anything happening in the evening not when it was as dead as this. But inside I thought if anything kicked off, I'd be straight out the door I am not being paid to deal with that kind of shit because Johnnie is off his tits. It went on and on and Johnnie didn't seem to come back down from wherever he'd gone.

Rudy then said "Will… I don't feel safe"! What we'd seen was indefensible and I said deflated "no, neither do I". I giggled to myself as I thought of that scene from the film Chicken Run, where the matriarch says, "we mustn't panic, we mustn't panic" and after a silent pause, all the chicken's scream in frantic panic.

Then I saw two bobbies in high vis jackets passing by and given we were so quite they peered in through the window and started to U-turn as though they were going to come inside. By this time Johnnie was flopping about trying to roll a cigarette, so I quickly walked to the main entrance and the police were speaking with security. They asked me "you guys' not busy tonight" to which I replied we'd been dead all night. Making small talk I rambled on as I do in a bid to bore them to death in the hope they'd want to get on their way.

The police weren't interested in small talk and asked if we'd had any bother. I said no, but security said, "yes a little earlier" and explained he'd kicked out the three guys for being abusive and doing drugs in the toilet. They seemed content the matter had been handled and they went on their way saying, "you know where we are if you need us". I thought that sounds ominous!

As I went back inside a guy followed me in. As I got behind the bar and stood next to Rudy in anticipation to serve him, he asked "tell me, and be honest, what's upstairs"? I thought if tonight couldn't get any weirder, so I repeated, "upstairs"?

"Yeah, what's upstairs" he enquired a second time. "Tables, chairs and a bar" I said. He looked at me puzzled and I thought 'we got one here'! "No, I mean what's upstairs"? He asked for a third time. "Tables and chairs, you can go up and have a look, the bar up there is open" I replied.

"Ok, so it's Wednesday night, what should I do? What would you recommend"? He was now asking us, so I said, "go home and put your feet up"! "Really"? He asked seemingly disappointed with my recommendation. I elaborated further by saying we'd been dead all night and given Soho is known for its vibe. He was best going home and coming out on a Friday or Saturday when there is always an atmosphere come rain or shine.

He then asked, by now trying my patience "one more question"! To which I said in a jovial tone "do I look like google! My colleague will answer any more questions you have, he can serve drinks too" as I went off to serve a waiting customer who mustered just about enough energy to say, "another one in their mate".

We managed to get to the end of the shift pretty much unscathed and we waited for Johnnie to come down from the office. As we waited patiently and given Johnnie was usually down and ready to go before now, I asked the others what happens once the 'high' wears off. Based on the assumption it did wear off as he'd been acting this way for a few hours now. I said we could be stood around waiting like dick heads and Johnnie could be sprawled over the office desk fast asleep or maybe dead on the floor!

The boys giggled once again at my naïve concern, although I couldn't care less of Johnnies welfare! I just wanted to go home and before the clock ticked onto 'unpaid' time! The boys collectively shared their experiences and the effects of the drugs they alleged Johnnie would have taken. As I looked on, Alex stated in response to the look of scepticism on my face, "Johnnie has offered all of us drugs from the first day we started"! As they nodded in agreement with Alex, Bobby and Rudy both stated the same. "Johnnie keeps asking me to do drugs with him! He says I should not do drugs alone and that he will help me," said Rudy.

I was truly, lost for words. I jokingly said, again, "he's never invited me" intimating that I was perhaps too old or not deemed 'cool enough' for an invitation. Although I suspect given my personality alone, let alone my professional background that I was not perhaps young and impressionable to be preyed upon.

Just as the boys were getting excitable in sharing their individual stories of Johnnie trying to push drugs onto them. Johnnie made an appearance and was still totally incoherent. He proceeded to roast each one of us which didn't offend nor land as none of us had a clue what he was saying. You could understand words, but it was just jumbled and slurred words and then he would burst out laughing. We only laughed because it was so bizarre which only encouraged him to carry on.

Rudy was sharing with the rest of us while Johnnie was fumbling around in his bag, that he'd gone to get his haircut today at a Kurdish barber. Upon entering he remarked how the place smelt strongly of fish. One of the barbers told Rudy to sit and wait while the barbers all sat on the floor in a circle. A large pan was placed on the Barber shop floor where the lid once removed bellowed with a burst of steam and the waft of fish.

Rudy waited for his haircut while the barbers all sat for their lunch. Well, we all fell about laughing that only Rudy would sit and wait and not perhaps find another barber or call back at a more convenient time. We asked if Rudy was offered a place at the table, but no invitation was forthcoming he said. Although he said he didn't have time to go home and shower and had to come to work with the smell of fish in his hair.

Johnnie kept butting in but was so incoherent and ruined the moment for Rudy. It was sad as Johnnie was good at giving a commentary to someone's story and you could be in stitches but sadly not this time.

I asked several times if we could go because I was starting to get pissed off with the floor show and we were now in unpaid time. As all four of us walked to Tottenham Court Road tube station, me walking on home to Islington. The boys shared that Johnnie, and a group of regular customers often talk about a place they go to in Kings Cross where they go for "chem's and chill". I asked if it was like 'Netflix and chill' and was told it was nothing like that at all.

It was a place you go to take drugs and then chill out. I said, yeah like watching Netflix and then chilling' to which the boys laughed, and shared Netflix and chill is a euphemism for sex. I said I didn't know as I don't even have Netflix but have heard the phrase a million times. And there was me the other week inviting Jack to come to mine for Christmas and knowing he watches everything on this Netflix, I said, "I'll subscribe to this Netflix, and we can watch Netflix and chill"! I was now mortified at this renewed understanding of this euphemism and what Jack must of thought I was suggesting!

All three boys shared as we approached Tottenham Court Road tube station their experiences of Johnnie trying to peddle his drugs onto them. I asked if his persistence meant he was dealing and was perhaps on commission. Is it like a 'refer a friend' loyalty scheme? Rudy said he wanted to state on record to me that he doesn't do drugs, alcohol is his limit. Alex and Bobby said they do their "business" [drugs] with friends they know and trust and only declined Johnnies constant invitations as they didn't want to fall into Johnnies group alongside Adam and Kenzie.

The boys wondered how Johnnie managed to cash up and lock up the pub in the state he was in. I said, "who cares, let's go home and forget tonight ever happened. Although I'll never forget "popcorn and rice""!

A couple of days later I was working with Jack on the opening shift. We were chatting about our family backgrounds and the similarities in our upbringing.

We had both experienced similar situations and yet had both approached them in different ways but had, had successful outcomes. Jack started talking about addiction and again his battle with alcohol. He shared again that he used to sit in the pub after closing and down a bottle of vodka by the DJ booth while crying his heart out. Jack shared this as he stood slicing the limes and I immediately couldn't help but think how tame Jack's story seemed compared to Johnnie peddling drugs at work. I thought I'd throw it out there, "who's Derek"?

Jack turned and looked at me and I knew, he knew, who I was referring to. But he played it down, so I gave a description of Derek as I'd interacted with this Derek and Jack said "ah, he's a DJ at a few of the London clubs". I said, "oh right, ok". And while I knew what Jack was going to ask next. I was not quite sure how much I should elaborate, when Jack asked, "why do you ask"?

So, I just came out with it "is he a drug dealer"? Jack hesitated in replying, as he temporarily paused butchering the limes, staring at the chopping board. Jack turned his head to look at me and said, "I don't think so"! It was not a firm denial and given the way Jack looked at me it seemed he was perhaps disappointed in himself that he was perhaps being a little disingenuous with me. It was unusual for Jack not to become neurotic and ask why I was asking such a question or making such an assertion. So, Jack's silence that followed was deafening.

I suspected it wasn't unknown that team members were doing drugs and the more I thought about it the more the pieces slotted together. From the team making passing comments and even those I suspected of substance abuse making self-deprecating comments. About the state they'd find themselves in both, in and out of working hours. Alex once told me when I asked where he'd disappeared to for so long, on shift, "I've been down in the cellar" with a manager "keying coke"! I innocently assumed he meant he was being shown or trying to change the coke syrup box for the soda gun. Confused, I replied, "you don't need a key to change the coke, it just unscrews"! Naturally he pissed himself laughing and taking the piss at my naivety before explaining what 'keying coke' [cocaine] meant.

It seemed I was truly the last to know as even customers would point out to me members of the team they deemed were "high on drugs". Some regulars used to sell 'little plastic bags' to the team at work by passing it through the beer taps in exchange for a cash note retrieved from their tips glass. Some customers would beckon me over just to ask me "is she high again" referring to a team member, often supervisors and management. My toes used to curl in my shoes, and I'd just shrug my shoulders in response and walk away. While I perhaps knew the customers observations were accurate. I have always been of the view that an unfounded allegation and/or assertion remains as such until proven, even in everyday mundane life. And I had seen no evidence of the team 'consuming' illegal substances to confirm nor deny if they were, as the customers stated "high"!

But who'd of thought it, me working in a dilapidated back street 'crack house' in Soho under the guise of a pub! Proper thrill-a-rama!

NO PRIDE

Both customers and colleagues were confused over what was happening over London Pride weekend. The pride parade had been cancelled due to covid-19. The organisers sent out a relatively last-minute message saying they could not meet the strict guidelines being imposed by Westminster Council. These were cited as necessary for public safety, although it didn't take the old queens long to start sharing conspiracy theories. The main one being touted was that this was a deliberate attack on the 'gay community' by the local authority. And as customers pointed out the parade was an outdoor event in the open air. But venues like pubs could remain open where everybody would pile inside and potentially spread the virus indoors.

But for venues, we'd been left hanging as nobody knew if we would still have the usual fun and frolics that usually takes place during and after the parade. Would there be the footfall if there was no parade and no draw for people to come into Soho. Word was many neighbouring venues would host small intimate pride celebrations within the parameters of their venues being covid secure.

But this quickly turned out to be a load of old shit, nobody was planning anything! Adam had this morning attended a meeting in the area where the council stated explicitly that venues should not hold events that would encourage a crowd and should not allow customers to congregate on the pavement outside the pub.

In preparation for Pride, I decided to do something I had been thinking about for a couple of years but never got around to it, having both ears pierced. I had one done as a teenager, but my mother made me take it out when she said I looked like a traveller child in her best Hyacinth Bucket voice! So, during my twenty-minute break I shot on over to Tattoo 13 just off Old Compton Street and where I'd had my chest tattoo done in 2012. I had a chest ribbon which in French reads 'Croyez-vous en la vie après l'amour' – Do you believe in life after love. Yes, I was a massive fan.

There was a bit of a queue as people were sat signing consent forms and I was greeted by a very nice chap with long grey greasy locks. He looked as if he'd been on the lash the night before and would have had no idea what day it was let alone who the current Prime Minister was if I'd asked. But I found that thrilling, plus I'd been there before so knew they were top notch.

"We can have you done in fifteen minutes fella. Its twenty for each ear and ten on top if you want to upgrade to the black studs". I agreed and he directed me to the cash machine around the corner and given covid regulations asked me to wait outside by the door and he'd come and get me when they were ready. I was called down with my fifty quid in hand and signed the consent form as a constant stream of people came in for piercings. I was taken around a corner and sat in a seat with the guy to talk me through the piercing process. He placed two dots on my lobes and asked me to look in the mirror to make sure I was happy before he speared me with a needle.

He said going through the closed hole wouldn't hurt as much as the fresh bit of meat on my other perfectly formed lobe. I think he lied because the old hole stung like a bitch but was bearable. Time was ticking and my twenty-minute break was over, and I had to dash back to work before they noticed I was late. But the piercer was making such a fuss of how "bad ass" they looked, I guess part of the customer service. He asked me to look in the mirror and said, "what do you think"? Short for time I had a quick glance and said, "yes lovely, do I pay out there"? A bit like when the barber shows you the back of your head and you must be all enthusiastic about a part of the haircut you'll never get to see anyway. I felt awful, because they looked ace, and I was proper buzzing.

I was only late give or take a minute or two but Johnnie was managing the shift so he wouldn't of minded. Truth was I was starving an all, compounded by feeling a little faint over the piercer talking me through the needle process when he laughed and rolled his eyes when I asked "have you got a gun" as if it was a branch of Claire's accessories!

Johnnie said inquisitively "there's something different about you" to which didn't take him long to notice.

The team had a half-hearted approach to dressing up for the Gay Pride weekend. Something the pub had traditionally done for every London pride and was the highlight of the calendar for the team. Many asked if I was dressing up and while I had not planned a costume given, I overheard Adam a while back say he was purposely holding back the 'flower' theme set by Carl saying to Johnnie "don't tell these cunts [newbies] the theme, let's keep it between ourselves" (the 'originals').

The conversation went on that not telling the newbies the theme would mean they wouldn't have time to make, buy or prepare a costume or outfit for the pride theme. I didn't share what I had overheard in case it was a set-up as it seemed to of been deliberately said in my presence. But as pride was cancelled so was the theme although it was never revealed what the theme would have been, and I wasn't interested to ask.

So, when others asked if I'd dress up, I shared I'd dig out one of my original and vintage uniforms, most likely my Royal Navy sailor outfit that I wore on my 30th Birthday. To a degree this felt sentimental given it was one of the few items of clothing that the last I wore it, I was not living with HIV.

Many of the 'newbies' said if one of us dressed up then they would too. I wasn't sure if I actually would but thought I'd encourage them as they had said privately, they didn't want to be judged by the 'originals' for dressing up or not, which I found to be outrageously sad and told them to merely 'fuck em'!

I was going to drag up, spurred on by others who knew I'd done drag for 10 years but I thought I'd leave that to our resident "geish" [sic] Ben. Others said they would drag up but when they shared images of their outfit it seemed to be less drag and more exploration of their sexuality which I thought was equally as fabulous.

Alex had purchased a short mini skirt, paired with a sexy piece of male underwear but this was somewhat curtailed by Adam who said it was rather revealing and inappropriate. Alex himself had seen the images of the previous pride where a staff member wore just a G-string, so Alex's confidence was knocked given we knew Adam was just being a bell end. Bobby said he was coming as a Fox which I must admit from his descriptions I was intrigued how he'd pull that off.

So, I picked up my Royal Navy Seamen No 2 dress from the dry cleaners and carefully squeezed it, along with my hat into my rucksack. I had customised a tally ribbon for the hat which spelt out the name of the pub in diamantes just to add a bit of sparkle. To make the uniform less formal, I was not wearing the white under shirt, so my chest was exposed under the jacket.

I was a little worried if I'd overheat on my 12-hour shift given the uniform is pure wool. I ditched the heavy army boots and opted for navy trainers as my bell bottoms covered them and I wanted to be comfy while on my feet. I'd also brought my work vest that was diamante encrusted and a pair of denim shorts to change into in the evening.

I was surprised at how quite Soho was as I walked into work. The weather was glorious, it was the perfect day for a gay parade but alas it was not to be. The end of week and into the weekend it seemed quieter than usual and as I quickly debated if I'd dress up or not, I didn't decide until I got into the staff room. I thought I'd go for it just for the other lads as they really wanted to dress up and were still sharing, they were nervous in the group chat.

I changed in the staff room and made sure I was presentable. I took a selfie in the toilets and posted it in the private group chat. The boys got all fired up which exited me that they'd come to work and have a giggle even if it wasn't as busy as previous years. I went downstairs to the main bar to start my shift and while I felt a little overdressed, Johnnie and Adam hadn't dressed up although Adam had a leather harness on under his vest. He said he might go topless later if he got the bottle. He complained his harness was digging in and chafing and I said just take your top off given some of the customers had dressed up and seemingly dunked themselves in glitter!

Kenzie was dressed up in an alternative outfit that could only be best described as a giant doily, which he looked fab in, and I shared as much with him. He complimented me on my outfit and through gritted teeth I engaged in casual conversation.

While pride had been cancelled, I felt it was still a day for the 'community' at least to put its differences aside and embrace each other and the foundations our peers before us had laid for us! And for me, with the AIDS it felt a little poignant to forgive and forget and have a pleasant day, preferably with some crudeness and hilarity!

So, with that I went about the entire shift embracing, the one person I didn't particularly want to embrace. I said to Adam, "come on whip the vest off and get ya tits out" to which he replied coyly "I will later"! I felt he was fishing for a compliment, so I bit and said, "Oh don't be daft, if you've got it, flaunt it". I did one of those mini sicks in my mouth, you know the ones you have no choice but to swallow. Although it did look as though he had a nice chest on him, so I was being entirely sincere, it just pained me a little to be nice to an arse hole.

I was trying not to clock watch, but I was keen for some of the others to start their shift, so I didn't feel a complete bell end. We got busy quick as it goes, and it was a sea of sequins and glitter. Two guys were telling me the influx of customers had been around the corner at a Pride party. I tried three times to ascertain what the event was and where, but they were so drunk, as were the others, I never did find out. They asked when I was clocking off to which I said I'd just started and they replied "shame, you look so shaggable in that uniform we were going to invite you back to ours". Whilst not a prude and secretly enjoying the compliment, two drop dead gorgeous hunks wouldn't give me the time of day out of uniform so I quickly moved on to another customer who was waiting to be served. I hoped he'd be my Jack to my Kate Winslet and save me.

Well, once he told me what he wanted to do to me which blew my mind he eventually placed his order. He gave me a twenty-pound note tip which made me feel slightly uncomfortable because it felt somewhat seedy. He stood back in the crowd and for over an hour stood there watching my every move and pursing or licking his lips trying to be alluring. I wasn't enjoying the attention but told myself I should have known better to wear what I was wearing with this crowd.

If I heard the phrase "oi oi sailor" once I heard it a thousand times. I was totally disappointed given there were a thousand 'seamen' jokes to be had, to which I only got once "will there be more seamen on the bar later"? To which

I replied, "no, but try the toilets, you usually don't have to wait long"! Keith who was stood close by said "for fuck's sake Will! Don't encourage them". Looking all gormless I said "what"!

As I moved around in a vain attempt to collect glasses, I constantly had my bum pinched. It was cheeky. I guess we now live in an era where this kind of behaviour wasn't to be tolerated. But for me there wasn't a 'pinch' that felt like someone was explicitly gratifying themselves sexually. It was a bit of cheeky 'Carry On' frivolity while people were in good spirits, and I quite liked it as I received positive feedback with almost every pinch.

I stood on the door trying to attract attention, not to me, but the venue in the hope we could draw in a few more customers as Old Compton Street was now heaving. As I stood in the doorway posing for photos with customers and passers-by, me now being the obstruction on the pavement. I turned and Jack had arrived and was stood in the doorway looking subdued and uncomfortable. He'd not dressed up and I really wanted to ask if he was ok, but it was far too busy for a conversation so kept it to the usual pleasantries.

Jack looked me up and down and nervously said "you look nice" with a forced smile as though he was about to cry. I said "thanks"! I asked how he'd been, and he said he was good and that was that. He didn't say anything else and was so miserable, and he remained so all day.

As I did move around the floor of the pub, I did overhear plenty of conversations around AIDS and HIV. Even a debate over which royal did more to help raise awareness and tackle stigma around AIDS. Princess Diana or Princess Margaret where the two nominees. As I leant in to collect glasses, with the sole intention of earwigging, one chap was broadcasting that he in some capacity worked for Princess Margaret. He passionately stated that she had done a lot more than Princess Diana in the fight against AIDS.

But Princes Margaret deliberately chose not to seek publicity while she did all this tremendous work against stigma around AIDS. I couldn't help myself and as I reached for an empty Guinness glass I said, "but was that not rather counterproductive? Why carry out work for a cause for the purpose of 'fighting stigma' if you're not going to publicise that work where the stigma exists"?

"Yes dear! But your probably far too young to of even lived during the AIDS pandemic" he sniggered to his two mates. As I departed their table as their dedicated glass collector I said, "but not too young to be living with the disease today"!

As I walked away, one of the group reached out and tried to grab my waist to no doubt offer some pity. But I didn't turn back as I didn't need any. But it was humbling to hear those conversations around AIDS/HIV are just as relevant today as they were then.

A short while later a conversation with two at the bar sounded more like a competition between the UK and the USA in who had the most damning AIDS campaign. The American conceded after watching for the first time on a mobile device at the bar that the UK had the most hard-hitting AIDS television advert with the falling tombstone and the slogan "Don't die of ignorance"!

Ben arrived in Drag. He'd made his costume "my gran gave me this dogs tooth fabric". I don't know what came over me as I said under my breath "definitely dog alright" to which Ben barked "sorry, Will"!

To be fair he'd done an excellent job sewing wise and I complemented him on his skill and presentation. It was an improvement; however, it was still not 'drag' for me. His face make up was as monotone as the fabric his costume was made of. He said he was going for city glam in his executive Karen look. He had a turban on his head, from a fancy dress shop with an emblem on the front that had about 4 plastic diamonds. It was weak for someone who continually boasted he was this massive sensation with a 5-year illustrious drag performing career behind him.

Elias was back in London but not yet back working in the pub, so it was fab to catch up with him dressed in drag as a bumble bee and being asked to constantly pose for photos with customers and passers-by. Both Johnnie and Adam made catty remarks they had shared with me previously that Elias often did drag for pride and other events but spent the whole night on the door getting pissed while the others worked their backsides off.

That may be the case I thought, but having someone dressed up on the door sets the tone for what's inside and usually draws people in. Being a 'door whore' not that I ever had to stoop so low during my ten years, although I'd spend 10 mins doing meet and greets to get punters in the mood, is both physically and mentally draining.

Bobby should have won a prize for best dressed as he looked super cute and pulled off a leather harness, small white shorts with a furry foxtail hanging out the back. He said it went down well with the customers, but the others just chatted shit behind his back which was a shame.

Keith was scheduled to work the upstairs bar which as I've mentioned nobody liked working. He too had not bothered to dress up at all. Not so much as a bit of glitter around the eyes. I was gobsmacked when I went to help him set up the bar and he stated "Will! You'd like to work up here wouldn't you"! Adam his house mate was stood the other side of the bar looking at me for my response. "Nope, I was up here last night, and I am back up here tomorrow"! I said confidently. I thought 'don't be taking the piss out of me mate. I didn't come up the Thames on a curly wurly'!

"Fair enough, it wouldn't be fair to ask you then" Keith said. I don't think anyone could argue that I had not done more than my fair share of working in the attic. I had to giggle to myself, because Adam had no ground to tell me to work the upstairs bar given it was him who had not only assigned Keith to work upstairs on Pride, but had assigned me, the one most likely to work in the attic the day before Pride as well as the day after.

Lurch arrived and I've hardly seen him of late. He looked fab in his quirky goth-kink outfit. It was simple but so effective! He'd paired black trousers and a black jacket with nothing underneath except a cross of black duct tape across each nipple. It looked as though he'd washed his hair and done face make up and he looked sensational, and I told him so.

Keith must have asked Lurch to swap with him upstairs as Lurch said to me "Keith's got a bloody cheek, he just asked me to swap with him upstairs! He hasn't even made the effort to dress up"! I concurred with Lurch; it was a cheek.

A short while later, I think complimenting Lurch on his outfit must have been mistaken for something else. I was tonging some limes when he passed me and to be fair the space in the bar is tight but if you shuffle sideways, you can pass with ease. Occasionally we might cock bash or bum each other as we navigate the bar when its busy and nobody bats an eyelid, and we take it as accidental. But as the others had mentioned to me a short time back, Lurch as he passed seemed to deliberately rub his cock against my thigh.

I knew he'd done it deliberately but thought I'd let it pass this once and give him the benefit of doubt. Not 10 minutes or so later I was in an open part of the bar, and he passed and did it again, except I felt his cock on my butt cheek! It wasn't anything to write home about which made me giggle. At least when Rudy cock bashed me as I was bottling up and he brushed past me, his 6-inch flaccid meat hurt so much I even checked for a bruise the next day!

I was a little taken aback with flashbacks to being assaulted when I was infected with HIV back in March 2020. Low and behold, Lurch did it a third time and this was as I was slicing limes. Quick as a flash I turned around with the steak knife in my hand. Pointing it in his direction, some distance away, I said "Oi! Fucking cock bash, me again I'll fucking chop it off, you hear"! Needless to say, he didn't do it again.

Other than that, it was a good night and we all seemed to have a good time considering. I'd changed into my diamante vest, denim shorts, pride socks and my pride themed converse. I kept the sailor hat on at an angle for extra campness and didn't do too badly in cash tips £147.

I was talking to Kenzie, just small talk when I spotted Jack stood looking down from the upstairs bar. We had direct eye contact, but he didn't smile or acknowledge me. I wondered why he was so glum and perhaps I should have asked him, but I didn't want to be intrusive. I wondered what he thought about me chatting to Kenzie after what Jack knew.

I'd shared with Jack people always kick me in the teeth and I don't let them get away with it, but if I forgive them or perhaps overlook it too easily. It doesn't mean they get away it as they go on my 'keep distant' list as someone I can't trust. But my personality and skill from my years in the hotel sector is that of 'diplomacy'. And I tend to implement this in my personal life, plus having had the usual stuff to deal with in life from perhaps a younger age than the average person. You mature quicker and weigh up what truly matters in life, and what doesn't. I don't ponder nor stew on things, I bin it and move on.

Having a bit of banter with Kenzie in this instance was to maintain a pleasant working environment not only for myself but my colleagues. I wanted to stab the bastard in the eyeballs with bamboo straws, but that's illegal, apparently. So, you just have to be nice and attentive, kill them with kindness as the adage goes. Jack then solemnly walked back upstairs looking lost as he lethargically dragged himself up each step, too many bagels probably.

The vibe slipped away at a decent hour and the crowds slowly disappeared admitting they'd drank enough, and they'd called it a night. We were all exhausted but had, had a good night and those that dressed up were pleased they had. The only sad thing was there was no team photo to commemorate the event, but I managed to grab a couple of selfies with some of the 'newbies which is what really counted.

I was hoping to catch Jack to see how he was and wish him goodnight, but he'd already gone before we closed apparently.

LIAR, LIAR, PANTS ON FIRE!

It is always hard to gauge Adam and what mood he will be in. Others used to throw shade as they termed it, by making fun that he never smiled and seemingly had no facial muscles, ravaged by years of drug abuse they alleged.

I said he looked like the American animated character 'Droopy' the dog and of course these bitches asked "who"? Like Adam who also spoke in a monotone and deadpan manner. Often as the others highlighted, incoherent as his mouth rarely moved to coherently form words so we'd all shared we nodded in acknowledgement to Adam but rarely understood what he had said.

My relationship with Adam wasn't so much frosty, we spoke convivially but it was kept to a minimum and the basic of pleasantries. I was still hearing crap he was saying behind my back, and I just didn't trust the guy.

We'd sometimes have awkward moments on the bar with just me and him and no customers to serve nor tasks for me to complete. We'd stand awkwardly staring at the fruit machines or the folk sat on the pavement slurping tea in the shop across the road. I'd often be the one to initiate a conversation but at times he did too. It was almost like we both really wanted to speak to each other, but perhaps our pride was getting in the way from the whole fiasco around me being accused of being covid-19 positive. Due to that I lost any trust I had in Adam and for him, well, I wondered if it was embarrassment given, he had seemingly jumped to conclusions over the covid incident. Alleging I was covid-19 positive which was proven unfounded when I insisted Jack conduct a lateral flow test on me which was negative for covid-19.

In one of these lulls in trade Adam shared "I had a call from the pub down the road. The manager was asking what you were like to work with as he said your CV was amazing in application for Deputy Manager".

I didn't want to ask, but just to make conversation and with my toes curled in my trainers I said "Oh really. I hope it was all good"?

"Yes, I said you was wasted here and was most likely bored. That knowing your CV and years in management you would be ideal for the role" Adam said.

I asked when this was, and Adam confirmed "about two weeks ago". Nervously laughing I said, "he hasn't rung me yet"! I was under no illusion that Adam hadn't given me a positive reference, I couldn't be sure, but the pub never called, and they immediately rejected subsequent applications when they kept re-advertising the same role.

Adam continued to share elements of his manager training that he's been struggling with. Given my experience I hoped I was sharing some useful advice but assured him not to stress it. "When you move into management you have a lot of skills and experience, even if doubt yourself. And like anything in life that's new, we sometimes make it up as we go along, you'll find what works and defines you and your style of management which always comes down to personality". I shared with Adam reassuringly.

Johnnie and others said Adam is not good at managing people, particularly both internal and external customers. He flits between good cop, bad cop but generally implements them the wrong way round.

Adam also has a habit of playing team members off each other. An example of this was Adam promoting the divide Kenzie always referred to as the 'originals' which consisted mainly of Adam, Johnnie, Keith, Bagel Boy, Kenzie and recently recruited Blair.

Versus the 'newbies' which comprised of Rudy, Emre, Bobby, Alex, Lurch and me. Other colleagues were essentially homeless floating between the two depending on how favourable they were at a given time. It was noted Ben being a new starter was somewhat of a 'snake' and in chats was referred to merely with the snake emoji. He seemed to float between the two groups carrying messages back and forth to each camp, shit stirring essentially.

He wanted to be with the 'newbies' as it was relatively drama free, and we were intent on having a good time as opposed to bitching and backstabbing. But he also believed kissing Adam's arse was a method of networking to 'start' his drag career on the London gay scene. Ben would often be seen on nights out with Adam and the originals. When some of the newbies queried this Ben would say he just coincidentally bumped into them. And then Ben would stand outside smoking with the newbies dispensing advice as though he was Adam's campaign manager.

Jack was very much not part of either group. The newbies stated they found Jack "dull" and "boring" and the originals who knew Jack relatively well just slagged him off continually and at times shared intimate and grotesque details about his former addiction to alcohol and his sexual escapades. Jack once said to me "I've heard them say worse about me. I don't really care"!

Pride being cancelled meant there was not so much of a post 'pride high' but the continuing pandemic there were post pride blues! And the mood was about to get even worse when a surprise bombshell was casually dropped into the group chat by Carl the manager.

Carl revealed he was leaving to manager another pub and Adam was replacing him. There was a small caveat, this seemed to be a trial for around 4 months. I guess it was part of Adams management training to demonstrate practical implementation of the fast-track training scheme he was on.

I arrived at work an hour after the message was posted and had deliberately ignored the flood of incoming messages by not opening them. The staff room key was not hanging behind the bar meaning someone was in there. I walked in to find Emre, Rudy and Bobby semi naked as they changed into their work gear. "Oi oi bitches" I yelled upbeat and jovial.

The mood was sombre, the air damp with precipitation of tears to the recent revelations. I said "Jesus, who's died"? My heart went out to them as they individually turned to look at me all sombre yet saying nothing. Their eyes saying all I needed to know, they'd not taken the news well.

I've worked long enough to of been in their young shoes to understand change can be daunting and at times unpopular. You'll always find someone who wants or tries to resist change in the workplace and at times I have often disagreed with change but always gone along with it.

This was the first time in 23 years I felt the change was a car crash in the making, but the bitch in me fastened my seatbelt and was looking forward to the ride. Deep down I hoped Adam made a success of it, I truly didn't want him to fail. I would in the capacity of my very junior role support Adam in his role. But this wasn't a career for me so either way I didn't really care.

"Come on guys it's not that bad, it just means you'll have to start arse licking like the others" I said optimistically. They were young, for two it was their first serious job since leaving school, so they had to learn work isn't a social club, its cutthroat sometimes, albeit in a back street pub.

But I did feel for them as I had a greater understanding of how this was a disaster. I tried to sugar coat the news by saying "look! Carl did say it was only for a few months, so it'll all be over soon. Some of you will probably have moved on to work somewhere better by then. Or maybe you'll of been fired by Adam"!

Emre chipped in with "yeah look at it this way guys! Thank fuck it wasn't Jack"! As I pulled my work gear out of my bag I said, "ironically you'd have nothing to worry about if it was Jack"!

Emre quipped again with the same old flannel that he found Jack to be "dull" and "boring" to substantiate his previous remark! Laughing, I asked, "and Adam is the definition of 'fun and frolics? Guys, managers aren't here to be popular, they're here to 'manage'. Take 2 mins to compare a shift managed by Adam and a shift managed by Jack and get back to me"!

Emre sat on the staff fridge pondering what I just said when Rudy shared "but Will! Jack is so strict! You can't be late back from break; you can't drink a beer when you finished cleaning at the end. He won't even allow my friends to wait inside the pub while you finish cleaning at the end of the shift"!

Changed and checking myself in the mirror I opened the staff room door, turned back to Rudy, and said, "now that sounds like an amazingly competent manager to me"!

As I left Rudy came shuffling behind me "no! Will! Wait…" I turned to him and politely said "Jack has nothing to do with this. Adam is in charge and really there is nothing you can do about it except, be smart and knuckle down".

Rudy knew I was referring to the points he just raised. He was regularly late for his shift, wasn't always productive and would, legitimately drink wastage (wrongly poured drinks) on shift which I had seen myself. Of which had been encouraged by Adam, as Adam and others drank deliberately poured and accidentally poured wastage. I'd told Rudy previously, to be 'careful' and explained the consequences of his actions at work as the legend that is, Judge Judy states when she refers to the 'doctrine of clean hands'!

I started to hear on the grape vine that Adam was bizarrely openly discussing with random colleagues that I was lying about being HIV positive.

I couldn't comprehend how someone would be so brazened to make such an allegation, so I immediately disregarded it as perhaps a miscommunication, a Chinese whisper. It came back up again when all the 'newbies' had inadvertently shared it. As they were slagging off Adam, they each separately shared this same piece of information with me as they were collectively all present at the time Adam was making this statement. I therefore took it to be credible.

I truly didn't understand why Adam would say such a thing and for what purpose? I wasn't a threat to him or his career so it could only be to serve as a malicious act. Imagine to be so bolden to tell your subordinates that a team member who has been forced to share his HIV status after receiving malicious messages threatening to expose his status. Is now, making an unfounded allegation that this person is "lying" about living with HIV. The more I thought about it the more dangerous the environment felt.

What if one nutter decided to cause me harm for lying about such a thing? I have to say, while I liked and respected most of the team, some of them were clearly, severely unbalanced and didn't have a true grasp on reality. You don't have to be a specialist to work that out from the things I have witnessed and what they have individually shared, that you need to have eyes in the back of your head.

If Adam had come to me, I would be quite happy to show him proof of my status via the NHS App where I can access my medical record. I can bring in for a little show and tell the six bottles of meds I collect twice a year to keep me alive and well.

But, although perplexed by this revelation, it was Adam, so I asked myself why I was so surprised? Talking like this with subordinates both personally and professionally just highlighted why Adam was not fit for the role nor responsibility he'd been given, and I was just utterly disappointed by his behavior.

I had a sneaky feeling this came about after Johnnie laid into me the other day when he had an audience. Jack came and shared with me that he was demoting himself from deputy manager to take on more studies. Adam has put his title as 'glass collector' on the new Rota which I suspect is Adam having a dig as I have heard and seen recently that the two are not getting along.

While we were all in the main bar Emre made a passing comment, trying to be funny, I think. About how Carl is never on site to manage and instead out buying Sushi or getting his hair cut. Johnnie took the moment to stand on a stack of glass trays as though he was standing on a soapbox!

"Now she" referring to Jack, "is out the door and Carl is out the picture you'll all see some amazing changes around this place. For one, you'll all have better hours, you'll have managers that are supportive, that will actually be on the floor and will actually do some work instead of being laid up at home".

Johnnies body contorting uncontrollably from side to side as he gave his speech in support of his friend Adam. Then wiping the frothy saliva from the corners of his mouth with his thumb and for finger.

I have always been a great believer in never saying anything behind someone's back that you're not prepared to say to their face. While I liked Johnnie tremendously, I recognised he was a bit snide in that area, but then to his credit he wasn't a confrontational person.

So as always, and sincerely, I shared my opinion to add balance to the tirade I had just witnessed. "I have always found Jack to be a very reliable manager, he has always been there when I have needed him and have never had to look very far to find him". And I was genuinely referencing to work related issues, such as manager approval on a till, refunds, customers that needed kicking out etc.

Well, if looks could kill as the saying goes. I could hear the bitches stood around me, take a sharp intake of breath. It was like the scene in the film 'The Devil Wears Prada' when Anne Hathaway makes the "this stuff" comment and Meryl gives it to Anne with both barrels in front of a group of people.

"Darling! She [Jack] was hopeless, if you class sitting in the office your entire shift watching YouTube videos then we can see why you're working in a bar and not as a hotel manager anymore! And if you think for a second, Jack was helping you with the HIV stuff for your benefit, think again! We all knew she [Jack] was only doing it to show head office how fantastic she thinks she is, because that's all that mattered to her 'getting that pat on the back' or had that escaped that tiny little brain of yours"!

My immediate thought was 'wow, that truly was well executed' as Johnnie was very good at throwing shade. If I'd of heard the director shout "cut, that's a wrap" I'd have showered Johnnie in roses and screamed "Bravo, Bravo"! But reality hit, my trainers were fixed to a sticky pub floor, the faint waft of warm urine filled the air from the gents and my colleagues had seemingly scattered and I was stood alone.

Johnnie stepped down from the trays while maintaining eye contact and rolling my eyes I just said, "what a load of old shit"!

Truth was, as I stood next to Bobby resting on the beer taps looking out onto Old Compton Street, I felt physically sick. Bobby nudged my elbow and said "don't worry about it. He's on one because he's high"!

As I continued to stare out through the window as people passed by, I said "I didn't think the scabs all round his mouth was impetigo"! Bobby laughed as he knew I was referring to a conversation I was having with Johnnie the other day. I was concerned by these scabs on his face and all around his mouth. I said it might be impetigo and he should get it seen to and stop picking at it. Kenzie passing by interjected "it might be drugs". Others found it funny that despite being nearly forty years old, I was mistaking the effects of substance abuse as a mere fungal infection.

So, it made me wonder if this interaction with Johnnie had got back to Adam and he was peeved that I'd declared I found Jack to be a good manager. Which may have come across as me not being supportive of Adam in his new role. But did that warrant him telling others I was "lying about living with

HIV"?

I decided it was time for me to leave this place, but I felt I had not had the fun that I perhaps expected to have working in a London gay bar in Soho.

So, I got together with Alex, and we started to go to the pub during our split shifts or running up to Tesco during our break. Buying wine and spirits with the intention to, what he termed, "neck it" with a view of getting tipsy to get through the shift. I'd never behaved like this in work, but thought, 'what the heck! If I'm going, go with a bang'!

We weren't plastered, in the proper sense, we were still functional. But I must admit not being a big drinker it didn't take much to get me lubricated. Me and Alex were 'necking' around 4 pints in the hour and copious shots of Sambuca before chomping on chewing gum and returning to work.

The first time we staggered back from China Town nearly getting flattened by a black cab on Shaftsbury Avenue. Johnnie and Blair both cottoned on as they looked at us both pissing and falling about laughing. Johnnie scowling inquisitively "Will! Are you ok? You seem happier than usual" which had me in stitches. I didn't care for the consequences and replied, "just a liquid lunch" as a hint to what we'd been doing. I guess like Kenzie, nothing could be done to discipline me because, I too 'knew too much'.

I mean what could they say? Snorting substances at work, popping pills on the premises compared to a few beers off site. In time between two separate shifts didn't make much for a disciplinary. Although coming to work intoxicated was gross misconduct as outlined in the staff handbook. I did feel emboldened to be more fun, caustic and cutting with customers and colleagues and they all lapped it up. I was able to recognise how behaving like this could easily become addictive but knew I didn't intend on staying long for it to become a serious concern.

At the weekends when I was working the main bar, which was more frequently now that I deliberately let slip to Adam that I loved working upstairs and "absolutely hate downstairs with a passion"! The rota changed and it was rare in the weeks that followed that I was even put upstairs once a week.

I thought Adam was smarter than to fall for that, but clearly not which did disappoint me. But at the same time, it only confirmed I was being allocated the upstairs bar based on his personal prejudice towards me. I dug out my other hats after a regular customer kept complementing me on my baseball hats and then said he was getting turned on by my Sailor hat at Pride.

I have a genuine Police Custodian helmet so dug out my rolls of diamantes and vajazzled the police emblem on the front to avoid getting into trouble for imitating an office whilst making it camp. I also dug out my Royal Air Force dress hat and added some camp glamour to that too.

I wore them on weekends, generally Friday, and Saturday nights to add to the vibe. I paired handcuffs with the police helmet, and this saw cash tips flood in. But I am continually asked to pose for selfies with customers which is a little embarrassing. But surely it is promoting the pub's sense of LGBT community and adds to the experience and atmosphere. It is all a little bit of fun and the team also lapped it up, to my face. I am sure the 'originals' have things to say behind my back, not that I care.

It was bizarre whenever I had a hat on, Ben would merely look me up and down with his top lip upturned and his nostrils flared and would say nothing. The diamonds were sensational, when the disco lights and strobes hit them, they'd reflect right across the pub like a mirror ball. I used to look in the mirror opposite the bar and just be dazzled by the sparkle, it was quite hypnotic.

I saw Ben staring at my glistening jewels and given I was only wearing a hat and a hoodie, I had more of a presence than he did in his plain and dreary "geish" and I could see the little green eyed monster in him. I thought 'if he hadn't been so quick to burn his bridges with me, I could have given him some pointers of where and how to pick up these inexpensive jewels' to elevate his drag. The drag queen DJ asked where I sourced them, and I was more than happy to share.

Jack used to make me laugh, as I'd bump into him back of house and he would stand frozen on the spot staring, often in my way. I wasn't sure if he was perhaps excited by the uniform, bedazzled by the vajazzle or just trying to comprehend why I was intent on having a good time while looking a little crazy. As he stood seemingly lost for words but with a cheeky smile on his face, we'd both make awkward grunts and groans to get by and proceed on our way.

LEMONADE-GATE

As I was in the main bar a lot more, I have to admit I was missing the upstairs bar. You worked harder as you worked alone but you were totally autonomous and could pretty much set the pace of the shift.

Jack sent me up to cover Rudy's break who was working the upstairs bar. Rudy complained he'd only had a handful of customers in the last 2 hours. I had earlier gone up to check on him and keep his morale up as he was sulking for being placed upstairs. He was still sulking come his break that he was missing the atmosphere in the main bar as it was much livelier and more importantly the cash tips.

I found his constant winging confusing as when he works the main bar, he incessantly moans about actually having to do some work. Customers are a major disposition to him, and I have often said hospitality is not a career for him. So, the upstairs bar where he could kick back and relax and essentially not be inconvenience by paying customers of which he loathed, was perfect for him.

Me and Rudy get on well and he has openly said to me and others, that he appreciates that I am direct and honest with him and others, unlike some of the other snakes. While I always tried to be diplomatic and sensitive in my approach. I am never afraid to share my opinion even if I know it isn't what the person wants to hear.

He was being a prima donna about being stuck upstairs and seemed to be taking it out on me, although I didn't bite and told him to go on his twenty-minute break. "I am taking 40 minutes darling, for being inconvenienced in this shit hole"! I knew Rudy well enough to know he wasn't joking, and his statement of his deluded self-entitlement was to be taken seriously as opposed to face value. The bitch would take forty minutes if not challenged so I quite bluntly stated that he would take twenty like everybody else and reminded him that his break had already started, alluding to how bored I was of his whining!

"You can finish my design for me" Rudy said while pointing at the receipt paper on the bar. I picked up the piece of paper and looked back to Rudy who was deliberately strolling to the staff room. He came back and was complaining he had to go out for food because he said he'd lost his appetite for what he'd brought to work for dinner. I said, "stood here complaining is eating into your break, your already 4 minutes in, you've 16 minutes left"! It wasn't my place to keep breaks on track and I wouldn't have minded if he came back a few minutes late. But I was due to take my break after and was merely trying to get him to 'go'!

He said with such rage and anger "Will! You are a fucking cunt"! before he stormed off. I looked around the bar and it was a state! He'd left empty glasses on several tables where customers had left. There was a stack of washing on top of the dishwasher. He'd left bottle caps strewn across the bar back and foil wrappers from bottles etc. I thought, 'to say he claims he hasn't had many customers, the pace is a shit tip'.

I didn't want to touch any of it and was happy to leave it for his return, but my OCD got the better of me, so I cleared it all up, but I was livid inside.

Rudy went outside and came back eating a salad and was nine minutes late and even then, came on the floor chatting to his friend on his mobile phone pleading "come to the pub and sit with me, I am so bored! I will buy your drinks, please, I can't cope"! I went downstairs and confirmed with Jack I was going to the chippy for my break. He asked, "is everything ok up there" and I knew Jack was referring to why Rudy was late. I said, "yeah all ok"! Jack looked at me in a way that indicated he knew I was resisting being a snitch.

The next morning Rudy's bad housekeeping came to bite him in the arse. Adam posted in the group chat a photo of Rudy's doodle with the caption "so who's the artist"? It was clear as there was no emojis to signal it was a bit of banter and Adam had taken the time to take a pic and post it in the group chat. Adam was querying the productivity of a colleague. The photo showed under the doodle someone had written, "do some work"! Of which that someone was me!

I replied saying it was me that wrote the comment but not the one who did the doodle. And in an email Adam said he was just having a bit of 'banter' by sharing the photo with the group to which was wholly disingenuous. Adam did, somewhat, have a bit more of a mature sense of humour than that. I was honest in my reply stating I found the bar in a shit tip and while Rudy was having a sulk and took liberties with his break that selfishly delayed everyone else, including me. I also didn't appreciate being called a "cunt".

I ended the message with a bit of tea by stating, "management may wish to focus less on doodles and more on stock, including the liberal squirting of lemonade".

I thought no more of it and although Carl had gone, he posted a message in the group chat a few days later, saying there had been a noticeable discrepancy of 'lemonade' and that any staff caught pouring themselves a lemonade would be dealt with as per policy. I pissed myself laughing sat at home when I read it, but for me, it was right. Company stock is stock no matter how inexpensive it may seem and taking what isn't yours is theft, end of!

I knew Ben was helping himself to Lemonade and spirits while on shift. Others had shared they took lemonade from the soda gun because they could pass it off as soda water, which was free and could be consumed by staff. They even traded tips with each other, as the syrup from the lemonade tended to froth up which was a giveaway to eagle eyed management as soda water doesn't froth. The Syrup held more bubbles from the gas, so you had to knock them out while pouring, but this made the lemonade flat. Who knew there are so many pitfalls to stealing lemonade?

I used to say to these bitches, "if you're going to run the risk of getting caught and fired from a job, that surely, you'd want to make it worthwhile and take something more iconic than lemonade". I wasn't encouraging them to steal, I was trying to highlight if you get sacked, which will follow you to your next job do you want to risk your new employer being informed you faced disciplinary for taking a soft drink.

Anyhow, conversation in our private group chat ensued and it was hilarious! There was mass panic over how Carl had established Lemonade was missing and how they were being watched. They argued that Lemonade was inexpensive so why the fuss? But to their credit they worked out that a box the syrup was quite expensive and in terms of how much revenue this syrup made, it was a substantial loss to the company over a period of time with them all frequently helping themselves.

When they did their calculations and conceded it was a significant loss in revenue, not one of them hesitated to state they would throw Ben under the bus as the most prolific lemonade thief if shit hit the fan.

Alex and Rudy said they'd also share Ben was pouring clear spirits such as vodka and gin deliberately and then placing them on the side as wastage and drinking them with lemonade to pass it off as H2o.

Emre then dropped a bombshell and implicated Rudy that while Ben was doing this, so was Adam and Johnnie. And only the other day Rudy poured Gin and Vodka accidentally and Adam told them both to top it up with a mixer from the gun and drink it. Adam and Johnnie too had their own wastage set aside already and this was a regular occurrence.

This made sense, as Johnnie used to reprimand me for chucking wastage drinks that were sat by the sink and the dishwasher. I could never tell if they were drinks that were at the end of their life and discarded or collected as empties from customers. So, I would sling what looked like dregs into the sink and get the glasses washed. Sometimes they would be ten glasses plus with spirits in sat along this worktop. Johnnie used to come over and say "Will! Have you slung the drinks that were here"? And I'd say gormlessly "yeah"! He never said anything more, although am sure he was raging inside. I had mentioned to him a few times in the past that, drinking wastage encourages 'deliberate' wastage and wasn't on. And that I was surprised the company didn't have a tighter procedure to record and offset wastage.

And there was a noticeable distinction in being high on substances and high with a few drinks inside them. Kenzie used to just blatantly pour himself a cider from the taps and sit it on the back of the bar without even attempting to hide it.

Rudy stated he once "accidentally" hit lemonade when he went to pour himself a soda water. He said he continued to fill his pint glass with lemonade to avoid wasting it. This made me giggle because he wasn't concerned about wastage, he was just too lazy to walk to the sink to empty his glass when realising his mistake. Rudy then in the chat shared that he found the lemonade too sweet so instead would opt for coke which made me laugh, 'Dumb, Dumb & Dumber'. Or the 'Lemonade Three' as I dubbed them.

Emre who is naïve was very blasé about it and said management wouldn't waste their time watching CCTV. Hence why Ben and others got away with claiming drinks at the end of shift as tips by collecting random receipts. Given they knew management would never query or go to such lengths to verify the CCTV with till transactions when redeeming these illegitimate 'drink tips'.

It was also stated that CCTV could not of played a part in what was now coined 'Lemonade-Gate' because surely eagle-eyed management would have picked up on the skimming of cash from the till as opposed to who was squirting lemonade.

Management knew spirits were unaccounted for, particularly vodka and gin as we were individually and collectively reminded to minimise wastage and it was touted that 'the new guys' were perhaps giving customers doubles instead of singles, by accident.

The reality is the guys pouring themselves wastage with these two particular spirits that they themselves shared, are clear in nature so can be passed off as water was why stock was short. I was puzzled as to how the odd few bottles a week that were missing weren't greater. Guys had shared how they were stealing bottles of spirits from the spirit room bypassing CCTV outside the spirit room. This was sometimes with the aid of the mop bucket and sometimes with the aid of cardboard refuse both leaving them retrieving the bottles by offering to walk the rubbish to the roadside on leaving the building to go home. I only came to learn about it when we dumped the rubbish on the roadside, they opened the bin liner to retrieve their bounty.

The ghost in the cellar, seriously we have a ghost, is knocking back the bottled Peroni like there's no tomorrow! I keep finding empty and open bottles dotted around the cellar. Oh! And empty crisp packets, well, who doesn't get a touch of the munchies after a drink or two! I figured I knew who it was as I spotted Blair in the cellar fingering his molars in a bid to dislodge food. I mean, who brings their lunch to the cellar? But then I was thrown when I saw Jack doing the same, in the bowels of the cellar. Maybe it was the 'ambience' or just the uncontrollable urge for a fried potato-based snack!

Although I was stumped on who was partial to the Ready Salted flavour as its very plain, if not vanilla! But then looking at the two of them, one with his knitting circle and the other who just witters on and on, it's a hard one to call!

Rudy sent a series of messages in the private group chat one of which was a letter that Adam had presented to Rudy by hand. Rudy said he walked into the staff room in preparation to start his shift when Adam followed behind him. Handing over an envelope mumbling and no doubt slurring, "Rudy, I am giving you an invitation". Rudy responded excitedly "Oh thanks, is it for a party"? Rudy said he thought Adam was inviting him to some sort of company party. Rudy opened the letter tearing at the seal and it turned out upon reading it that Rudy was under investigation and invited to attend a formal disciplinary.

The letter stated Rudy was under investigation alleging "theft of Lemonade". Alex and Emre both said in the group chat they too would get one given they had privately alluded to helping themselves to the company's stock and they were right, all three now had a disciplinary letter alleging gross misconduct for the theft of lemonade.

The three of them were understandably nervous and furious when it was confirmed that only the three of them were in receipt of a letter. Ben was on annual leave and the boys were eager to establish if he would be receiving a letter and Adam bizarrely confirmed with the 'lemonade three' Ben was not facing any disciplinary. Private chats went wild, all three plotted that they would chuck Ben under the bus as they felt he was the worst offender. He helped himself to the lemonade, spirits, claimed random receipts as drinks bought by customers to consume at the end of shift and allegedly, he was skimming the till of cash.

Ben gloated in the private chat that he wouldn't be under investigation as he had been booked to put on a drag show at the pub for Halloween 2021. I thought Adam had to be commended for his choice, I couldn't think of anything 'scarier'!

Rudy was called in earlier than his disciplinary letter stated and myself on annual leave was asked if I could come into to work by Adam, to which I agreed. Rudy was swiftly taken to the office shortly after my arrival and re-emerged 40 minutes later all puffy eyed saying he had been "fired" and was leaving. He was sobbing and dripping snot all over the bar. He seemed lost as he didn't know what to do and making a fuss with regulars. Therefore, management should always escort people off site in these situations, as it was embarrassing for the company and for Rudy.

Rudy spent some time outside on the pavement, crying and being consoled by the regular customer before beckoning me outside. He said "Will! How can they do this" and I said this is not the time nor place and that I'd speak to him when I get my break.

He asked for me to tell Alex to go out and see him to which I said, "leave Alex, don't get him involved when there's eyes watching him"! I went back in, and Kenzie was talking to Alex, and I interrupted and said "Alex, erm, oh Jesus, what's his name, erm" as I pointed to Rudy stood in the pub doorway. Kenzie said, "Oh Will, you shady cunt"! I said I genuinely forgot his name in the heat of the drama but continued "wants to speak to you". Alex knew this was a bad idea and refused and Rudy went on his way.

Adam emerged from the office and pulled Alex to one side, "we're sorry you got mixed up in all of this, but just to let you know that we won't be investigating you, it's all over for you". Alex turned and thanked me for speaking to Adam earlier that afternoon. I'd shared with Adam that I had never seen Alex helping himself to anything other than water at work. Whether he had or not without me seeing is another matter.

It turned out that Rudy had not been fired, but he had been suspended pending further investigation. Rudy shared that Adam and Johnnie had shown him CCTV from a recent event where he and Emre had been working the upstairs bar. Emre serving a customer who had purchased a single vodka coke, but Emre poured two separate vodkas and kept one in reserve and gave the other to the customer.

Rudy said he was seen on CCTV coming back behind the bar where Emre then hands Rudy this drink and Rudy took a sip of it before handing it back to Emre. Adam had checked the receipt of the customer to confirm that one drink was purchased but two of the same drink was prepared.

I knew nothing of this event although the date I recall I was working downstairs. Jack was the only one who was helping Rudy and Emre upstairs that day. As Rudy was not behind the bar when the customer ordered he just assumed when he returned, and Emre handed him this drink that it was just wastage.

The only people who didn't drink wastage was me, Jack and Simon (pronounced See-mon), with the latter two not touching alcohol at all. But it was commonplace for others to either consume genuine wastage and deliberately make wastage that went unrecorded and unchallenged.

Rudy thought he was in the clear, and stated to Adam that if he was 'stealing' something would he stand in plain view of the CCTV and consume it? While Rudy was right, and it was commonplace I highlighted that the staff handbook states drinking alcohol on duty is gross misconduct. So was helping yourself to the companies' assets, i.e. stealing stock.

Rudy was heartbroken at the prospect of losing his job and when I advised there were plenty of jobs out there, he stated he didn't want to be anywhere other than Soho. He somehow felt this was where he belonged and felt safe.

I was upfront with Rudy and said he didn't have a leg to stand on, unless he explained to head office that others do the same and he alone should not take a bullet for the entire team, including management. Rudy wrote a letter naming all those that drink wastage and deliberately create wastage in order to consume alcohol freely. This included Ben, Adam and Johnnie. And most recently with witnesses present, Adam encouraged Rudy to consume some of his own wastage during his shift, even telling him to pop in a mixer for good measure.

Rudy was reluctant at first saying he didn't want to get on the wrong side of his colleagues for 'grassing' to which I stated he was about to be dismissed on the grounds of gross misconduct so what did he have to lose?

While I was on the phone to Rudy, Johnnie was calling him. I told Rudy to hang up, take the call and see what he wants, as this was very bizarre. Rudy called back to say that Johnnie was advising Rudy to resign to ensure he got a good reference.

Rudy was sharp and sent me an earlier email communication from the company that stated they didn't do refence requests nor confirmations of employment. So, Johnnie's advice was slightly disingenuous and only served

THE LOST BOYS OF SOHO

to highlight something underhand was going on. Rudy said Johnnie was so nice, telling Rudy "It's not fair that you take a hit for the team for this"!

Rudy asked me why Johnnie was apparently being so nice to him, to which I stated it was obvious. Johnnie was ensuring he saved his own skin given he knew Rudy, if not all of us, know far too much. One way to stop someone dobbing you in on their departure is to keep them sweet so they find it impossible to spill the tea.

Rudy said as the conversation progressed, Johnnie was getting frustrated with Rudy and his tone changed. Rudy saw an opportunity, although I think he'd quicky seen through Johnnie. Rudy exclaimed "I've made an email already for human resources Johnnie. In it I have named you, Adam & Ben as helping yourself to wastage drinks and encouraging others to drink them".

Rudy said Johnnie hit the roof and got aggressive with him. "You might want to think twice before you do that, I suggest you think again"! Johnnie continued "you want to be very careful as there will be consequences"! Johnnie threated.

With that Rudy said he had no alternative but to send the email and Johnnie ended the call by saying "well, you might want to look at who shared screenshots of your private group chat before you start grassing on others"!

Rudy shared this insight in the private group chat which consisted of Me, Bobby, Emre, Rudy & Ben. The boys noticed that Ben had remained pretty much silent with the recent developments over the last couple of days. It was quickly determined that as Ben had always gloated about helping himself to spirits, that he was perhaps feeling guilty that the others were facing dismissal while he sat cushty. I didn't think that and stated Ben didn't care about anybody but himself, he is a vile creature.

While nobody asked me if I had shared any information from our group chat with management, I took the opportunity to share with Carl in a private message. That Johnnie seemed to be overstepping the scope of his role as a supervisor. That Johnnie was also communicating with a member of staff who has been suspended pending an investigation which could jeopardise the integrity of the investigation.

I also shared with Carl that Johnnie had shared the source of some of the evidence regarding lemonade but had not revealed that I was the one who shared the screenshots but alluded to exposing me. Not that I was arsed.

There were only four screenshots of each of the boys in one way or another incriminating themselves while making light of the situation. I only felt compelled to share given the boys were discussing how hilarious they found it and how they had got away with it.

At the time of the messages, I'd also been taken aside by Adam in a private face to face chat. I would manually log into the till system instead of using a fob key which took ages. In doing so I would always punch an extra number which meant I would inadvertently add a drink to the customer's order by accident. I didn't realise pressing delete, not void, was logged and management viewed excessive use of the delete button as suspicious. Apparently, I was the 3rd worst with a total of over £700 of deleted transactions.

Adam said this was not acceptable and I said I would stop manually logging in with my finger as this was the cause. Although I had entered, somehow sixty odd bells whiskey which came to about £300 of that £700. Adam said, "no worries, but we have also noticed a lot of vodka on your account and that could look suspicious as we are always down on vodka and gin"! My reasoning for this was working upstairs with the 'straight crowd' who would ask for a Vodka, especially the ladies and I'd punch in the house vodka. Guys wanting to impress or flashing the cash would upgrade their vodka to a better brand meaning I had to delete the house vodka that Adam was correlating with the missing bottles from stock.

My conscious was clear, so it didn't bother me, too much. I wasn't the only one pulled to one side either, but still, it made me feel a little seedy and as though my professional integrity in this back street pub was being viewed under a microscope.

But the more I thought about it, these bitches are helping themselves to vodka and gin and think it's hilarious, that's why the stock is missing. Not because I am pressing 'delete' (not void) and now they have been warned about Lemonade and think that's hilarious too. So, I shared what was being said.

Blair was Rudy's choice to be his companion to attend the disciplinary after I said while on annual leave, I didn't want to see the cesspit. They both arrived but the disciplinary was cancelled, citing, a last-minute clash of diaries. Rudy said Blair shared that all was not well in the management office and Blair wasn't enjoying it.

Blair openly shared with Rudy that there was a lot of animosity towards Jack, and this seemed to be purely malicious. Adam had that day announced Keith who works ad-hoc and around 4 hours in a week, if he works at all, had been promoted to supervisor. Rudy said he asked, "don't you think that's suspicious, especially as Keith and Adam are housemates" and apparently Blair smirked and said, 'it does look suspicious doesn't it'!

In the end it was shared that head office received the email from Rudy and informed Adam to give both Rudy and Emre a verbal warning to save face. Nobody is allowed to accept drinks as tips anymore and as I recommended a wastage sheet has been introduced and all wastage signed off by a manager and poured straight down the sink. And for a period, nobody was drinking on shift and the atmosphere was noticeably different as they were sobor, ish! Then those that couldn't abstain from the drink started bringing in their own reusable bottles that didn't allow you to see the contents, but it was safe to say, it wasn't water nor a soft drink they were consuming, and the atmosphere returned to normal.

"JUST A FRIENDSHIP FOR ME"

There came a point while keeping Jack updated over text message when he said he would come into work after his shift at the vaccination centre and catch up with me. I told him it could wait be he insisted that he come in to speak to me. I think given the update with external proceedings he was keen now push to 'officially' identify who sent the malicious messages.

I was working the main bar and saw him come in, in his uniform and Adam, of all people, approached me and said, "Jack wants you in the office".

We sat down in the office and after the usual pleasantries of 'how you are'? I stated I was tired but pleased I now had a sense of closure given the police had on my advice decided to give Kenzie a caution. In some respects, the toxicity on a whole at this place of work, was having more of an impact on me than those malicious messages.

Sharing this view with Jack, while he agreed with some of what I expressed, he felt a caution from the authorities was not entirely justifiable. He kept stating "me and Carl would like to dismiss the individual after an investigation". While he was right, at the back of my head I couldn't help but think Jack was using me and this incident to get rid of someone he didn't like. No matter how many times I told myself, this was unreasonable for me to think such a thing. Johnnie had sown the seed of doubt in my view of Jack's intentions. Which was a kind, caring and good-natured chap to be perhaps malicious and disingenuous himself.

I appreciated Jacks time and as we both talked, I got emotional as I shared what I was expecting from my time at this pub. I was expecting a jovial carefree environment where us, 'the gays' had gone through enough shit to know not to bring it to our own door. That working at the pub would be an escape of the mundane reality of life. A place where camp banter, shade and even tea would make coming to work enjoyable.

I just managed to hold back the tears as I shared why I specifically applied for the job at 'this' pub. That being amongst my own 'community' after being punched unconscious, raped and infected with HIV that I would somehow be amongst those that would cheer me up. Overall, I'd had a good time, but it was marred by others who seem to thrive on being malicious, sadistic and vitriolic in a bid to disguise their own faults, habits and/or insecurities.

The messages only served to highlight that stigma still exists and there may be another time I will face this level of stigma in the future. But I guess, I have had a shot of immunity should I no doubt face the same again in my lifetime.

Jack pushed for me to share the name and while he was giving a speech to convince me I just blurted it out "Kenzie, it was Kenzie"! A few tears rolled down my cheek as Jack leaned back into his chair. I had already decided I was I leaving, but I intended to work my notice and knew if Jack shared this revelation that Adam and Johnnie would treat me with contempt as I had seen on social media the three of them were super tight.

Jack said with such warmth and empathy "would you like a hug" and I replied "No"? I was truly tired of hugs; I was tired of giving this a second thought if I was honest.

As we wrapped up the chat Jack didn't say what he was intending to do with this information, and I didn't ask as I was not remotely interested. Jack looked absolutely knackered and he spoke about his shift at the vaccination centre and said he had become so passionate about vaccinating and helping people that he began to cry.

I thought 'oh for fuck's sake, now what shall I do' so I stood up, I stretched out my arms and we had a hug and I said "you should be so proud of yourself, I hardly know you and I think it's fantastic what you have done! I am so proud of you!". He seemed to perk up a little, but he looked absolutely burnt out.

I left the office and was drained, I truly hoped this was the end of the matter. I will be living with HIV for the rest of my life, my medication a daily reminder, I didn't need some pathetic arse wipe reminding me of 'my AIDS'.

So, I hoped I didn't need to give it another thought, and my resignation was on my phone in PDF format, and I planned to submit it after this weekend, to depart at the end of next weekend. This gave me two weekends to have a laugh and be a total tit.

I wanted to mark the end of mine and Jacks time in and out of the office, the tears, hugs and sometimes the laughs on the floor with a little something, but not a gift.

I was often known for doing quirky things for hotel guests during my years as a guest relations manager. Such as making personal messages on mirrors in their room and treasure hunts. I thought the latter would be easy to do and put together. I made a series of five postcards that had inspiring slogans on the front such as 'Born to stand out' and 'you're limited edition' etc. On the reverse I'd written quotes and messages before popping them into envelopes labelled for each day of the week. I made a video with my arm outstretched holding the envelopes in a fan and on a trail placing them in the cellar behind the cleaning products to the Mission Impossible theme tune.

The following day was Monday, and I was stood on the door of the pub watching life go buy on Old Compton Street. Jack appeared out of nowhere tapping me on the arm "hi Will! How are you"?

He noticed I had a new button badge on my sweater of drag icon Lady Bunny, "She always comes in here for a drink when she is in London. You can always recognise her as you always hear her voice before you see her" Jack reminisced. Bizarrely, don't ask me how, Jack got onto the meaning of life and alternative therapies. I thought as I do, I'd take the piss and said "those buildings across the road. They were built in the past, but are they still in the past or are they here in the present"?

I thought Jack would be pushed for time and would perhaps say 'oh piss off, taking the piss'. Well, Jack made space in his diary, and we mulled over theories of time of the past, present and future. I found it interesting, but I could hear others such as Johnnie in my head saying "you got her started now! You should know better Will you've been here long enough"!

But low and behold, I was saved. Jack jumped as his spirit guide reminded him, he needed to pass the cable he was clutching in his hand to the DJ who was trying to set up.

I sent Jack a message with the video titled 'Your mission should you choose to accept it'! I explained he needed to collect the envelopes and follow the instruction which was to open one envelope daily. The envelope titled 'Monday' had the following card with the slogan 'No one is you and that is your superpower'. On the reverse I had quoted the Dalai Lama in gold pen "There are only two days in the year that nothing can be done. One is called yesterday, and the other is called tomorrow. Today is the right day to love, believe and mostly live".

Jack sent a photo of him holding the card and sent me a message saying "this is so lovely" with the blushing hearts emoji and a second "Thank you" with pray hands emoji. I felt this perhaps meant more to Jack than a gift and was a little bit of fun, given my hotel guests said it would brighten their day when doing something similar.

I bumped into Jack an hour or so later and he said to me "are all the cards for me or do I have to share them out with others". I was taken aback slightly as I had made no mention of sharing them, so I clarified "they're all for you". I sent a further message saying they were to be opened daily as the envelopes suggested and not to be opened all at once. I joked "unlike an advent calendar when you just want the chocolate". He replied that he would open one every day.

By the end of the week, I had not given my one weeks' notice but intended to do so after the weekend. Given it was Friday me and Alex were both working a double shift and had the same hour off in the afternoon so decided we would get absolutely pissed in Leicester Square and have a wicked Friday night with the drag queen DJ who played cheesy pop mash ups that we both liked.

We first went to Ku Bar and did Sambuca shots and downed a couple of pints before moving to O'Neil's and doing the same. We weren't drunk to the point we couldn't do our job but, I did stumble down the stairs and Alex pissed all over his shorts.

We were noticcably merry and very hungry! We both drooled as we pledged to have battered sausage and chips from the chippy down the road. Johnnie said, "I want whatever you two have had" and I replied without thinking "Why is Derek on his holly-bobs"?

As I served a customer I went over to the optics where Jack was seemingly aware me and Alex were a bit pissed. Jack grinned at my sense of mischievousness, but I could tell he didn't approve. "Are you OK Will"? Jack enquired. "Yeah, I'm fine thanks, it's me medication, other than that I feel fine" I replied imitating that disastrous interview of Kerry Katona slurring on This Morning with Philip Schofield. Jack laughed uncontrollably.

"I opened the last of the cards today and I'd like to have a chat with you" Jack said. I said yeah ok. But felt the need to add "as long as you know there was nothing sexual about them, I know you wouldn't have thought that, but…"! Jack paused looking at me, I thought 'oh me and my gob'.

And I genuinely knew, or did I really know? I guess I hoped without thinking too much about it that Jack would not have looked at it as anything but a friendly gesture. There was nothing suggestive in there anyway, not to my mind anyway.

"God no. Not at all"! Jack replied, and I jokingly said "phew" before staggering off with my double vodka red bull for my customer. Me and Alex had a fab night, he had battered sausage and chips and given the queue for the chippy on my break I had to settle for a supermarket club sandwich. But by the end of the night, we both said, 'that was the best atmosphere we've experienced since we've worked here'! And it wasn't because we'd had a drink given, we'd sobered up by the time the drag queen DJ started.

The next day having thought about what Jack had said I sent him a text in short, I was merely trying to say that while Jack had qualities I liked about him, I didn't see features or qualities that I found sexually attractive. But I was keen, perhaps too keen to have Jack as a friend given, we got on so well and conversationally had so many interests and similarities.

I had never met someone like Jack before who seemed so closely aligned to me. We'd both discussed our childhood and family life and we had so many similarities. Let's put it this way every time me and Jack have a conversation one of us would say "oh my god, me too"! And it seems spooky that we had so many similarities which meant we could understand and relate to each other with ease.

I do think in my text message to Jack I was in parts incoherent and my two thumbs doing the typing had a case of 'verbal diarrhoea'. I think with Jack, he was very much unobtainable. He would speak to you in work and keep conversation pretty much at work. I remember I was stood on the door back in the summer and saw him walking down the pavement with 3 friends.

As he approached, he looked at me and I said smiling, "Hi Jack" and he ignored me and continued walking. I said under my breath "fucking arse hole" and Johnnie had heard me as he approached from behind and said "yeah, she's two faced that one! Especially when she's with her "friends"! Drops you quicker than you can say Louise Woodward"!

A couple of days after I was outside wiping a table and Jack was passing again. I had my head down as he approached and said "Hi"! to which I looked up smiling thinking it was a customer enquiry, most likely asking if the table, I was cleaning was available as was common. "Hi! Oh, it's you"! I said to Jack as my smile slowly disappeared. Jack seemed offended and I had to explain "no I meant it as in I thought you was a customer, so I was doing the whole 'tits and teeth'. But it's nice to see you, how are you…" I reluctantly enquired.

But I respected this in Jack as I too have always kept work and private life separate and never go to team get-togethers. I didn't add colleagues to social media or the like and I didn't meet up with them outside work. As I intended to leave and Jack had been, it seemed supporting if not carrying the weight of my HIV also. I was keen to keep Jack as a friend.

I often shared with Jack that I don't let guys into my life so easily in an intimate scenario and the same was said for 'friends'. I like to keep people at a distance and often got called Miranda Priestly played by Meryl Streep in the movie The Devil Wears Prada and on rare occasions, I don't know why, I'd get called Hitler.

Jack replied to my message a short time later and said, 'let's have a catch up' and we arranged to meet at a juice bar in Soho before we both started our shift at the same time. Re-reading my message I knew what Jack was going to say, he'd not read into anything I'd written but I could see where I was so keen to establish a friendship with Jack that I'd overstated my feelings.

It was a hot day; I made every effort to dress down and as I arrived first. I resisted texting him to offer to buy him a juice because he was coming to tell me that from my text message he was 'friend zoning me'. This killed me, because I knew what was coming and I really had to bite my tongue and just take it on the chin. Not the rejection, just that my eagerness to establish a friendship I'd made Jack feel I was hoping for more. Biting my tongue was not something I could do easily, but I thought I'd give it a try.

I'd said a lot in the message and Jack had a right to reply so I told myself not to butt in and let Jack speak.

I was sat downstairs on the sofa although I was looking for a more formal style of seating like a table and chairs, so we had the table between us. I started by sitting on the sofa all proper, like I was at a job interview but had to give in and slouched with my right ankle tucked under my left thigh.

Jack arrived and there was a queue at the bar, so he came back down, and I gave him my bottle of unopened water. We got the usual pleasantries over with and he very quickly said "I like you a lot, I think you're really cool, but it's just a friendship for me. I've got so much going on in my life now, I am not even considering a man in my life".

By this moment I had sweat beads running down my forehead, my arsehole had eaten half the sofa and I'd rolled my tongue to the back of my throat to stop me saying a single word.

I was absolutely mortified, and I wanted the sofa to swallow me whole! But then I thought maybe Jack would be flattered with my 'perceived' schoolboy crush and the attention. Jack said himself he was "needy" when it comes to men, so I guess it all worked out in the end. And I was amazed at how restraint I was in just taking it on the chin when I was absolutely bursting to have an opportunity to restate my comments and ambitions were in a bid to establish a 'friendship' and nothing more.

But Jack handled it graciously and when he said 'friends' I knew that meant just work colleagues and nothing else. No friendly drinks after work so I just went with it. Once we established that, Jack then decided to have a post-mortem on the cards I had sent and why he had stated when he saw me next that he wanted to have a chat.

"I knew when I opened the card about dinner, I said to myself 'oh god" to which with a raised eyebrow I said, "is the prospect of a friendly dinner with me so hideous" to which we both laughed and Jack said neurotically "god no"!

The card he is talking about had the slogan 'Born to stand out' and I had written in gold pen on the reverse "Wise-man say meal deal is 'not' good for mind, body and soul. Dinner with me is good for 'mind, belly and soul, wise-man say"!

Jack had shared he wasn't a great cook and had been living off the supermarket meal deals which mainly consisted of a sandwich, a snack such as crisps and a soft drink. My offer of dinner was merely that it would be a good home cooked meal which would give him brain power for his studies, be good for his belly as in he'd be full of substance and soul in that he'd eaten something fresh and more nutritious.

I am not sure how someone would see that today, in the 'old fashioned' sense "dinner". I mean it didn't have to be at my house, we could have grabbed something out and about, for me it always was with a view of just a friendship. I have been single for 6 years and now I am living with HIV I am very much still at the 'nobody wanted me when I was normal, nobody will want me now I have the most stigmatic gay disease out there'. I am sure that will pass, but not just yet. Although I am happy and content as I am for the moment.

Me and Jack chatted for 20 minutes, mainly about him to which he apologised. I told him not to apologise, it was, after all nice to listen to him for a change than him having to listen to me. We headed off to work, and as we walked down Old Compton Street, I just told myself to swallow my pride, if I had any left.

It wasn't an hour into my shift when I got a message from Emre asking what I was doing coming out of the juice bar with Jack which was followed with some gifs of two guys kissing. There was nothing to defend so I didn't even reply.

On my lunch break I sat on the fire escape eating my usual battered sausage and chips which was smothered in chip shop curry sauce. Jack came down the fire escape and said, "Sausage and Chips" and I retorted sarcastically "yeah! I am literally eating my emotions" as I stuffed a forkful of chips in my gob.

Jack turned around so innocently and with puppy dog eyes said with such empathy "oh Will". I spat out my chips to reassure him by shouting "I was taking the piss, I'm joking for fucks sake"! I knew he was somewhat naïve but come on!

The only thing that had been playing on my mind was that I had remained silent when I wanted to say I was only ever pursuing a 'friendship'. By the end of the shift, I'd forgotten the 'chat' completely and was the last one out of the building. Adam and Jack were stood by the fire exit we used to leave the pub. I bid them both goodnight and was quite buoyant as I had to get home to sort out friends coming for afternoon tea the following day.

As I was leaving Jack was stood in front of Adam and again raising his inner brow to give those puppy dog eyes and slightly sticking out his bottom lip he said softly "Will! Goodnight, I hope you're ok" and without thinking of others being present I said, "goodnight, Jack! I am fine, honest"!

As I left the pub and walked up Old Compton Street, I thought 'Jesus, get over yourself Jack'! I sent a quick reassuring text message to Jack saying, "It's all cool, honest" [smiley emoji].

GAGGING FOR 'IT'!

It was incredibly sad that the days that followed our chat in the juice bar Jack kept his distance. We even had shifts together where we didn't even speak to each other. I'm not backwards in coming forwards but couldn't get my head around why this was. I said "hello" to Jack and he seemingly ignored me but made a point of talking to others that he didn't usually spend a lot of time with.

I have an ability to just cut people out of my life with ease. Although I had not let Jack into my life beyond the scope of being work colleagues. Despite sharing intimate details of my HIV, him behaving this way didn't matter to me. I just wondered if I'd done anything to upset him since he said he wanted to be just friends but was seemingly being unfriendly.

I didn't really care so I stayed out of his way. I did overhear Ben who was now leaving the pub to pursue a career in drag said he felt there was a special connection between him and Jack. And Ben, when challenged by Emre said his initial view that Jack was boring had now changed after taking the time to get to know him more.

A few days later I messaged Jack and asked if I could come in and observe him cleaning the cellar as I felt this would support my recent applications for manager roles within this sector of hospitality. I'd been shown how to do it in 2005 but as manager it wasn't my domain, so I didn't pay attention. I said it didn't have to be in depth and that he knew he could tell me straight if he didn't have the time.

He said he didn't have the time. I thanked him for his reply.

On that day I came in at 10am as expected and Jack was sat fiddling with some papers and I got to work removing all the glasses from the shelves to sanitise the shelves. He came over and asked if I was ok as I seemed quiet.

He knew me well enough by now so I just said quite sarcastically, "I just can't be bothered shouting to you all the way over there". Point being, I wasn't going to have a conversation all the way from behind the bar when he is sat some distance away.

I thought now he is lingering around the bar I'll make conversation so asked how his studying was going. I enquired to a few things he was struggling to arrange with his studies the last we spoke. He shared he still hadn't managed to find a solution. He got onto elements of his practical study that requires him to speak to people who have suicidal tendencies. I said, "you would be amazing at that. You'd bring the suicide rate right down, because if they don't top themselves, you can bore them to 'death'"!

Jack smiled and then giggled as my quip finally landed. I felt mean but couldn't resist and I hoped he knew it wasn't my view that he was boring but one he'd heard time and time again, although not with the malicious sentiment it was expressed behind his back by those claiming to be his friends.

There was a small queue outside of red-faced regulars waiting for the pub to open. Jack let them in and one group who I'd not seen had apparently been barred from other pubs for being aggressive towards staff according to Jack.

They placed an order with me of around 6 drinks. With each order I repeated back extra carefully their chosen mixer to ensure there could be no discrepancies. This was pointless with people who are alcohol dependent because you still can't argue when they claim you got their order wrong.

Low and behold, one who asked for Vodka and ginger ale, said when I presented it that he'd asked for vodka coke. I apologised and took it back, but it didn't end there, the customer said in the most condescending tone, "you're having a bad day, you've made a mistake, don't worry about it"!

I took the opportunity to remind him that I had not only listened to his order but repeated each drink back to him. His order of which was the same on the previous occasion, the drink in question being a vodka and ginger ale. I even asked him to slow down so that I could enter each drink that his crew shouted across the pub into the till. So, I had not made a mistake.

Jack came over and asked what was wrong and as I went to prepare his now amended drink, I said "he's being a bell end" to which Jack said "how about you take your break now" as though I was the problem. I didn't argue, I just went on break. When I came back from break, I thought I'll flip if Jack patronises me further with anything along the lines of 'have you calmed down now'. But he didn't and he left shortly after without saying goodbye as Johnnie came on shift. I told Johnnie and he said, "you're not the first, nobody likes that group when they come in here, they are horrid"! So not just me then.

But I guess Jack was perhaps ensuring that I didn't piss these guys off by standing up for myself and starting a fight. Johnnie explained a barman was glassed in a pub down the road for back chatting them.

The weekend came and I had still not got around to handing in my resignation although it was written and ready to go, in truth I'd written it a couple of months back, so it was always ready to go. The Saturday night was Adam's birthday and he had reserved the whole of the upstairs bar and to everybody's surprise has requested that Lurch work the bar. Nobody was put out, just surprised as Lurch always served customers with one hand in his pocket and had no sense of speed or urgency when serving.

I was wearing my police helmet this night and bumped into Adam in the staff room and wished him a happy birthday. Although he had been a twat with me my birthday wishes were genuine, I am never one to hold a grudge. Elias was in the building too as he was soon to start back at the pub after spending time studying his master's in media.

It was just a shame that he was coming in as I was intending to leave. I shared as much with Elias and he told me to stay as it would be fun the pair of us together. I agreed it would, but it wouldn't be often that we'd get to work together with his days off and me being banished to the Attic like Anne Frank. The main bar was busy for a Friday night and again my choice of headwear got the usual "nice helmet" gags and drunk women wanting to pose for selfies. But in all it was a laugh, and the drag queen DJ was playing some proper camp tunes! Adam had placed a sign on the stairs that stated access was only permitted to "invitees only". The guest list seemed to only consist of regular customers and close colleagues of Adams who had been given the night off to make up numbers.

I overheard two regulars state separately why each of them was not upstairs as they had been invited. One replied, "it's dead up there" and "it's boring"! I instantly felt embarrassed and thought I can't walk upstairs because if I see it, I will be even more embarrassed. I had brought my own lunch but decided to go to the chippy instead to avoid having to pass the upstairs bar enroute to the staff room. As I saw people walking up the staircase towards the sign, I was willing them to proceed beyond the sign meaning Adam had friends and they'd received an invite. But the vast majority who started to climb the stairs, turned, and came back down given they had no invitation.

I did see Adam down in the main bar three times and each time as I was dancing around like a bell end in my helmet and handcuffs hanging off my shorts. Adam smiled and winked. I thought 'ok! That's weird'. It was odd for Adam to be that nice to me. I wondered if he was merely approving of the tone, I was setting in my diamond encrusted police helmet. As it seemed closely aligned with the vision, he said he had to make the pub the number one gay venue as it once was in his new, interim general manager role.

The following day I was scheduled to work the Fetish social event and given the nice weather despite it being October, I wore my diamante work vest, denim jean shorts just above the knee and my Royal Air Force hat that had some diamante on the motif. Adam and Keith were sat in the upstairs bar as I got it prepared and Keith declared he was more hungover than Adam despite him being the birthday boy. Shortly after they left the fetish event started to arrive and pretty quick the bar was manic and you could not move on the floor. I was pretty sure we had breached the capacity and did worry having tried to collect glasses as we ran out that people were being crushed and not only that but being so packed in with covid-19 still being prevalent and cases on the rise.

Emre came up to help and the new girl Cara who is from Muff, a village in Donegal, Ireland. And get this, she is also a self-proclaimed "muff muncher"! You couldn't make it up. She is such a lovely person and a real breath of fresh air.

We hit it off the moment we met, and we both traded banter with no regard for political correctness. She asked what the rest of the team was like, and I said "I wouldn't trust some of them as far as you can throw them! When one of them found out I had the AIDS…"

Cara screamed and said "fuck Will! You can just throw that into conversation"! We are a perfect match, and she really has made working in the pub a joy, she is hilarious and runs rings around some of these bitches!

Cara setting her eyes on this fetish social for the first time was an eye opener and she didn't believe half of what I told her goes on. I was relived for my break and struggled to make my way across the floor to get to the staff room. Adjacent to the staff room door was the gents and I was bursting for a pee so popped in as we had no staff toilet. There was a small group of guys in there in rubber and leather in what is already a small room. I walked over to the vacant cubicle but didn't bother to shut the door given you had to walk all the way in, and breath in for the door to close. I'd just unzipped my shorts when from behind I felt someone violently grab between my legs which was the crushing sensation of my testicles through my jeans. It was so forceful I was knocked forward while he seemingly tried to lift me off my feet!

I turned around and saw a guy dressed head to toe in leather including a leather hat. "What the fuck do you think you're doing"! I said in total disbelief. "Come on you bitch, dressed like that, you're gagging for it"! I wasn't sure why, but my first line of defence was "you do know I fucking work here"! Trying to highlight that I was not part of their group and was not consenting to whatever the pub 'turns a blind eye to'. I had only dressed up, well, compared to what I usually wear for work I added the hat after being encouraged by the organiser in previous weeks to add to the ambience of the event behind the bar.

I made a speedy exit as there were 3 guys all looking at me and as I left the gents I said, "don't fucking touch me again, arse hole"! As I was leaving one of them kicked me on the back of my leg. As I turned the organiser was stood outside the staff room door and I said, "excuse me" to unlock the door. Seeing me flustered and upset he said, "are you ok"? To which I replied, "I am not here to be molested or groped by your group"! His response was "Mm you're such a top"!

I thought 'fuck off' and entered the staff room locking the door behind me. I looked at my leg which was stinging and noticed I had been cut and that it was bleeding. I cleaned up the cut which turned out to be more a scratch but was bleeding heavily, and me with the AIDS, imagine! Then busting for the loo, I took a piss in the sink in the staff room. The week prior the ladies was backed up and shit was backing up out of the sink, so I figured it was all going down the same hole. I made sure I washed my hands after.

I had brought a work hoodie with me in case the weather changed, and the venue was cold, so I changed into that and put my baseball cap on. Blair was the manager on duty and given he is new to the role of supervisor and scared of his own shadow, and completely useless in every sense. I knew he'd be incapable of doing anything and this proved to be the case when I told him after my break. He said meekly "oh are you ok Will"? Not, who was it? Point them out to me they need removing! I just gave him a raise of my eyebrow as if to say, 'are you for real' and he quickly ran off.

The organiser came and asked if I was ok and if he could buy me a drink, a drink he suggested I placed on his tab. A tab that the pub writes off as wastage. A little like offering to buy someone a drink when you're on an all-inclusive holiday! I politely declined but was in a foul mood for the remainder of the evening but was occasionally picked up by some of the attendees who pointed out that we were working hard and doing a good job.

The next day when I came on shift Johnnie asked how I was and how the fetish event went. He stated the takings for the event were extremely high which was hardly surprising for how packed and busy we were. I shared what had happened in the toilet and he was shocked and said that was unacceptable. He enquired "did you tell Jack"? I said Jack wasn't working and when asked I said, "Blair was on" to which Johnnie just said "ah". Alluding he knew Blair didn't have the experience nor ability to confront a customer and potentially ask them to leave the premises having sexually assaulted an employee.

It was hilarious watching Blair clear the pub after closing, meekly and politely requesting customers to finish their drinks. I couldn't see him approaching a 6-foot big burly man head to toe in leather and asking him to 'leave'. Johnnie finished his shift and again I was left with Blair managing the pub for the remainder of my shift which took me to closing.

"SAY PLEASE"!

It was bouncing down with rain in Soho and the streets were deserted. With Johnnie having finished his shift leaving me once again with Blair there was at least something to look forward to!

It was Rudy's first shift back after Lemonade-Gate. Blair's attempt at camp humour was to ask us all to "ignore Rudy when he comes in, it'll be so funny"! I looked at Blair and said "no, that's victimisation, that's what that is"!

Rudy came back and flung his arms around me first, I responded as I usually do "ew! Get off me, this is dry clean only"! As the team welcomed Rudy back a customer asked me for a pint of Guinness to which I rung up in the till, picked up the glass and started to pour the Guinness. Presenting the customer with the credit card machine I respectfully said, as I always do "that'll be £5.50p please".

During the pandemic we were a business that still accepted cash and none of us had any issue with handling cash in terms of transmission of the covid-19 virus. Many customers stated that many pubs and businesses had stopped taking cash altogether and we were one of a few still accepting cash.

It was default to present the customer with the credit card machine as even the old boys had finally got to grips with contactless card payments. I had also, as a very observant person, noticed the customer trying to pull out of his wallet a card marked 'Banco'. As a speaker of Portuguese, I recognised this to be most likely a Spanish card as I lived for a time in Barcelona with my ex and recognised the logo. And the big give away, the customer himself had a Spanish accent.

The customer took exception to me presenting the credit card machine and stated I should have first ascertained if he was paying by cash or card. I assumed as he was making this protest that he didn't wish to pay by card and therefore wanted to pay cash. This wasn't a problem, so I replied, "Yeah if you want to pay cash that's not a problem" and I simultaneously cancelled the transaction on the till and as I continued to pour his Guinness saying "£5.50p please".

As I checked to see how his Guinness was settling, he said "£5.50p please" assuming he was merely repeating back what I said as perhaps someone who was not a native speaker of English, I replied, "yeah five pounds fifty".

I assumed he was doing, without looking, what many of us do when handling cash. Repeat back the amount as you fish around your wallet for loose change while keeping the cashier waiting.

I then caught his eye and he said "£5.50p 'please', you need to say please". Slightly confused I said, "I said please". Anyhow this went back and forth, and he said, "I am sick of immigrants coming to this country and not bothering to learn the language"!

As the customer said this, I was naughty and immediately turned to look at Rudy, our resident Italian and proud self-confessed 'immigrant'. I was quite wrongly assuming the customer must be talking about Rudy and couldn't possibly be referring to me, an English native with a recorded family history going back to the year 1411. The customer said, "no, I am talking about you"! In disbelief I reconfirmed the customers statement "me, an immigrant"?

To which the customer said "yes, you!".

I was dumbfounded and thought, if he wasn't dead Jeremy Beadle is about to walk through those doors.

I stated I found his comments extremely offensive, "my good man, I was not only born and raised in this country from a long line of English forebears recorded as far back as the year 1411, but I am also a confident, native speaker of the English language along with commanding the very basic of good manners and common courtesy".

The customer stated my use of the word "native" was me being racist and he went on to state I should have been removed from the UK when Brexit came into effect and that he was taking his money elsewhere. I advised that I was not willing to serve him as I found his behaviour "of serious concern" if not "discriminatory"!

He then challenged me stating I didn't have the power to refuse him service. I advised him I did on three counts. One being the company does not tolerate any form of abusive behaviour towards its staff and pointed out the big bold sign hanging next to him on the wall. Two, to uphold the licencing objectives of the premises licence such behaviour as his was a breach of the objective. And three, in my own right as a personal licence holder I was authorised to take action to ensure the licencing objectives were upheld.

He walked off, seemingly to his two friends who had pint of Guinness in their hands already. One of his friends came over to me and asked how I was able to refuse him service as he was under the impression the pub was a "free house". I stated public or free house, no pub is exempt from upholding the licencing objectives, one of which was to not permit abusive behaviour. He tried to defend his friend by saying "but he's not drunk" to which I replied, "I agree, he doesn't appear to be drunk, but you don't have to be drunk to be verbally abusive".

I was pleased the friend didn't push me further because this discussion had already gone on for some time which goes against the personal licence training where your advised to avoid long debates, be firm and stand by your decisions. Because in my opinion this customer had a screw lose. The customer then came over and said to me "I will find out where you live" to which to show I wasn't fazed by his threat I gestured wafting my hand for him to 'go away', to 'leave'.

Blair came over and asked what was going on just as the customer had returned to argue some more. I had been looking for security on the door but couldn't see him, then I saw security coming down from the upstairs bar. But then I was distracted as I tried to tell Blair, but he was forcefully pushing me in the chest up against the beer taps which was quite painful. I politely asked Blair to take his hands off me to which he ignored while he tried to speak with the customer over my head.

I asked Blair a second time to take his hands off me to which he did while apologising. I allowed the customer to speak and of course, the customer missed the beginning and middle of the story and started from the point of me refusing him service. He then said I gestured by wafting my hand and verbally said "Shoo, like a dog". Blair shocked turned to me and said, "did you do that"? to which I replied, "I gestured yes. I didn't say "shoo""!

When the customer finished, I said, "How about we start with the beginning and middle of the story and not just share the end"? The customer gestured for me to go ahead, and I briefly outlined what had happened. To the customer's credit, he agreed with everything I said. This left me looking at Blair and saying, "there ya go…"! And without surprise, the customer said to Blair and his friends "leave it, let's go". The customer knew me retelling the story was not at all favourable to the customer and he realised his behaviour was wholly unacceptable.

Bizarrely, Blair said, "no wait, let me speak to you" and Blair went from behind the bar and spoke with the three customers who were then joined by a fourth customer who was also of Spanish origin. This fourth customer was stating I was rude "your colleague is refusing to serve this man. He said he had a right to refuse to serve him but gave no excuse [sic] why"!. A few minutes later Blair came behind the bar, finished the Guinness I had started to pour and took the credit card machine around to the customer who paid for his drink by card, not cash. Blair came to me and said, "I am so sorry Will! Are you upset with the way I handled it"?

I was dumfounded and said "so after all that, the customer didn't want to pay Cash given you just had him pay by card. Surely that tells you there is something wrong there. You've also served a customer who was in breach of the licencing objectives, and I am led to believe as are you despite only just gaining your personal licence".

As I spoke with Blair the customer looked over and smirked at me "and now he is deliberately trying to goad me, so when he has finished that pint, you just served him after I advised he needed to leave for being abusive. Who's to say he isn't going to feel empowered to plant that glass in my neck. What will you explain to the court when you're up for manslaughter as a result of your bizarre intervention"?

Blair kept apologising and his solution was not to look at the customer which was ludicrous as the pub is fairly small with nowhere else to look! Nor should I be made to feel uncomfortable in my own workplace. I went and stood in the bar ready to serve the next customer and the customer in question came up to me, lent across the bar, smirked, and walked off back to his friends.

I went back over to Blair who had seen what had just happened, "That's it Blair, I am out of here, your unable to guarantee my safety so that's it, I am done. I was sexually assaulted last night with no intervention when I told you, so I am not sticking around to find out what this customer intends to do, if anything.".

Blair said "ok, no problem" of course he was relieved that he didn't have to deal with any potential situation. Me walking out resolved it for him.

I walked upstairs, gathered my belongings from the staff room and left. I stepped onto a wet Old Compton Street and the waft of the drains and the wet rain I instantly felt relieved to be out of that place.

I sent a quick email while walking down Old Compton Street to Carl stating I was having to resign without notice as I was concerned about my safety to which Carl replied 3 minutes later with "Thank you for your time and wish you well in the future".

There was a slight sadness, but on reflection I had enjoyed my time with the people I enjoyed working with. It had perhaps not entirely lived up to my expectations but then I wonder if my expectations were too high. I sent Jack a message saying it was unfortunate that I didn't get to say goodbye in person. But I thanked him for making what was a bizarre, toxic and at times odious place of work, somewhat fun and bearable. I thanked him again for all his support with the AIDS messages whilst going on to say it was truly a joy to work alongside him, Rudy, Alex and Cara.

Jack had seen my message within the hour but never replied. Two days later I was back in Soho for my 6 monthly bloods at the HIV clinic. As I entered the waiting room on the HIV floor with my covid-19 mask on I saw three customers from the pub. As I sat down, I thought, 'wow, I never knew, you, you and you had HIV'.

After my bloods and collecting my 6 months meds, I walked down Old Compton Street and as I waited to cross Wardour Street I saw Jack standing outside the Duke of Wellington pub putting up his hood. As he headed towards China town waiting for traffic to pass, our eyes met across the road.

I took out my wireless earphones in anticipation of a quick 'hello'. It was like a remake of the final scene in the film 'The Devil Wears Prada' where Anne Hathaway spots Meryl Streep leaving her office and getting into her car. I smiled at Jack, he gave me an icy glare and looked away.

Like Anne Hathaway, I rolled my eyes and laughed to myself. As I crossed Wardour Street putting my earphones back in I accepted what I perhaps already knew. Jack assisting and helping me was entirely disingenuous and was only motivated by his own self-interest. This only seemed to be reinforced by what Johnnie divulged in his diatribe while stood on the glass trays that day. And retrospectively Jack had seemingly distanced himself from me once he obtained the information he sought.

For a brief second I questioned if I'd been too trusting of Jack before telling myself "bah! Fuck it, you'll know for next time! There won't be a next time"!

As I walked down the cobbles of Winnett Street my playlist was now playing Paloma Faith: I've Gotta Be Me. I kid you not! As I blinked, a tear fell out and rolled down my cheek. Wiping it away I said to myself "tears of joy, tears of joy"! And without any regard for who was around me, like any talented ex-drag queen I puckered up for a lip sync "I want to live, not merely survive. And I won't give up this dream, of life that keeps me alive. I gotta be me, I gotta be me"!

It all sounded like the perfect ending to a movie, except I tripped on a cobble on the road, and I stumbled three times before righting myself. I don't think anybody noticed!

ABOUT THE AUTHOR

When I received the first malicious message relating to me living with HIV [sic] ("AIDS"). I shared the event with other PLWHIV in an online forum. The thread was titled "diary of working in a London gay bar". Along with the malicious messages I also documented the conversations I had already overheard and/or taken part in relating to HIV. I felt documenting my experience and time at this Soho gay pub would give a glimpse into the life of a gay man living with HIV in a LGBT work environment.

To add balance, humour and positivity I shared stories in weekly entries which meant I was introducing colleagues and in turn sharing their backgrounds and my interactions with them at work. With each entry followed the thoughts and opinions of other members of the forum living with HIV. I was able to take their responses as advice and/or perhaps an indication as to what was post worthy for the audience and future entries.

When I made my final post in the forum once I left the pub I was flooded with messages of regret and dismay. Not entirely that I had walked out of my job, but that there would be no more diary entries from this "soap opera"! Many shared they only logged into the forum to catch up on my weekly posts and some stated they logged in to "binge read" several weeks posts. It was suggested that I share my story with a wider audience in the form of a book.

I am not a natural writer nor an experienced 'author' but I have always believed in verbally sharing my experiences with honesty and integrity. The only aspect of this experience that makes me nervous, but not embarrassed, is to openly share my HIV status so publicly. But I do so in the hope that I have documented the progress we have made in treating and managing HIV. Although my experience sadly shows within the LGBT community especially, that such progress has not been entirely matched in terms of stigma around HIV. Although my experience documented here highlights most people, I worked with are not suck in the 1980's with a misguided nor backward view of catching "AIDS" (HIV) through touch alone. Given they were aware of advances made in both HIV medication and education.

My story is a mere glimpse into working life as a gay man living with HIV in the heart of London's gay village. But it is the untold stories of millions of others that should be researched, shared, and remembered when the day comes that HIV no longer exists.

What did I do next? Well, despite Carl's message the company said they wanted to retain me and so transferred me within the company to another property close to Soho. The manager of this pub said he once lived with Jack "…in the days we did drugs together"! I messaged Jack to say I was now working for an old acquaintance of his who was asking after him, but Jack never replied. On my first day the manager picked up a water bottled and asked who's it was and when I declared it was mine, he tossed the bottle in the air like a hot potato while stating "ew I don't want HIV"! The next day he gave me a dead rose from the vase at the end of the bar to toss into the bin. I pricked my finger on a thorn which started to bleed. He made another HIV reference.

He was eastern European and had made several outdated and discriminatory remarks to other colleagues also especially to their ethnicity under the guise of 'humour'. Unsure if Jack had shared my status with him in their 'catch up' or if this was just outdated homophobic humour I never found out. I resigned on my 2nd day given this and other observations made me uncomfortable. I reported this incident and others I had witnessed in my two days to the two numbnutts in human resources and the 'district area manager', neither ever replied in response to these serious concerns.

Shortly after I was hired in a pub back in the very heart of Soho and am enjoying myself with a new team who are anything but 'lost'. In general conversation a colleague while talking about his gout randomly stated, "there's a cure now for HIV". He is heterosexual and seemingly being in Soho had heard about PrEP. I took the time and opportunity to share this wasn't a cure but a means to stop transmission of HIV. This naturally led onto medications for PLWHIV although my knowledge didn't seem to arouse suspicion, or maybe it did?

I keep in touch with some of the 'lost boys' but conversations with some have fizzled out as they live a life preoccupied with sex, drugs and drama. Me and Rudy keep in touch regularly and if we talk about the pub I often reminisce of my time there while he grows ever more disillusioned with the place. Cara too has been to see me in my new pub and we keep meaning to hook up for drinks and giggles! I walk past daily on my way to work or to our sister sites and I try not to look in. On the odd occasion I have and seen the boys on the door or behind the bar like caged animals pacing, I feel nothing but pity for them.

Ben's big drag career didn't quite work out. He quickly became known on the scene for wearing the same costume and speaking with a few queens' venues decided not to re-book him again for a long list of reasons, "no talent" being the main one cited. Alex became besties with Kenzie, yeah that's right the unicorn killer. I walked past Kenzie on Pentonville Road heading towards Kings Cross just before New Year 2022. He had eyes like saucers so clearly too spaced out to perhaps recognise me. Sharing this encounter with the lost boys Emre said he was most likely going to the 'chems and chill' in Kings Cross as Emre himself had received an invite that night.

Kenzie approached Rudy and complained that Jack had told Kenzie he needed to "show more compassion towards people". Apparently, this was Jack merely imparting friendly advice to Kenzie. I smiled as I perhaps, maybe even delusional, made a correlation with the final scene in 'The Devil Wears Prada'. Where Anne Hathaway calls Emily Blunt, asking her to take the clothes off her hands. Where Emily Blunt ends the call, smiles reminiscently before turning to the new assistant saying, "you have some very large shoes to fill! I hope you know that"! It felt like Jack had perhaps made this statement to Kenzie with me in mind given Jack knew what Kenzie had said and done to me.

I didn't receive another instruction to isolate by NHS test and trace for covid-19 after leaving the pub despite still working in the same environment in busy Soho. I did, however, have a positive lateral flow which was confirmed by a PCR as being positive for covid-19. This came after I had a 3rd full vaccine given, I am a PLWHIV as opposed to a booster jab. Both the vaccine and covid-19 made me incredibly ill but didn't stop me carrying out my first and second edit of this book. My HIV is still below 20 copies meaning I am still U=U which isn't set to change if I remain on effective medication which is my one tiny pill a day.

Printed in Great Britain
by Amazon